Sir Gaston Camille Charles Maspero

**Life in Ancient Egypt and Assyria**

Sir Gaston Camille Charles Maspero
**Life in Ancient Egypt and Assyria**
ISBN/EAN: 9783337231569

Printed in Europe, USA, Canada, Australia, Japan

Cover: Foto ©Andreas Hilbeck / pixelio.de

More available books at **www.hansebooks.com**

# LIFE IN ANCIENT EGYPT AND ASSYRIA

G. MASPÉRO,
LATE DIRECTOR OF ARCHÆOLOGY IN EGYPT AND MEMBER OF
THE INSTITUTE OF FRANCE.

With One Hundred and Eighty-eight Illustrations.

*TRANSLATED BY ALICE MORTON.*

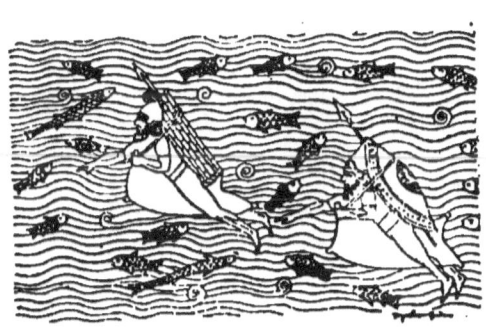

LONDON:
CHAPMAN AND HALL, Lᴅ.
1892.

# PREFACE.

THIS will not be an unbroken history of the ancient Oriental dynasties and nations: the order of events, the lines of the kings, the movements and invasions of the peoples may be found fully related in my *Ancient History*, or in its abridged edition by Van den Berg. I only wish to give the readers of this book some impression of life under its various phases amongst the two most civilised nations which flourished upon our earth before the Greeks. I have chosen for each of them the epoch we know the best, and of which we possess the greatest number of monuments: for Egypt, that of Rameses II. (fourteenth century B.C.); for Assyria, that of Assurbanipal (seventh century). I have acted like those conscientious travellers who do not like to enter a new country without some preparation, who study its customs and language before they start; then I journeyed—or at least I believed so—two or three thousand years back, away from our present era. Once there, I looked round and endeavoured to see as well and as much as possible. I walked through the streets of the city, glanced through the half-opened doors, peered into the shops, noted down the remarks of the populace that I chanced to overhear. Some famished masons went on strike: I followed them to the house of the Count of Thebes to see what happened. A funeral passed with a great clamour: I accompanied the dead man to his tomb, and learnt the chances of life granted to him in the other world. A marriage was being celebrated: I took advantage of the facility with which Orientals open their houses upon festival days to be present, at a distance, during the reading of the contract. When Pharaoh or the King of Nineveh passed by, I joined the loungers that followed him to the temple, the palace, or the hunting-field; where custom and etiquette prevented me from entering, I penetrated in the spirit by conversations or by the texts. I have read upon a clay cylinder the prayer which Assurbanipal addressed to Ishtar in an hour of anguish; an important and loquacious scribe has related to me the travels of an Egyptian soldier in Syria; twenty basreliefs have enabled me to be present, without personal danger, at the wars of the ancient world; at the recruitment of its armies, at their marches, their evolutions; have shown me by what energetic efforts Rameses II. triumphed over the Khita, and how an Assyrian general prepared to attack a city.

I have reproduced in Assyria the majority of the scenes described in Egypt; the reader, by comparing them together, will easily realise upon what points the civilisations of the two countries were alike, and in what respects they differed. The illustrations which accompany the text render this difference visible to all eyes. There are a great many of them, but I would have added to their number if I could. Our scholars, and even their professors, are sometimes much embarrassed when they wish to picture to themselves one of these ancient men whose history we are relating, how he dressed, what he ate, the trades and arts which he practised. These drawings by M. Faucher-Gudin will teach them more on these points than any long description. They have been executed with remarkable fidelity; it is the Egyptian and the Assyrian himself that they show us, and not those caricatures of Egyptians and Assyrians which are too often seen in our books.

G. MASPERO.

# CONTENTS.

## EGYPT.

| CHAP. | | PAGE |
|---|---|---|
| I. | THEBES AND THE POPULAR LIFE | 1 |
| II. | THE MARKET AND THE SHOPS | 17 |
| III. | PHARAOH | 37 |
| IV. | AMEN, THE GREAT GOD OF THEBES | 55 |
| V. | THE RECRUITMENT OF THE ARMY | 75 |
| VI. | LIFE IN THE CASTLE | 93 |
| VII. | ILLNESS AND DEATH | 113 |
| VIII. | THE FUNERAL AND THE TOMB | 133 |
| IX. | THE JOURNEY | 153 |
| X. | THE BATTLE | 172 |

## ASSYRIA.

| XI. | A ROYAL RESIDENCE: DUR-SARGINU | 194 |
|---|---|---|
| XII. | PRIVATE LIFE OF AN ASSYRIAN | 215 |
| XIII. | DEATH AND THE FUNERAL | 233 |
| XIV. | THE ROYAL CHASE | 252 |
| XV. | THE ROYAL AUDIENCE: PREPARING FOR WAR | 271 |
| XVI. | ASSURBANIPAL'S LIBRARY | 287 |
| XVII. | THE SCIENCE OF PRESAGES | 303 |
| XVIII. | THE WAR | 318 |
| XIX. | THE FLEET AND THE SIEGE OF A CITY | 337 |
| XX. | THE TRIUMPH | 359 |

# LIST OF ILLUSTRATIONS.

|  | PAGE |
|---|---|
| The Pool of Luxor | 2 |
| Brick-making | 3 |
| Man of the People | 6 |
| A Bastinado | 8 |
| A Woman of the People | 11 |
| Sandal | 12 |
| Collar | 12 |
| A Little Boy | 14 |
| A Young Girl | 15 |
| A Necklet for some Onions | 18 |
| Some Perfume for a Necklet | 19 |
| Sale of Perfumes—sale of Fish | 19 |
| The Fish-hooks and the purchase of a Necklet | 20 |
| Weighing the *Outnou* | 21 |
| The Pastrycook at Work | 23 |
| The Cookshop | 24 |
| The Cook roasts a Goose | 24 |
| One of the Customers in the Cookshop | 25 |
| The Barber and his Customer | 25 |
| A Shoemaker's Workshop | 26 |
| The Goldsmith at his Crucible | 27 |
| The Carpenter making Chairs | 27 |
| The Carpenter's Adze | 28 |
| Women at a Loom | 29 |
| An Egyptian Citizen | 32 |
| The House of Psarou, seen from the Street | 35 |
| Pharaoh | 38 |
| The names of Rameses II. | 42 |
| Amenophis III. and his Double | 43 |
| The Great Sphinx buried in the Sand | 51 |
| Pharaoh (Amenophis IV.) and his Escort | 53 |
| The Queen in her Chariot behind Pharaoh | 54 |
| Entrance to the Hypostyle Hall of the Temple of Amen at Karnak | 57 |

## LIST OF ILLUSTRATIONS.

|  | PAGE |
|---|---|
| The Royal Throne | 59 |
| The Granaries: Registering and Storing the Grain | 61 |
| The Ark of Amen, borne by his Priests | 64 |
| Offering Red Water to the god Amen | 67 |
| The King lassoes the Sacrificial Bull | 69 |
| The Priests throw down the Bull after the King has lassoed it | 70 |
| The King gives the Death Signal | 70 |
| Cutting up the Victim | 71 |
| The Priests bring the pieces of the Victim | 71 |
| Before the Scribes | 80 |
| The Manufacture of the Chariots | 82 |
| The Wrestling Match | 83 |
| Distribution of Weapons to the Recruits | 84 |
| Royal Cuirass | 84 |
| Shield | 84 |
| War-dance of the Archers | 85 |
| The Light Troops Marching Past | 86 |
| The Line Infantry Marching Past | 86 |
| Saluting the Prince | 86 |
| The Soldiers fetching their Rations for the Campaign | 87 |
| A Shairetana of the Guard | 88 |
| The Cattle crossing the Ford | 94 |
| An Egyptian Villa | 95 |
| A Vine: gathering the Fruit | 97 |
| Pressing the Grapes | 98 |
| The Balance for drawing Water: the *Shadouf* | 99 |
| Fishing with a Double Harpoon | 101 |
| Fowling with a Boomerang upon the Pond | 102 |
| Fishing with Nets | 103 |
| Fowling with a Net | 104 |
| Preserving the Game in Salt | 105 |
| The Valley of Apu | 107 |
| Hunting in the Desert | 109 |
| The Monsters that live in the Desert | 110 |
| A Pillow | 112 |
| The god Bisou | 112 |
| The King (Amenophis IV.) and his Family throwing Golden Collars to the People | 115 |
| Postures of Adoration before Pharaoh | 117 |
| The Scribe registering the Golden Collars | 117 |
| Slaves bearing the Jars of Wine | 117 |
| Psarou congratulated by his Family | 118 |

## LIST OF ILLUSTRATIONS.          xiii

|  | PAGE |
|---|---|
| Anubis and the Mummy of Osiris | 125 |
| A Mummy's Head in the Coffin | 127 |
| A Mummy's Head: the King Seti I., from a Photograph taken from the Corpse preserved in the Museum at Boulak | 129 |
| Wrapping up the Mummy | 130 |
| The Master of the Ceremonies reciting Prayers during the Swathing of the Mummy | 131 |
| The Mummy finished | 132 |
| The Funeral Procession: Slaves bearing Offerings | 136 |
| ,,       ,,       Carriage and passage of the Chariots | 136 |
| ,,       ,,       The Furniture | 137 |
| ,,       ,,       The Weapons and Jewels | 137 |
| ,,       ,,       The Mourners and the Priests | 138 |
| ,,       ,,       The Catafalque followed by the friends | 138 |
| ,,       ,,       The Mourners' Bark | 140 |
| ,,       ,,       The Bark of the Dead | 141 |
| ,,       ,,       The Friends' Boat striking the Sloop | 143 |
| The Funeral: the Farewells before the Door of the Hypogeum | 145 |
| The Dance of the Almahs | 148 |
| The Harpist | 149 |
| The Sycamore of Nut | 151 |
| The Judgment of the Soul at the Tribunal of Osiris | 152 |
| A Syrian Fortress | 154 |
| The Tyrian Ladders | 161 |
| A Phœnician | 164 |
| A Syrian from the North | 165 |
| An Egyptian Ship, Sailing and Rowing | 166 |
| The Egyptian Camp before Kadesh | 173 |
| The Guard at the Gate | 174 |
| Scenes in the Egyptian Camp | 175 |
| The Spies are beaten | 178 |
| Rameses holds a Council of War | 179 |
| Rameses II. in his Chariot | 180 |
| The Legion of Ptah entering the Field | 182 |
| The City of Kadesh | 185 |
| Collision of the Chariots | 187 |
| Registry of Hands cut from the Prisoners | 189 |
| Rameses II., from a photograph of the Corpse | 192 |
| The Royal Sacrifice | 197 |
| One of the Gates of Dur-Sarginu | 198 |
| Transport of the Bull | 199 |
| A Winged Bull | 200 |

xiv   LIST OF ILLUSTRATIONS.

|   | PAGE |
|---|---|
| Assyrian Houses | 201 |
| The Royal Palace of Dur-Sarginu (from Perrot and Chipiez) | 203 |
| Triumphal Gate at the Entrance to the Palace (from Place) | 204 |
| One of the Gates of the Harem at Dur-Sarginu (from Place) | 206 |
| A Bedroom in the Harem at Dur-Sarginu | 208 |
| The King's Rolling Throne carried by two men | 209 |
| The Tower of the Seven Planets at Dur-Sarginu (after Place) | 213 |
| A Slave kneading Dough | 217 |
| The South-west Wind: a bronze statuette | 219 |
| A Scribe, from the figure restored by M. Heuzey, in the Exhibition of 1889 | 223 |
| Assyrian Cylinders | 226 |
| Death and Hell | 242 |
| Chaldean Coffin in Baked Earth | 244 |
| Round Chaldean Tomb | 245 |
| Interior of a Chaldean Tomb | 246 |
| Hunting the Wild Ass | 255 |
| Assurbanipal and his Suite | 255 |
| The King crosses the Stream in a Boat, the Horses swim behind | 256 |
| Foot Soldiers blowing out their Swimming Skins | 257 |
| Crossing the River upon the Swollen Skins | 257 |
| The Royal Tent | 258 |
| The Royal Stable | 258 |
| The King kills the Auroch with his Poignard | 260 |
| The King giving thanks to the goddess Ishtar for his sport | 261 |
| The Dog used for hunting the Lions | 264 |
| The King shoots an Arrow at the Lion whilst in full gallop | 265 |
| Death of the Lioness | 265 |
| The Wounded Lion | 266 |
| The King kills the Lion with his Lance | 266 |
| The Lion attacks the Royal Boat | 267 |
| The Lion taken back to the Camp | 268 |
| The Lion leaving its Cage | 269 |
| Fragment of an Assyrian Embroidery, from a bas-relief reproduced by Layard | 273 |
| The King's Necklet | 275 |
| An Assyrian Sword | 276 |
| The King in his State Costume | 276 |
| The King upon his Throne | 277 |
| An Elamite Nobleman | 279 |
| Gistubar Strangling a Lion in his Arms | 302 |
| An Assyrian Standard | 323 |
| Assyrian Cavalry charging | 324 |

## LIST OF ILLUSTRATIONS.

XV

|   | PAGE |
|---|---|
| The Assyrian Cavalry fighting in a Mountainous Country | 325 |
| Elamite War-chariot | 326 |
| Elamite Archers | 327 |
| The City of Susa | 327 |
| The remnant of the Elamite Army thrown into the River | 329 |
| Death of Teumman | 331 |
| Reception and Registration of the Heads | 332 |
| Teumman's Head carried through the Assyrian Camp | 333 |
| The Elamite Musicians marching to meet the Assyrians | 334 |
| The Assyrian General presents Ummanigas to the Elamites | 335 |
| Prisoners going to Assyria | 336 |
| A Phœnician Galley | 340 |
| Hea, the Fish-god | 343 |
| An Encounter between the Assyrians and the Inhabitants of the Marshes | 344 |
| A Family of the Chaldeans taking Shelter in the Reeds | 345 |
| The Towers with their extra Defences | 348 |
| Prisoners impaled by the Assyrians | 349 |
| Entrenched Camp of the Assyrians | 350 |
| Three Tents in an Assyrian Camp | 350 |
| The Assyrian Slingers | 351 |
| The Archers behind their Bucklers | 352 |
| The Siege of a City | 352 |
| The Battering Rams opening the Breach in the Wall | 355 |
| Scenes from a Siege | 356 |
| The Assyrians felling Trees in an Enemy's Country | 357 |
| A Griffon in the Egyptian style | 362 |
| The Horses being led past | 363 |
| A Camel and his Drivers | 363 |
| A Prisoner being flayed alive | 367 |
| The King's Guests at Table | 369 |
| Slaves bringing Fruit | 370 |
| Slaves bringing Wine, Cakes, and Fruit | 371 |
| The Cup-bearers taking the Wine from the Large Bowl | 371 |
| The Sentinels, Cup in hand | 372 |
| Assurbanipal drinking with the Queen in the Gardens of the Harem | 373 |

# ERRATA.

Page 135, line 16, *for* Canoptic *read* canopic.
Page 135, line 19, *for* cynophelus *read* cynocephalus.
Page 136, line 16, *for* Canoptic *read* canopic.
Page 147, line 22, *for* Canoptic *read* canopic.
Page 164, lines 35 and 36, *for* Acheans and Daneans *read* Achæans and Danaäns.
Page 167, line 30, *for* Acheans and Daneans *read* Achæans and Danaäns.
Page 168, line 11, *for* Tyrinthe and Mycenea *read* Tyrinthé and Mycenæ.
Page 171, line 9, *for* Dardenians *read* Dardanians.

XVIII

# LIFE IN ANCIENT EGYPT AND ASSYRIA.

## CHAPTER I.

### THEBES AND THE POPULAR LIFE.

The suburbs—The mud houses—Brick-making and the construction of houses—The furniture of the poor—Thieves and the urban police—The family: the man and the handicrafts—The scribe and his chances of fortune—The administrative formulas—The woman and her household: water, bread, fuel—The children at home and at school: their respect for the mother.

THOSE parts of Thebes which extend over the banks of the Nile between Luxor and Karnak present the dull, sordid aspect which, as a rule, belongs to the suburbs of a great city. They are not regularly formed districts, so much as a collection of grey huts, joined, together at every imaginable angle. Narrow, crooked paths wind amongst them, as though left there by chance, broken at intervals, by a muddy pool, from which the cattle drink and the women draw water (Fig. 1); by an irregular square shaded by acacias or sycamores; by a piece of waste land encumbered by filth, for which the dogs of the neighbourhood dispute with hawks and vultures. Most of the houses are miserably built of earth or unbaked bricks, covered with a layer of mud. The poorest of them consist of a simple square cell, sometimes of two little rooms opening directly into each other, or separated by a small court. They are covered by a thin roof of palm-leaves placed side by side, which is so low that a man of medium height, rising incautiously, would pierce it with a blow from his head. The richer inhabitants have a solidly built ground-floor, surmounted by a terrace and two or three rooms, reached by a staircase placed against the wall of the court. The small, dark rooms below are used as stables for the cattle, sleeping-rooms for the slaves, and storerooms for the clothes and

Fig. 1.—The Pool of Luxor.

household provisions; the family live in the upper story. The roofs and floors are made of the trunks of palm-trees, simply split in two lengthwise and laid side by side, a bed of beaten earth being then spread over them.

Rain is rare in Upper Egypt, but once or twice in a century the heaven opens its cataracts, and absolute waterspouts pour for eight or ten hours upon the plain of Thebes. The slightly thatched roofs are perforated and broken in a few minutes, the terraces give way and fall into the lower story, the walls become diluted and flow away in muddy rivulets;

where populous districts were seen in the morning, uneven heaps of black paste are found in the evening, with broken beams and pieces of half-melted walls projecting here and there from the mud. Elsewhere such a catastrophe would entail utter ruin; here one or two weeks of labour suffice to repair it all. As soon as the rain has ceased, the whole population—men, women, and children—exert themselves, and hasten to draw from the rubbish the wood, provisions, and utensils that have resisted the inundation, then from the diluted mud of the old buildings they make new huts, which the sun quickly dries and cracks in all directions. Two days later no traces of the accident remain.

Fig. 2.—Brick-making.

A little more time and labour are required to rebuild the houses of the better classes. Two or three labourers go down into the nearest pool, and collect pailsful of mud from the bottom, heap it upon the bank, knead it, mix it with gravel and finely chopped straw, and press it into wooden moulds, which an assistant carries away and empties out into the sunshine. In a few hours the bricks are ready for use, and the building is commenced (Fig. 2). No one thinks of clearing the ground or of digging foundations; the people are satisfied with levelling the rubbish, and placing the first bricks loosely upon the kind of bed they have thus prepared. A fortnight later the ground-floor is closed and roofed in, the family re-enter the dwelling with their cattle, and live in it whilst the upper story is being completed. The new house is exactly like the old one, only it is built upon a higher level. Whenever an accident forces the landowners to rebuild their houses, the soil is raised several feet, and the district, as though upheaved by a perpetual movement, rises above the level of the surrounding plain. At the end of some centuries it is perched upon a regular mound, which contains the accumulated remains of all the former buildings.

There is no furniture, or at least very little, in the homes of the smaller folk. No seats or beds, but a few very low stools, some mats of rush or of fibres of the palm, with curved edges, provided with sharp prickles to keep off the scorpions and protect the sleepers from their attacks; one or two wooden chests for the linen; some large flat stones for grinding the corn; in one corner a bin made of beaten earth, which contains the corn, oil, and provisions; some tin pots, saucepans, and bowls; lastly, against one of the walls stands a small figure of a god, in enamelled stone, wood, or bronze—a kind of domestic fetish, to which a short worship is offered, and which drives away evil spirits or venomous beasts. The hearth is usually placed near the back wall; a hole is left in the roof just above it, through which the smoke escapes. It is a serious business to procure fire if no one in the neighbourhood has a light or will give one; it is then necessary to strike two pieces of flint together until a spark is obtained, which sets light to a heap of dry leaves or fibres prepared beforehand. The women, therefore, always leave some fuel smouldering beneath the ashes, which can be easily fanned by the hand or revived by the breath. The fire is regularly extinguished once in every year, upon the Feast of the Dead, or again when any member of the family dies; the new flame is then kindled by means of a spark from the sacred fire, borrowed from the nearest temple. Furniture, utensils, linen, provisions, tools, everything that the house contains, is of so little value that most people leave the door open night and day, even if they absent themselves for a long time: their poverty defies theft. Those who have something to lose guard their property by large wooden locks and bolts, which they secure by a little mud, sealed with a stamp. To break a seal is a crime severely punished, but fear of the punishment does not always keep evildoers away. On the first of the last Epiphi, Nsisouamon was robbed by a band of thieves who are still undetected, but he suspects that they came from the workyard of the master-mason, Nakhtmout. They entered his house whilst he was at his business, and took from it two large household loaves, as well as three votive cakes, which were piled in a corner; then perceiving the flasks of scented oil, which they could not easily dispose of, they broke them, pouring the contents out upon the floor from pure malice. They then attacked the bin, and took two pots of the fruit of the jujube-tree. When Nsisouamon returned home in the evening he discovered the theft, made a formal complaint, and left it to the police to detect and punish the culprits. But he reckoned, so they say, without his host. The captain of the Libyan soldiers, the Maaziou, who is entrusted with the supervision of the district, has married Nakhtmout's sister and feels no inclination to quarrel with his brother-in-law. The robbers, sure of their impunity, determined to punish Nsisouamon for having dared to complain. The 13th Epiphi is a day of solemn festival in honour of the deceased Pharaoh, Amenophis III.; the workshops were closed, the shops shut, the workpeople had a general holiday, and Nsisouamon took advantage of his leisure to pass the afternoon with his father. The scoundrels entered his shop and stole three great loaves, eight cakes, and a plateful of macaroons; they then poured the palm brandy into the beer to make it turn sour.

The poor man is ruined, and heaven only knows what would have become of him if his masters had not come to his assistance, and out of their own money refunded to him all that he had lost.

Although polygamy is authorised by law, the men of the lower classes and the small tradespeople have only one wife, who is frequently their own sister or one of their nearest relations. The family is very united, but the husband rarely stays at home during the day; his trade necessitates his absence. He leaves very early in the morning, at sunrise, barefooted, bareheaded, or merely wearing an old felt cap which tightly fits his skull, his only garment a pair of cotton drawers which scarcely fall below his hips (Fig. 3). He carries his food with him—two cakes of dhoura, baked under the ashes, one or two onions, sometimes a little oil in which to dip his bread, sometimes a morsel of dried fish. Towards noon the work stops for an hour or two, which is used for eating and sleeping; it ceases entirely at sunset. Each trade has its disadvantages, which the poet enumerates in the following lines:—'I have seen the blacksmith at his work in the heat of his forge; he has the fingers of a crocodile, and is black as fishspawn. The artisans of all kinds that handle the chisel, have they more rest than the peasant? Their fields are the wood they shape, their profession is the metal; even in the night they are called, and they work again after their labour of the day; even in the night their house is lighted up and they are awake. The stonemason seeks his work in every kind of hard stone. When he has completed his orders and his hands are tired, does he rest? He must be in the workyard at sunrise, even if his knees and spine break with his toil. The barber shaves even

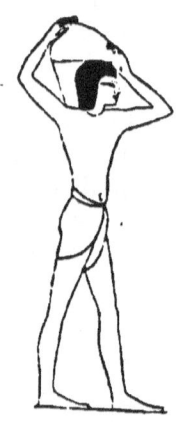

Fig. 3.—Man of the People.

in the night; to be able to eat, to be able to lie down, he must go from district to district searching for customers; he must overwork himself, as well as his two hands, to fill his belly: thus the honey is eaten only by those who make it. The dyer, his fingers stink with the odour of decayed fish, his two eyes ache with weariness, his hand never ceases renewing pieces of stuff, until he detests the sight of stuff. The shoemaker is very miserable, and is for ever complaining; his health is like that of a dead fish, and he has nothing to eat but his leather.'

The wages, so laboriously earned, just suffice to maintain the family. They are usually paid in kind—a few bushels of corn, measured by a parsimonious hand, a few measures of oil, some salt provisions, and, on festival days, one or two jars of wine or beer. The overseers bear a stick as their insignia, and use it freely. 'Man has a back,' says the proverb, 'and only obeys when it is beaten.' It was the stick that built the Pyramids, dug out the canals, won victories for the conquering Pharaohs; it is now building the temple of Amen, and aids the artisans of every trade to manufacture the linen, jewels, and valuable furniture which constitute the wealth of Egypt, and for which foreigners compete at high prices in the markets of Asia, Africa, and distant Europe. It has, therefore, entered so completely into the daily life of the people, that it is looked upon as an inevitable evil. Small and great, all are equal before it, from Pharaoh's minister to the least of his slaves; and it is a phenomenon worthy of admiration and of quotation in an epitaph, if any one, even of the nobility, have lived all the years of his life 'without being once beaten before a magistrate' (Fig. 4). The workman, resigned beforehand, patiently labours under the rod that threatens him, with intelligence, even with gaiety. His mind is naturally lively and his repartee quick; he instinctively seizes the pleasant side of things, and knows how to give a piquant turn to his slightest witticisms. The smallest incident in the day's work—an awkward apprentice cutting his finger, a comrade sleeping over his task whom the overseer lashes to awaken him, an ass suddenly braying in the quiet street outside—anything serves as a pretext for amusement: laughter breaks the silence, then tongues chatter, scoffs and merry jokes pass round, the stick vainly interferes, at least an hour elapses before quiet is re-established.

The writer, the scribe, escapes these discomforts, at least so he boasts. 'There is nothing like being a

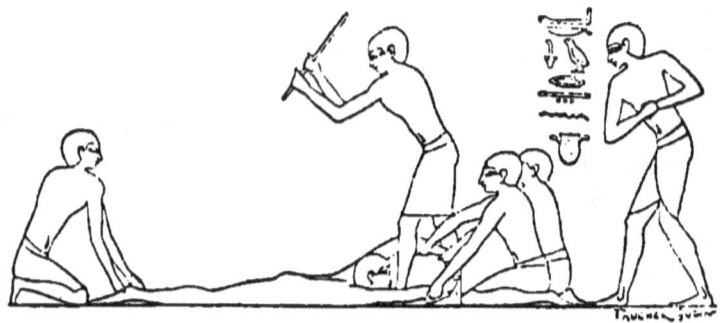

Fig. 4.—The Bastinado.

scribe,' the wise say; 'the scribe gets all that is upon the earth.' But we must not be dazzled by this assertion, or always expect those who boast of learning to be skilful authors in verse or prose—wealthy, influential personages. No doubt there are some scribes of very high rank. Prince Amenhiounamif, the eldest son of Pharaoh, the designated successor to the throne, and his brothers are all scribes. Nakhtminou, the hereditary lord of Akhmim, is a scribe; so is also Baknikhonsou, the high priest of Theban Amen, and the greatest religious dignitary of the kingdom. But so are Thotimhabi, whom the architect Amenmosou employs to register the workmen in the building-yard every morning; Hori, who passes his days in counting heads of cattle and entering the numbers in his books; Ramisou, the keeper of the accounts to the master-carpenter Tinro; Nofirronpit, who runs about drawing up petitions or writing notes for illiterate people who require such aid—these are all scribes, and they bear the same title as the son of the sovereign or the most powerful barons of the kingdom. The scribe is simply a man who knows how to read and write, to draw up administrative formulas, and to calculate interest. The instruction which he has received is a necessary complement of his position if he belongs to a good family, whilst if he be poor it enables him to obtain a lucrative situation in the administration or at the house of a wealthy personage.

There is, therefore, no sacrifice which the smaller folk deem too great, if it enables them to give their sons the acquirements which may raise them above the common people, or at least ensure a less miserable fate. If one of them, in his infancy, displays any intelligence, they send him, when about six or eight years old, to the district school, where an old pedagogue teaches him the rudiments of reading, writing, and arithmetic. Towards ten or twelve years old, they withdraw him from the care of this first teacher and apprentice him to a scribe in some office, who undertakes to make him a *learned scribe*. The child accompanies his master to the office or workyard, and there passes entire months in copying letters, circulars, legal documents, or accounts, which he does not at first understand, but which he faithfully remembers. There are books for his use full of copies taken from well-known authors, which he studies perpetually. If he requires a brief, precise report, this is how Ennana worded one of his:—' I reached Elephantine, and accomplished my mission. I reviewed the infantry and the chariot soldiers from the temples, as well as the servants and subordinates who are in the houses of Pharaoh's l. h. s.* officials. As my journey is for the purpose of making a report in the presence of his Majesty, l. h. s., the course of my business is as rapid as that of the Nile; you need not, therefore, feel anxious about me.' There is not a superfluous word. If, on the other hand, a petition in a poetical style be required, see how Pentoïrit asked for a holiday. 'My heart has left me, it is travelling and does not know how to return, it sees Memphis and hastens there. Would that I were in its place. I remain here, busy following my heart, which endeavours to draw me towards Memphis. I have no work in hand, my heart is tormented. May it please the god Ptah to lead me to Memphis, and do thou grant that I may be seen walking there. I am at leisure, my heart is watching, my heart is no longer in my bosom, languor has seized my limbs; my eye is dim, my ear hardened, my voice feeble, it is a failure of all my strength. I pray thee remedy all this.'

The pupil copies and recopies, the master inserts forgotten words, corrects the faults of spelling, and draws on the margin the signs or groups unskilfully traced. When the book is duly finished and the apprentice can write all the formulas from memory, portions of phrases are detached from them, which he must join together, so as to combine new formulas; the master then entrusts him with the composition of a few letters, gradually increasing the number and adding to the difficulties. As soon as he has fairly mastered the ordinary daily routine his education is ended, and an unimportant post is sought for. He obtains it and then marries, becoming the head of a family, sometimes before he is twenty years old; he has no further ambition, but is content to vegetate quietly in the ob-

* *L. h. s.* **is the abbreviation of the words life, health, strength (in Egyptian,** *onkhou, ouza, sonbou*), **always placed as a wish after the name and titles of Pharaoh.**

scure circle where fate has thrown him. His children will follow in the path that he has traced for them, and their children after them; in certain administrations there are whole dynasties of scribes, the members of one family having succeeded to the same posts for a century or more. Sometimes one of them, more intelligent or more ambitious than the others, makes an effort to rise above the usual mediocrity; his good writing, happy choice of words, activity, obligingness, and honesty—perhaps, on the other hand, his prudent dishonesty—attract the attention of his superiors and secure his advancement. Cases have been seen of the son of a peasant or of a poor citizen, commencing by booking the delivery of bread or vegetables in some provincial office, and ending, after a long and industrious career, by governing one half of Egypt. The rooms of his barns overflow with corn; his storehouses are full of gold, valuable stuffs, and precious vases; his stable 'multiplies the backs' of his oxen, and the son of his first protector dare only approach him with his face bent to the ground, dragging himself upon his knees.

The Egyptian woman of the lower and middle classes is more respected and more independent than any other woman in the world. As a daughter, she inherits from her parents an equal share with her brothers; as a wife, she is the real mistress of the house, *nibit pi*, her husband being, so to speak, merely her privileged guest. She goes and comes as she likes, talks to whom she pleases without any one being able to question her actions, goes amongst men with an uncovered face, a rule quite opposed to the habits of the Syrian women, who are always more or less strictly veiled. She is dressed

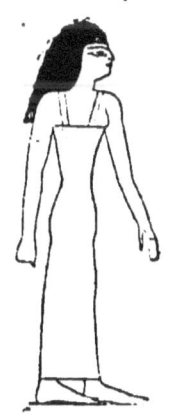

Fig. 5.—A Woman of the People.

in a short smock-frock, very narrow and clinging to her body; it only reaches her ankles and leaves the upper part of the bosom uncovered, being held in place by braces over the shoulders (Fig. 5). The forehead, chin, and breasts are covered with delicate and indelible tattooing, the lips are rouged, the eyes surrounded by a black band, which is lengthened on the temples almost to the hair. The powder used for this adornment is a mixture of antimony and finely powdered charcoal, which heightens the whiteness of the complexion, gives brilliancy to the eyes, and protects them from ophthalmia; the use of it is hygienically beneficial and coquetry

Fig. 6.—Sandal.

Fig. 7.—Collar.

also finds it advantageous. The hair, greased, oiled, and sometimes dyed blue, falls upon the shoulders and neck in very fine tresses, which terminate in balls of earth; since this arrangement requires several hours' work to complete it properly, the hair is not often dressed, once in every ten or twelve days, once a month, or even less frequently. The feet, arms, and neck are bare, but on festival days a pair of sandals, made of papyrus-leaves or of leather (Fig. 6), glass bracelets on the wrists and ankles, a large collar of beads or of tubes of enamelled faïence (Fig. 7), a fillet, and a flower on the forehead, complete the costume and correct the too great simplicity of ordinary days.

In truth, the woman is the mainspring that keeps

the whole household in movement. She rises at daybreak, lights the fire, distributes the bread for the day, sends the men to the workshop, the cattle to pasture under the care of the smallest boys and of the girls, then, once rid of her family, she goes out in her turn to the water supply. She descends to the river, canal, or nearest pool, exchanges with her friends the news of the night, washes, as she chats, her feet, hands, and body, fills her jar, and slowly reascends to her home, her loins bent, her chest forward, her neck straightened by the weight. As soon as she reaches the house she changes her trade of water-carrier for that of baker. She scatters a few handfuls of grain upon an oblong stone, which has a slightly concave slanting surface, and then crushes them with a smaller stone, shaped like a pestle, which she damps from time to time. For an hour or more she labours with arms, shoulders, loins, the whole body; the effort is great, the result very mediocre. The flour, several times repassed over the mortar, is uneven, rough, mixed with bran and whole grain, which have escaped from the grinding, dust, and splinters of stone. Such as it is the housewife kneads it with a little water, mixes with it, by way of leaven, a piece of stale paste kept from the previous day, and makes it into round cakes, as thick as a thumb and about six inches in diameter, which she spreads upon flat stones and covers with hot ashes. Wood is too rare and too dear for her to procure; she, therefore, replaces it by a fuel of her own manufacture. The dung of her live stock, with that of asses, oxen, and sheep collected by the children from outside, is vigorously stirred like an ordinary paste, and she then forms it into clods or bricks, which she stands against the outer walls of the house or places in the court, so that they may dry in the sun. This doubtful substance burns slowly, almost without smoke, with a light flame and a fairly strong smell of ammonia; it gives out a great deal of heat before it falls into ashes. The bread, slightly risen, often undercooked, retains a special flavour and a sour taste, to which strangers find it difficult to accustom themselves. The impurities which it contains at last triumph over the strongest teeth : one grinds rather than munches, and many old men have worn their teeth down to the gums, like horses.

In spare moments the woman cooks, spins, weaves, sews, cuts out and mends the clothes, goes to market to sell her poultry, eggs, butter, and the linen she has woven—doing all this without neglecting the little ones who cry, or the newborn infant that she is nursing. Usually married very young, a mother before she is fifteen, frequently a grandmother at thirty, children are always multiplying and swarming round her. A large family is a blessing from the gods, which is welcomed with gratitude, partly because its keep is inexpensive. There is no question of costume ; boys and girls sometimes wear a bracelet on the wrist or an amulet round the neck, as well as a thick tress of hair falling over one ear, but they remain unconsciously nude until puberty (Figs. 8 and 9). As soon as they can walk the mother employs them in little ways, sends them out to pick up dry branches and herbs, or to collect in baskets the materials for the fuel ; she entrusts them with the care of driving the geese to feed, and finally allows them to take the cattle to pasture and to drink. As soon as they are six or eight years old she sends them to school or makes them learn a trade, usually that of the father. Many never get so far, but die in infancy. Badly fed, indifferently cared for, abandoned to themselves for entire days, those who have any weak points in their constitutions die one after the other. The most nume-

Fig. 8.—A Little Boy.

rous families are, usually, but the remnants of still larger numbers. But, at least, those who survive are endowed with good health that resists every shock. The Egyptian people, weeded, so to speak, by this natural operation, contains only vigorous individuals, of robust, sturdy beauty, who can endure pain and fatigue. It includes few of those infirm, crooked, and ill-made creatures who swarm in other countries: ophthalmia is the only malady it has to dread. The action of the fine sand, with which the atmosphere is saturated, the insupportable glare of light, the influence of the serene nights and of the fogs which rise in the mornings, produce, amongst the labourers and city workmen, a number of eye diseases, which the doctors cannot always cure, so that the streets are full of the one-eyed and the blind, of red and purulent eyelids.

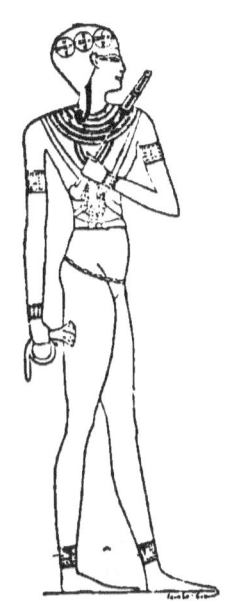

Fig. 9.—A Young Girl.

The woman of the lower classes fades rapidly through her work and fecundity; her face becomes hollow and wrinkled, her bust ill-shaped, her form bent. She is already decrepit at an age when other women are scarcely elderly. Her position in the family does not suffer in any way from this early deterioration: to the end she is 'the beloved of her husband' and the mistress of the house. The children display their affinity by her name rather than by that of the father. They are Khonshotpou, Ahmosou, Nouhri, born of Mrs. Banisit or Mrs. Mîmout, and not Khonshotpou, Ahmosou, Nouhri, sons of Mr. Nibtooui or of Mr. Khâmoïsit. The divinities themselves set a good example to men on this point, and the young Horus is styled Harsiîsit, Horus son of Isis, without any allusion to Osiris. The father, when necessary, encourages and reanimates by his counsels the children's affection for their mother. 'It is God himself who gave her to thee,' says one of them, the sage Khonshotpou to his son Ani. 'From the beginning she has borne a heavy burden with thee, in which I have been unable to help her. When thou wast born, she really made herself thy slave. During three years she nursed thee at her breast, and as thy size increased her heart never once allowed her to say, "Why should I do this?" She went with thee to school, and whilst thou wert learning thy letters, she placed herself near to thy master, every day, with bread and beer from her house. And now that thou art grown up, and hast a wife and a house in thy turn, remember always thine helpless infancy and the care which thy mother lavished upon thee, so that she may never have occasion to reproach thee, nor to raise her hands to heaven against thee, for God would fulfil her curse.'

# CHAPTER II.

## THE MARKET AND THE SHOPS.

The middle-class quarters of Thebes—The market: sale by exchange or the weights of metals—The bazaars and shops—The confectioner, the cook-shops, the itinerant barber—The shoemaker—The goldsmith—The carpenter—The weavers, the curriers, the potter—The beer-house and its customers—Appearance of the crowd—The masons' strike—Psarou, count of Thebes, and his house—The arrival of Pharaoh.

PEOPLE and houses, the whole aspect of both changes as we penetrate further into the heart of the city. The streets are neither wider nor straighter, but the buildings are more carefully constructed; they are more regular, and so high that, from below, the sky looks like a simple luminous band between two dark lines. It is evident, from a thousand indications, that the population is rich, or at all events very comfortably off, but it conceals its wealth instead of displaying it. The sides of the houses that face the street are dingy and silent. The outer windows are rare and highly placed, the doors are low and carefully closed; when one of them stands ajar the curious can only see through the opening the end of a dark passage, or the first steps of a staircase lost in shadow. A dog barks, a child cries in a distant chamber, a voice issuing from some unknown spot breaks the silence for an instant; two passers-by exchange a salutation, poor little asses, laden with straw, trot nimbly by under the driver's stick. Here, however, one house projects over the street and

C

joins the house opposite: we must grope the way for about twenty or thirty steps in a kind of suffocating tube, and then suddenly emerge into the full sunshine of a noisy little square, where a market is being held. Sheep, geese, goats, asses, large-horned oxen, scattered in unequal groups in the centre, are awaiting a purchaser. Peasants, fishermen, small retail dealers, squat several deep in front of the houses, displaying before them, in great rush baskets or on low tables, loaves or pastry, fruit, vegetables, fish, meat raw or cooked, jewels, perfumes, stuffs, all the necessities and all the superfluities of Egyptian life.

The customers stroll past and leisurely examine the quality of the commodities offered for sale; each carries something of his own manufacture in his hand —a new tool, some shoes, a mat, or a small box full of rings of copper, silver, even of gold, of the weight of an *outnou*,\* which he proposes to barter for the objects he requires. Two customers stop at the same moment in front of a fellah, who exhibits onions and wheat in a basket. Instead of money, the first holds two necklets of glass or of many-coloured earthenware, the second a round fan with a wooden handle, and one of those triangular ventilators which the cooks use to quicken the fire. 'Here is a beautiful necklet which will please you, this is what you want,' cries the former; whilst the latter urges, 'Here is a fan and a ventilator.' However, the fellah, quite unmoved by this double

Fig. 10.—A Necklet for some Onions.

* The average weight of an *outnou* is $2\frac{67}{625}$ ounces or 91 grammes according to Mr. Chabas.

attack, methodically proceeds to first seize a string of the beads for closer examination. 'Let me see it, that I may fix a price' (Fig. 10). The one asks too much, the other too little; from concession to concession they finally come to terms, and settle the number of onions or the weight of corn which the necklet or fan may be worth. Elsewhere (Fig. 11), it is a question of bartering a pair of sandals or a row of enamelled beads for some perfume. 'Here,' urges the buyer, 'is a very strong pair of shoes.'

Fig. 11.—Some Perfume for a Necklet.

But the seller does not require shoes for the moment, so he offers one of his small pots in exchange for a row of beads. 'It is delicious when a few drops are poured

Fig. 12.—Sale of Perfumes—sale of Fish.

out,' he explains, with a persuasive air. A woman thrusts under the nose of a kneeling individual two jars, probably containing some ointment of her own manufacture (Fig. 12). 'Here,' she cries, 'it smells sweet enough to entice thee.' Behind this group two men are discussing the value of a packet of fish-hooks (Fig. 13); a woman, box in hand, is a vendor of bracelets and necklets; another woman endeavours to obtain a reduction upon the price of a fish, which is being dressed before her.

When it is a question of a large animal, or of objects of considerable value, the accounts become intricate. For instance, Ahmosou sells a bull for a mat, five measures of honey, eleven measures of oil, and seven objects of different kinds. Now, imagine the calcula-

Fig. 13.—The Fish-hooks and the Purchase of a Necklet.

tions which must have been made before he succeeded in establishing such a complicated balance. Besides, the value in metal of each article was carefully noted, and is mentioned in the bill.* The mat was estimated at 25 *outnou*, the honey at 4, the oil at 10, and so on, the whole weighing 119 *outnou*, which is not too dear

* Twenty-five *outnou* equal 91 × 25 = 2275 grammes; 4 *outnou*, 91 × 4 = 364 grammes; 10 *outnou*, 91 × 10 = 910 grammes; 119 *outnou*, 91 × 119 = 10,829 grammes in weight, and, without alloy, 14,378 grammes, equal to about 143 francs 78 centimes, or 5*l.* 15*s.* in copper money. By repeating this calculation for each figure indicated later on, the value of objects computed in *outnou* of gold, silver, or copper is easily ascertained.

## THE MARKET AND THE SHOPS.

for a beast in good condition.* This custom of payment by one of the usual metals is so convenient, and dispenses with so many calculations, that it has been adopted even for the minor transactions of daily life. The butcher, the baker, the corn-chandler, all the small tradesmen prefer exchange for metal, which is of small compass and does not spoil, to exchange for objects, often bulky in size, which are liable to deteriorate if kept too long in the house. A pair of ducks is worth a quarter of an *outnou* in copper; a fan, a quarter; a bronze razor is worth a whole *outnou;* a pickaxe, two ; a goat, two ; an ox-head, half an *outnou* in silver ; a leather bottle of fine wine, three *outnou* of gold. It is true that often the rings or twisted wires which represent the *outnou* and its multiples do not contain the reputed quantity of gold or silver, and are too light. They are then weighed at every fresh market (Fig. 14). The parties interested take advantage of the excuse for quarrelling loudly; when they have declaimed, for about a quarter of an hour, that the scales are false, that the weight has been badly taken and should be tried over again, they get tired of war, come to an agreement, and go away quite satisfied with each other. The evil is more serious when too intelligent and too unscrupulous individuals falsify the precious metals, and introduce as much copper into the ingots as they can contain without detection. The honest trader who thinks that

Fig. 14.—Weighing the *Outnou*.

* This bill has been preserved upon a fragment of pottery (*ostracon*) in the British Museum.

he receives, let us say, eight *outnou* of fine gold, and upon whom are foisted eight *outnou* of an alloy exactly resembling gold, but which contains only two-thirds of it, then unconsciously loses one-third of his merchandise.

But for this danger of fraud, which every one naturally dreads, exchange for metal would have already superseded barter for miscellaneous objects. It will become the universal custom as soon as some method can be discovered which will free the public from the necessity of continual weighing, and will guarantee the purity of the ingots.*

Two or three commercial streets or bazaars open from the other side of the square, and the crowd hastens towards them when it leaves the market. Nearly their whole length is filled with stalls and shops, in which not only Egypt, but the majority of the oriental nations display their most varied productions. Beautifully ornamented stuffs from Syria, Phœnician or Hittite jewellery, scented woods and gums from Punt and the Holy Lands;† lapis and embroideries from Babylon; coral, gold, iron, tin, and amber‡ from far-distant countries beyond the seas, are found scattered pell-mell amongst the native fine linen, jewels, glass-work, and furniture. The shop is usually independent from the rest of the house, and is let separately. It is a small, square room, often a simple shed, widely open in front, and closed every evening by means of wooden shutters, held in place by cross-bars; with one or two mats, one or two low stools, some shelves fixed to the wall, which hold the goods;

---

\* This method was discovered in the early part of the seventh century before our era, some say by the kings of Lydia, others by Phido of Argos. By putting a stamp upon the ingots, an official mark which guaranteed the weight and value, the Lydians or the Greeks transformed them into pieces of money.

† Southern Arabia, the African coasts of the Red Sea and the land of the Somalis.

‡ I have found a fair quantity of amber beads in the tombs of the Ancient and Middle Empire, which I excavated in Abydos.

## THE MARKET AND THE SHOPS.

perhaps behind the shop one or two carefully closed rooms where the most valuable objects are stored. Most of the tradesmen are also manufacturers. They have apprentices or workmen who work for them, and they join them during the intervals between their sales. The handicraft they ply has no secrets which a curious customer may not see if he feel so inclined. Artisans of the same trade have usually a natural tendency to collect together, to dwell side by side in the same place—blacksmiths with blacksmiths, curriers with curriers, goldsmiths with goldsmiths, forming a small city in which objects of the same kind only are found: here the shops are of all kinds, and follow each other without any particular order.

The two which occupy the corner of the square belong, the one on the right to a confectioner, the other on the left to a cook. It is noon, the time for dinner and afterwards for the siesta; the crowd hurries towards them. Whilst the confectioner spreads out his preserved dates, syrups, and pastry made of honey and spices, his assistants at the back are pounding almonds and pistachio nuts in a mortar (Fig. 15), decanting and filtering mysterious liquids, and preparing as difficult combinations as those of a doctor making up a medicine. Over the way the cook and his waiters are quite inadequate to satisfy the requirements of their customers.

Fig. 15.—The Pastrycook at Work.

Quarters of geese, portions of beef, stews, vegetables, the patient work of the whole morning, only appear in order to disappear. Fortunately extra supplies are at hand; pieces of raw meat hang from the ceiling, awaiting their turn to enter the scene of action (Fig. 16). Two saucepans, full to overflowing,

Fig. 16.—The Cookshop.

are just boiling, and a cook is roasting a goose, which he holds upon a spit over the fire with his left hand, whilst he quickens the flame with a ventilator held in his right hand (Fig. 17). Some of the customers carry their purchases away, after they have paid for them, for the family dinner in their own houses. Others prefer to eat them on the spot. A citizen (Fig. 18), seated upon a stool, draped in his mantle, is prepared for a good meal, if we may judge of his appetite by the amount of food placed before him. A barber, roaming about the neighbourhood, has at last found a customer amongst all these diners, and is rapidly shaving his head before satisfying his own

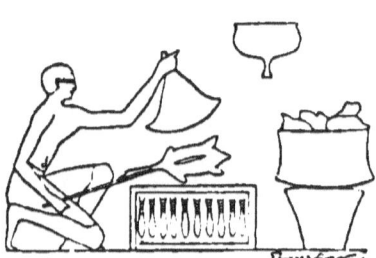

Fig. 17.—The Cook roasts a Goose.

hunger (Fig. 19). A shoemaker lives next to the confectioner, a goldsmith to the shoemaker, a carpenter to the goldsmith. The shoemaker appears to have the largest connexion, for he keeps four workmen continually employed (Fig. 20). One of them has fetched a skin from the back of the shop, and has cut it into bands of the width of a man's foot, which he lays upon a high bench, in order to make them supple and pliable by tapping them with a hammer. The three others, each seated before a low, sloping work-bench, upon which their tools are laid, work hard, whilst their master bargains with his customers. They do not make fancy shoes, sandals with curved points and many-coloured bands, high-heeled Turkish slippers, or soft leather shoes lacing in front, but footgear for use and hard work. This usually consists of a strong sole, shaped in a general way to the form of the foot. It has two ears at the back, through which pass leathern thongs; a third thong fixed between the great and the second toes is fastened to the two others over the instep. The workman in the centre pierces one of the ears with his awl, the one on the left bores through the sandal, and the one on the right draws the strap with his teeth to get it into place. Looking at them, one understands why the satirist said of the working shoemaker 'that he had only leather to

Fig. 18.—One of the Customers in the Cookshop.

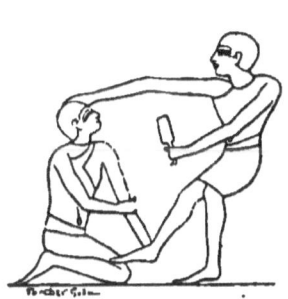

Fig. 19.—The Barber and his Customer.

cat.'* Sandals cut out, but not finished, hang against the wall, with half-a-dozen skins; but one single pair is entirely completed and ready for sale.

The goldsmith occupies less space than his neighbour, the shoemaker. A small anvil, some pincers, some hammers, a furnace with a reflector, and, as assistant, one single apprentice. A few dozen rings, some earrings, and bracelets in copper or in bad silver are laid out for show, but the valuable jewels are safely placed in a chest at the back of the shop, far from the eyes of the crowd, and, above all, far from its hands. The gold arrives in nuggets, in packets of a given weight, from the heart of Africa, where the

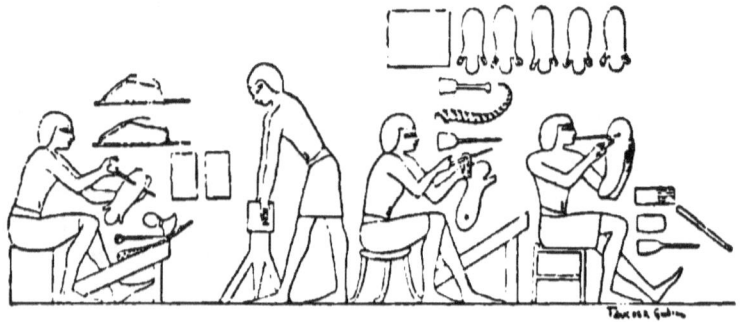

Fig. 20.—A Shoemaker's Workshop.

negroes collect it from the sand of the rivers; in bars and rings from Syria, or the deserts which separate the Nile from the Red Sea. Silver and *electrum*, that natural alloy which contains twenty parts of silver to eighty of gold, are brought by the Phœnicians and Ethiopians. Green (*mafkait*) and red stones, emeralds, jasper, olivine, garnets, rubies, cornelian, are found in Egypt itself. The lapis-lazuli is imported by Chaldean merchants from the unknown and almost fabulous regions bordered by Elam. Here a young woman has just given a slab of electrum to the goldsmith, and

* See on page 7 the passage in which this allusion is made.

she is waiting, chatting the whole time, whilst he converts it into a bracelet. He first carefully weighs the metal, then throws it into the fire. Seated before the crucible, his pincers in one hand, he quickens the flame by means of a blowpipe to hasten the fusion, or rather the softening, of the electrum (Fig. 21). As soon as the metal is hot enough, he withdraws it from the fire, beats it upon the anvil, reheats it, rebeats it, and finally reduces it to the desired thickness and length. He then bends it with a single movement, and rounds it until the two extremities meet, rapidly solders them, cleans his work with sand, pours a jar of water over it to cool it, and polishes it with his hand. This takes him at least an hour, during

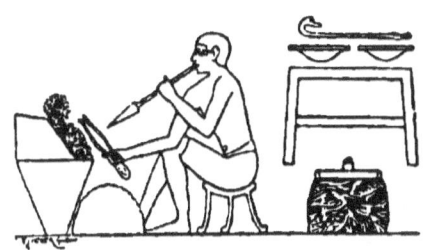

Fig. 21.—The Goldsmith at his Crucible.

Fig. 22.—The Carpenter making Chairs.

which time he has been disturbed perhaps twenty times by requests for rings, a pair of earrings, a chain, or an ankle-ring.

The same activity reigns at the house of his neighbour, the carpenter (Fig. 22), where, at the present moment, some state chairs in inlaid wood are being made. One of them is already put together, and the workman is drilling holes in the frame to which the lattice for the seat is to be fastened. The workman opposite is less advanced in his work; he has carved the four lion's feet which are to support the seat, and is now hastening to rub them down with pumice-stone. His adze is placed upon the block of wood which furnishes him with materials. It is formed of a short blade, usually of iron, attached by a lacing of straps to a curved handle (Fig. 23). The adze is the favourite tool of the Egyptian carpenter. He uses it to cut up his wood, to shape his planks, to cut and plane them; in his hands it is worth half-a-dozen different tools in those of any foreign carpenter.

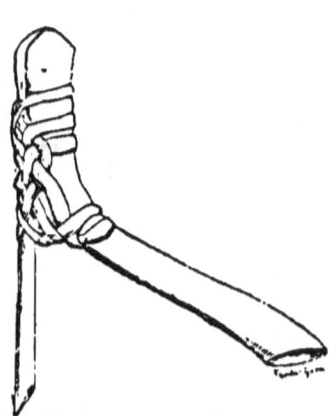

Fig. 23.—The Carpenter's Adze.

A clicking of shuttles, blended with the chattering of women, points to a room full of spinners and weavers in active work. One winds and twists the flax between her fingers, another smooths the thread, a third dresses it; two others, crouched on each side of a low loom fastened to the ground, are weaving a piece of linen (Fig. 24). A currier scrapes some skins with a paring-knife; a potter moulds some dishes in red clay; a maker of stoneware hollows and polishes the inside of a large alabaster horn with a kind of wimble. These are all honest industries which are openly plied. Further on a *beer-house* stands half-concealed at the corner of a dark alley. The Egyptian is sober as a rule, but when he allows himself 'a good day,' he never deprives himself of the pleasure of drinking, and has no objection to intoxication. The beer-house, openly frequented by some, secretly by others, always has an excellent trade; if the publicans be not as much respected as other tradesmen, they, at least, prosper well.

The reception-room has been freshly limewashed. It is furnished with mats, stools, and armchairs, upon which the habitual customers sit side by side, fraternally drinking beer, wine, palm brandy (*shodou*), cooked and perfumed liquors, which would probably seem detestable to us, but for which the Egyptians display a strong taste. The wine is preserved in

Fig. 24.—Women at a Loom.

large amphoræ, pitched outside and closed with a wooden or clay stopper, over which some mud is laid, painted blue and then stamped with the name of the owner or of the reigning Pharaoh. An inscription in ink, traced upon the jar, indicates the origin and the exact date of the wine: *The year XXIII, imported wine, The year XIX, wine of Bouto,* and so on. There is wine of every variety, white and red: wine from Mareotis, wine from Pelusium, wine *Star of Horus, master of heaven;* native growths from the Oasis, wines of Syena, without counting the wines from

Ethiopia, nor the golden wines which the Phœnician galleys bring from Syria. Beer has always been the favourite beverage of the people. It is made with a mash-tub of barley steeped in water, and raised by fermented crumbs of bread. When freshly made, it is soft and pleasant to the taste, but it is easily disturbed and soon turns sour. Most of the vinegar used in Egypt is not wine vinegar, but a vinegar made from beer. This defect is obviated by adding an infusion of lupine to the beer, which gives it a certain bitterness and preserves it. Sweet beer, *iron* beer, sparkling beer, perfumed beer, spiced beer—cold or hot, beer of thick, sticky millet, like that prepared in Nubia and amongst the negroes of the Upper Nile. The beer-houses contain stores of as many varieties of beer as of different qualities of wine.

If you enter, you are scarcely seated before a slave or a maid-servant hastens forward and accosts you: 'Drink unto rapture, let it be a good day, listen to the conversation of thy companions and enjoy thyself.' Every moment the invitation is renewed: 'Drink, do not turn away, for I will not leave thee until thou hast drunk.' The formula changes, but the refrain is always the same—*drink, drink*, and again, *drink*. The regular customers do not hesitate to reply to these invitations by jokes, usually of a most innocent kind: 'Come now, bring me eighteen cups of wine with thine own hand. I will drink till I am happy, and the mat under me is a good straw bed upon which I can sleep myself sober.'[*] They discuss together the different effects produced by wine and beer. The wine enlivens and produces benevolence and tenderness; beer makes men dull, stupefies them, and renders them liable to fall into brutal rages. A man tipsy from wine falls on his face, but any one intoxicated by beer falls and lies

---

[*] The remarks of the drinkers are taken from a scene of a funeral meal in the tomb of Ranni, at El-Kab. I have paraphrased them in order to render them intelligible to the modern reader.

on his back. The moralists reprove these excesses, and cannot find words strong enough to express the danger of them. Wine first loosens the tongue of man, even wresting from him dangerous words, and afterwards it prostrates him, so that he is no longer capable of defending his own interests. 'Do not, therefore, forget thyself in the breweries; be afraid that words may come back to thee that thou hast uttered, without knowing that thou hast spoken. When at last thou fallest, thy limbs failing thee, no one will help thee thy boon companions will leave thee, saying, "Beware of him, he is a drunkard!" Then when thou art wanted for business, thou art found prone upon the earth like a little child.' Young men especially should avoid this shameful vice, for 'beer destroys their souls.' He that abandons himself to drink 'is like an oar broken from its fastening, which no longer obeys on either side; he is like a chapel without its god, like a house without bread, in which the wall is wavering and the beam shaking. The people that he meets in the street turn away from him, for he throws mud and hoots after them,' until the police interfere and carry him away to regain his senses in prison.

Some are going to market, others coming from it; the crowd is divided into two streams of almost equal force, which meet at the street corners, blend together, or cross each other, showing, as they pass onward, a thousand varieties of costume and type. Nothing can be more mixed than the population of a great Egyptian city. Every year thousands of slaves are brought into it by the fortunes of war, its commerce attracts merchants from all quarters of the globe, and the foreign elements, perpetually absorbed in the old native population, form hybrid generations in which the features of the most opposite races are blended, and ultimately lost. Amongst twenty officers or functionaries who surround Pharaoh, perhaps ten are of Syrian, Berber, and Ethiopian origin, and Pharaoh himself has in his veins the blood of Nubian and Asiatic princesses, whom the fortunes of war have introduced into the harems of his ancestors. Dark skins predominate in the streets; Egyptian fellahs burnt by the sun and inclining towards red ochre, Nubians the colour of smoked bronze, negroes from the Upper Nile, almost nude but for the short cotton drawers round the loins; here and there a soldier of the Shairetana guard, or a Khita from the gorges of the Taurus, is rendered conspicuous amongst the surrounding crowd by his fair complexion.

Fig. 25.—An Egyptian Citizen.

Citizens, newly shaved and painted, with curled wigs, folded cloak and floating skirts, bare-footed or wearing peaked sandals, are gravely wending their way to business, a long cane in one hand (Fig. 25). A priest passes with shaven head, draped in a white mantle. A chariot, drawn by two horses leisurely makes its way through the crowd. Ladies of good family are bargaining in the shops in groups of three or four. They wear above the close-fitting smock-frock a long dress of fine linen, starched, gauffered, but almost transparent, which covers rather than veils the form.

Suddenly a great noise is heard at one end of the street, the crowd is violently opened, and about a hundred workmen, shouting, gesticulating, their bodies and faces covered with clay and mortar, force their way through, dragging in the midst of them three or four frightened, piteous-looking scribes. These are the masons employed in the new buildings of the temple of Mut, who have just gone on strike, and are now on their way to lay their grievances before Psarou, the count-governor of the city, and general superintendent of the king's

## THE MARKET AND THE SHOPS. 33

works. These small riots are not rare, they spring from misery and hunger. As we know, the greater portion of the wages consists of wheat, dhoura, oil, and rations of food, which the masters usually distribute on the first day of every month, and which ought to last until the first of the month following. The quantity allotted to each man would certainly suffice if it were economically used; but what is the use of preaching economy to people who reach home in a famished condition, after a day of hard work in which they have only eaten two cakes, seasoned with a little muddy water, about twelve o'clock? During the first days of the month, the family satisfy their hunger without sparing the provisions; towards the middle the portions diminish and complaints begin; during the last week famine ensues and the work suffers. If we consult the official registers of the scribes in the workyards, or simply the books of the overseers, we shall find notes in the end of each month of frequent idleness, and, at times, of strikes produced by the weakness and hunger of the workmen.

On the 10th of last month, the workmen employed at the temple of Mut, having nothing left, rushed from the workyard in a tumult, went to a chapel of Thothmes III. which stands near, and sat down behind it, saying, 'We are hungry, and there are still eighteen days before next month.' Is their pay insufficient, or have they eaten their supplies unreasonably quickly? According to their own accounts, the scribes give them short measure and enrich themselves by the robbery. On the other hand, the scribes accuse the poor fellows of improvidence, and assert that they squander their wages as soon as they receive them. No one could be astonished if both scribes and masons were found to be right. The malcontents were scarcely outside when the superintendent of the works hastened up, accompanied by a police officer, and began to parley with them. 'Go back, and we solemnly swear that we will ourselves lead you to Pharaoh, when he comes to inspect the works of the temple.'

Two days later Pharaoh came, and the scribe Pentoïrit went to him with the police officer. The prince, after listening to them, graciously delegated one of the scribes of his suite, and some of the priests of the temple, to have an interview with the workmen. The latter presented their request in excellent terms. 'We come, pursued by hunger, pursued by thirst; we have no more clothes, no more oil, no more fish or vegetables. Tell this to Pharaoh, our master—tell this to Pharaoh, our sovereign—that we may receive the means of living.' Pharaoh, touched by their misery, ordered fifty sacks of corn to be distributed amongst them, and this unexpected windfall enabled them to wait for the end of the month without too much suffering. The first days of Ephipi passed fairly quietly, but on the 15th the provisions fell short, and the discontent recommenced. On the 16th the men stopped work, and remained idle on the 17th and 18th. On the 19th the men endeavoured to leave the work-yard in the morning, but the scribe Pentoïrit, who overlooked them, had secretly doubled the guard, and had taken his precautions so wisely that the workmen could not get outside the gates. They passed the whole day consulting and plotting together in small groups. At last, this morning, at sunrise they assembled at the foot of an unfinished wall, and seeing the superintendent of the works coming to make his rounds they rushed towards him and surrounded him, making a great noise. Vainly he endeavoured to calm them with gentle words: they would not listen. Their shouts attracted other officials and several of the priests of Mut; the workmen immediately hastened towards them, and appealed to the superintendent to explain the matter. 'By Amen,' they said, 'by the sovereign whose rage destroys, we will not go back to work! You can tell this to your superiors, who are assembled down there.' At last, tired of protesting and of obtaining nothing, they suddenly decided to go to the Governor of Thebes, and to appeal to him for justice.

The distance is not great between the temple of Mut and the house of Psarou; ten minutes' walk through the streets, not without exchanging some blows with the crowd, which did not make way quickly enough, and the rioters have reached the gate. It opens in a long, low, crenellated wall, above which a large acacia lifts its leafy head, and it gives access to a large courtyard surrounded with buildings (Fig. 26). On the left stands the master's dwelling, built of freestone; it is narrow and bare, consisting of a rather high ground-floor, surmounted by two stories and a terrace; in the centre are two granaries for corn, rounded at the top; on the extreme right is a large vaulted cellar. The doorkeeper had put up the safety bars at the first noise, but the swing-doors yield under the strong pressure from without. The whole band simultaneously enters the court and waits there, a little uncertain what to do next. However, Psarou hurries forward, and his appearance alone suffices to impress the men, trained from infancy to bow before a master. At last one of them decides to speak; the others applaud, timidly at first, then they become excited at the tale of their sufferings. They refuse to listen when the governor endeavours to soothe them with promises. Words are no longer sufficient, they clamour loudly for actions. 'Will the overseers give us some corn in addition to the distribution already made? If not, we will not move from here.' At this moment a slave makes his way through the crowd and softly warns Psarou that Pharaoh left the

Fig. 26.—The House of Psarou, seen from the Street.

palace a quarter of an hour ago, that he is going towards the temple of Amen, and will pass the house; in fact, his escort has already reached the neighbouring street. Pharaoh coming upon a riot! Pharaoh himself hearing the workmen's complaints! Psarou rapidly decides upon his movements, and, interrupting the discussion, calls his steward, Khâmoïsit: 'See how much corn there is in the granaries and give it to the men!' Then, turning to the others: 'Go at once to the granaries with Khâmoïsit and take what he gives you.' The crowd, not knowing the motive of this sudden decision, attributes it to an impulse of natural generosity, and loudly expresses its thanks and praises. 'Thou art our father, and we are thy sons!—Thou art the old man's staff, the nurse of the children, the helper of the distressed!—Thou art a warm shelter for all who are cold in Thebes!—Thou art the head of the afflicted, that never fails the people of our land!' There is a profusion of thanks and gratitude. Psarou cuts these protestations short, hastens the departure of the men, and does not breathe freely until the last of the strikers has disappeared behind the granaries with Khâmoïsit. In five minutes the court is empty, and the street has resumed its usual appearance: Pharaoh may come.

# CHAPTER III.

### PHARAOH.

A royal costume—Pharaoh goes to the temple—Pharaoh is a god upon earth, a son of Ra—The dream of Queen Moutemouaït—The four names of Pharaoh—The double and the hawk's names—Pharaoh is adored as a god during his lifetime—His cabinet council: Rameses II. and the gold mines—The insignia of Pharaoh and his double royalty—Pharaoh is the intermediary between earth and heaven—The connexion with the gods: dream of Thothmes IV.—Pharaoh's escort and his passage through the streets.

THE king of the two Egypts, Ousirmâri-Sotpounri, son of the Sun, Ramsisou-Miamoun, who, like the sun, gives life eternally—usually called Sésousri (Sesostris) by his subjects—is anxiously expecting the arrival of a courier from Syria. The last accounts received from that country were bad. The *royal messengers* who go there every year to collect the tribute complain of being insulted, even ill-treated, by the inhabitants of the great cities; bands of the Shasu,* posted in the gorges of Lebanon, have recommenced robbing the caravans from Babylon and Khaloupou;† the princes of Zahi and Amaourou are drilling their militia and hastily repairing the walls of their fortresses; lastly, Motour, the old king of the Khita, has mysteriously disappeared in some palace revolution, and his successor, Khitasir, seems little inclined to respect treaties. Pharaoh, more anxious than he cares to own, has therefore resolved

* The Shasu are the Syrian Bedouins.
† Khaloupou is the ancient name of Khilibu, Alep.

this very morning to go to the temple of Amen, in order to see the god and to consult with him. He wears a state costume suitable to the occasion: short drawers of pleated linen gauze, ornamented at the back by a jackal's tail, and in front by a kind of stiff apron of gold and coloured enamel, a long robe of fine linen, with short sleeves, peaked sandals, a head-dress of white, striped with red, ornamented with the uræus (Fig. 27.) His equerry, Menni, waited for him in the great court of the palace, ready to drive him as usual. Rameses dismisses him with a gesture, and seizing the reins with a firm hand, he springs into the chariot. The large folding gates of the palace are at once thrown open, and the king drives through them at a gallop, or, to use the correct expression, 'shows himself under the gateway of lapis-lazuli like the sun when he rises in the morning in the eastern horizon of heaven to inundate the world with his rays.'

Fig. 27.—Pharaoh.

He is not compared to the sun without some reason for such a title. Ra, who created the world, was also the first sovereign of Egypt and the ancestor of all the Pharaohs. Since he quitted this earth for heaven his royalty was directly transmitted to the gods, from the gods to the heroes, from the heroes to Menes, and from Menes to the historic dynasties. However far back the history of the past may be traced, the genealogical chain remains unbroken between the present Rameses and the Sun; the Pharaoh is always a son of Ra, and through successive sons of

Ra we at last reach Ra himself. It is said that he sometimes condescends to come amongst us and to personally secure the direct succession of his house. Tradition relates that the three first kings of the fifth dynasty, Userkaf, Sahu-ra, and Kaka, were born from his union with the wife of a priest, in the small town of Sakhibou. Nearer to our own time, we know from authentic sources that he intervened directly in the case of Thothmes IV. to give him the son he wanted. One night when the Queen Moutemouaït was sleeping in the most beautiful room in her palace she suddenly awoke and saw her husband by her side, then a few minutes after — was it a dream, or reality? — the brilliant figure of the Theban Amen. As she cried out in alarm, the apparition predicted to her the birth of a son, who should reign over Thebes, and then vanished in a cloud of perfume sweeter and more penetrating than all the perfumes of Arabia. The child, who was afterwards Amenophis III., became famous as one of the most glorious sovereigns of his time. He killed one hundred and twelve great lions in ten years, subjugated the tribes of Ethiopia to the southern extemities of our earth, kept the Syrians, Phœnicians, Cyprus and the isles of the sea, the Khita, and all the peoples of the North, in a state of subjection, received the homage of Nineveh and Babylon, repaired the old temples of Thebes and built new ones. His funeral chapel is the most beautiful of those in the place of tombs on the left bank of the Nile, and the two granite colossi which flank its door are second in grandeur to the gigantic Sphinx of the Pyramids only.* The temple that he erected at Luxor in honour of Amen is a commemorative monument of the events that preceded his birth. A picture may still be seen, in a room

---

\* The chapel is destroyed, but the colossi are still standing. One of them, the most mutilated, is the celebrated statue of the *Memnon*, which sings at daybreak. Roman tourists went to hear the voice when they visted Thebes, during the first two centuries of our era.

adjoining the sanctuary, in which the nocturnal interview of the queen and the god is vividly represented. As a rule, the personal intervention of Ra or of one of the forms derived from him is unnecessary. The divine blood which flows in the royal veins is transmitted by natural inheritance to all his children, and if sons be lacking, daughters can transmit it; for even if the husband be the lowest of slaves, their children are born sons and daughters of Ra, and they can become kings through their mother.

In assuming the royal diadem, Pharaoh does not lose the name he received as a royal prince. He was Amenophis, Thothmes, Rameses, Harmhabi; and continues to bear the same name, adding to it an epithet, Miamoun, the beloved of Amen; Hiq-oïsit, the Regent of Thebes; Menephthah, the friend of Ptah. Since, however, it was necessary that his change of position should be visible to all men, a flat-bottomed elliptic oval, which we call a cartouche, is traced round the name of Rameses or of Amenophis, before it is placed the title Si-ra, son of Ra, which marks his solar descent, behind it an unvarying formula, in which he is complimented upon being the eternal life-giver, like Ra himself; this assemblage of words is henceforth inseparable and forms his usual name, the title which his subjects habitually use, and by which he is known in history.

The first kings were content with this, even the haughtiest amongst them—Menes, Seneferu, Kheops, Mykerinos; but towards the end of the fifth dynasty the custom was established of adding to this birth-name a coronation title, which was also surrounded by a cartouche. This was always a short phrase formed of three words, expressing that quality or privilege of Ra that was most desired for the new sovereign during his sojourn upon earth. For instance, the surname of Thothmes III., Menkhopirri, signifies *Steadfast is Ra*, and that of Amenophis III., Nibmâoutri, *Ra is the*

*Master of Truth.* Seti I., the father of Rameses II., was entitled Menmâtrî, *The Sun is steadfast through Truth;* and Rameses II. joined to Ousirmari, *The Sun is powerful through Truth,* the epithet Sotpouniri, *elected by the Sun.* There is little variation in the formulas adopted by the different princes of the same branch of the solar line, and the surnames of each dynasty bear a strong family resemblance that cannot be mistaken. That of Thothmes I. was Akhopirkeri, *Great is the soul of Ra:* Thothmes II. the son of Thothmes I. substituted the preposition *in* for the word *ka,* soul, and assumed the title of Akhopirnirî, *Great is Ra.* Thothmes III., who succeeded Thothmes II., suppressed the preposition and changed the term *âa,* to be great, for the term *men,* to be durable, Menkhopirri; but his son, Amenophis II., returned to the ideas expressed by *âa,* but placed the word *Khopri,* being, in the plural, Akhoprouri, *Great are the ways of Ra.* Lastly, Thothmes IV. adopted his grandfather's surname with the plural of *Khopir,* Menkhoprouri, *Stable are the ways of Ra.*[*]

This is not all: the full title of each Pharaoh commences by a third name, which is recognised by the oblong rectangle which surrounds it. This rectangle is terminated at the lower part by a collection of lines which represent a monumental façade, in the midst of which a bolted gate can sometimes be distinguished. Above is a figure of a hawk wearing a double crown and the solar disk. Kheops here called himself Hor maziti, *Horus, who crushes the enemies;* Thothmes III., Hor ka-naktou khâ-m-mâit, *Horus, the strong bull who rises through the Truth;* Rameses II., Hor ka-nakhtou miri-mâit, *Horus, the strong bull who loves the Truth* (Fig. 28). We read, at the end of the third name, a series of epithets which again commence by a hawk,

[*] The English forms of these titles are: Thothmes I., *Raakheperka;* Thothmes II., *Raakheperen;* Thothmes III., *Ramenkheper;* Amenophis II., *Raakheperoo;* Thothmes IV., *Ramenkheperoo;* Amenophis III., *Ramaneb;* Seti I., *Ramenma;* Rameses II., *Ranserma-sotepenra.*

Fig. 28.—The names of Rameses II.

but by a hawk placed over the golden sign, which designates the living Horus, Horus the conqueror. The comparison between the king and the Sun is then continued. Rameses II. thus boasts of being *the golden hawk*, rich in years, and very strong. In short, the complete designation of the Pharaohs includes four parts, always arranged in the same order: two, which may be called the hawks' names, the names of Horus, and two which bear the royal names surrounded by a cartouche. The scribes also insert between them as many phrases as the spirit of flattery can inspire, and as their space will contain. It is probable that this practice is favourably regarded in high quarters, but the four regulation names suffice for etiquette, and by themselves express the sovereign's personality. This personality is composed of two parts, like every human person—a soul and a body. The cartouches respond to the stages through which the body has passed, and which render it two distinct beings. The name takes possession of the man upon his entry into the world, and establishes his identity from the commencement to the end of his life; the surname follows the moment he is born into the sovereignty, and consecrates the aggrandisement he acquires in wearing the crown. The hawk names define the soul and its state. The Egyptians imagine that the soul is a subtile double of the man, which exactly reproduces the individual, with his figure, colour, gesture, and gait. When one of us is born into this world, his double, or to give it the native name, the *Ka*, enters it with him. Since this double is usually invisible, the painters and sculptors seldom represent it; when they attempt to do so, they depict it as the exact image of the being to which it is attached. The pictures at Luxor, in which Pharaoh Amenophis III. has reproduced the history of his childhood, is a good example of the fashion in which it should be imagined (Fig. 29). Amenophis is born, and his double is, like himself, an infant, whom nurses cherish with the same care; he grows, and his double grows with him. The double faithfully accompanies his prototype through all the vicissitudes of his earthly existence. After death it follows him to the

Fig. 29.—Amenophis III. and his double: the double is the second figure.

tomb, and dwells there near the mummy, sometimes hidden in the funeral chambers, sometimes escaping outside, recognisable at night by a pale light, which has won for it the name of Luminous, *Khu*.

The gods, both greatest and least, have a double as well as men, only they can divide it into many doubles, and diffuse it over as many bodies as they like without either diminishing or weakening it. If Ra, Horus, or Amen choose to send forth one of their own doubles, the object into which it enters—man or beast, stone, tree, or statue—at once assumes life, and participates in the nature of the divinity which animates it. Every royal soul is a double detached from Horus. Whilst the child predestined to reign is still a prince or a princess, the double of Horus slumbers within it, and it has apparently merely the same soul as other men.

As soon as the youth ascends the throne and acquires the sovereignty, the double awakens in him and transforms him into a living Horus, incarnate upon earth. The hawk names are those by which this Horus is distinguished from the Horii who have reigned before him, or who will succeed him in the exercise of the supreme power. The epithets preceded by the symbol of the conquering Horus depict him triumphant, during the term of his royal existence, over all the enemies of Egypt, just as Horus formerly overcame all the murderers of his father, Osiris. The name surrounded by the rectangle is the part of Horus, the double, destined to survive the king. The rectangle is the funeral chamber in which he will one day rest, and the closed door is the door of the tomb. He loses none of his power through this incarnation, and even retains the faculty of drawing new doubles from himself and of sending them to a distance to animate other bodies. Every statue of the king has one of these doubles dwelling in it, rendering it an animated effigy of the king, in spite of its outward immobility. When Amenophis III. built the temple of Soleb in Nubia, he wished to dwell by the side of his father Amen. He caused a statue of himself to be hewn out of rose-coloured granite, and by a prayer placed one of his own doubles in it; then he introduced it into the sanctuary, and offered before it the worship always celebrated at the enthronement of the gods. Even now we see him upon the walls of the temple, adoring his living portrait. The double once linked to his stone body never leaves it whilst it remains intact; to restore it to liberty the statue must be broken.

Pharaoh is then really a visible god, a god become flesh. He is called the good god, the great god, the living god, and no one approaches him without offering the words and honours due to a god. When he wakes in the morning he is the rising sun, and the members of his household salute him as they would Ra. 'Turn thy face to me, oh, rising Sun, which lightens the world with thy beauty; disk sparkling amongst men, that drivest away the darkness of Egypt. Thou resemblest thy father when he rises in heaven, and thy rays penetrate into all lands. There is no place deprived of thy beauty, for thy words rule the destinies of all lands. When thou art resting in thy palace thou hearest all that is said in every country, for thou hast millions of ears. Thine eye is more brilliant than any star of heaven, and sees better than the sun. If any one speak, even if the mouth that speaketh be within the walls of a house, its words reach thine ear. If any hidden action be committed, thine eye perceives it, oh! king, gracious lord, who givest to all the breath of life.'*

Each movement, each official act of the sovereign resembles an act of worship, celebrated midst the chanting of solemn hymns. If he grants an audience, the subject whom he admits to the favour of gazing upon his face approaches him with a formula of devout adoration. If he summons a council for any business, the nobles of the kingdom open the deliberation by a kind of religious service in his honour. Imagine Rameses II. seated upon his large golden throne, wearing a diadem adorned with two feathers, seeking for some means of facilitating the access of caravans to the gold mines situated in Nubia, between the Nile and the Red Sea. The convoys entrusted with the carriage of the gold humbly complain that they can find no spring, no pool, on the road they are forced to take. 'One half of them, with their asses, die of thirst upon the way, for they have no means of carrying sufficient water for the journey there and back.' The councillors enter the presence of the good god, their arms raised in an adoring attitude; they fall prostrate upon their faces, and remain

* This hymn to the king is addressed to Minephthah in the *Papyrus Anastasi*, No. IV.; to his son Seti II. in the *Papyrus Anastasi*, No. II.

in that position whilst the business is explained to them The desolate aspect of the country is graphically described, and they are asked whether it is desirable to dig wells at intervals along the road? Their reply is not long deferred: 'Thou resemblest Ra!' they all exclaim together; 'thou resemblest Ra in all that thou doest, therefore the wishes of thine heart are always fulfilled; if thou desire something during the night, at dawn it is already there. We have seen many miracles that thou hast accomplished since thou hast risen as king of the world, and we hear of nothing, our eyes see nothing elsewhere that can rival them. Every word that issues from thy mouth is like the words of Harmachis!\* Thy tongue weighs, thy lips measure more justly than the truest balance of Thoth.† What is unknown to thee? Who is there perfect like unto thee? Where is the spot thou canst not see? There is no foreign country that thou hast not visited, and thine activity hastens to a place if thine ears attract thine attention towards it. Now, since thou art the vicar of the gods in this country, thou rulest its destinies. Still in embryo, in thy dignity as child-heir, thou wast told all that concerned Egypt. A little boy, with the tress still hanging over thy temple, no monument was built without thy direction, no business transacted without thy knowledge, and thou wast the supreme head of the soldiers. A youth of ten years old, all the public works were made by thy hand, for thou laidest the foundations of them. If, therefore, thou sayest to the water, 'Come up upon the mountain,' the celestial water will soon flow at thy word, for thou art Ra incarnate, Khepera created in the flesh; thou art the living image of thy father Tmu, lord of Helio-

---

\* Horus upon the morning horizon and Horus upon the evening horizon: sunrise and sunset.

† Thoth weighed the actions of men before Osiris; he watched that the scales were correct, and adjusted the bar so that all error should be avoided.

polis; the god who commands is in thy mouth, the god of wisdom is in thine heart, thy tongue is the sanctuary of Truth, a god sits upon thy lips, thy words are accomplished every day, and the wish of thine heart realises itself, like that of Ptah when he creates his works. Since thou art eternal, everything acts according to thy designs, and everything obeys thy words, sire, our master!'

When the chorus of councillors have ended their speech, the Viceroy of Ethiopia, from whom the gold mines are held, speaks in his turn: 'The land is therefore in this condition, water has been lacking there since the reign of Ra; the people die of thirst; all the preceding kings have wished to dig wells there, but their efforts have failed; the King Seti I. even caused borings to be made for a well to a depth of one hundred and twenty cubits, but it was left unfinished because no water was found! But thou, if thou sayest to thy father the Nile, father of the gods, "Raise the water to the height of the mountain!" he will obey thy words, even as all thy projects have been accomplished in our presence, although no one had ever heard of such deeds, even in the songs of the poets, for thy fathers, the gods, love thee more than all the kings that have existed since Ra.' Rameses, convinced by this speech, gives his orders, labourers are set to work, and a well is dug at a suitable spot.* This is one example amongst a thousand of suitable language to be used when any one has the perilous honour of raising his voice in Pharaoh's presence; no business, however unimportant it may be, can be brought before him without a lengthy memorandum of his superhuman origin and of his personal divinity.

The other gods reserve heaven for themselves.

---

\* These speeches and the history of the well are taken from a *stèle* of Rameses II., dated the third year of his reign, and erected at Kouban at the entrance of the road which leads from the Nile to the mines of Etbaye.

Pharaoh possesses the earth; not only the land of Egypt, but the whole earth. If, beyond the valley of the Nile, there be peoples who claim to be independent, or kings who refuse to bow before him, they are rebels, 'children of rebellion,' who will be punished sooner or later, and who will pay for their hour's liberty by eternal ruin. Their chiefs are styled vanquished, their country vile. In the deeds of the royal chancellery the current expression for the prince of the Hittites and the small kingdoms of Ethiopia is the *Conquered Khita* and *Cush the vile*. But the earth is not integral; it is divided by the course of the sun into two equal parts, or, rather, into two earths, the Northern, or night earth—the Southern earth, or earth of day. Egypt is the same. Tradition relates that in the ancient days it was at first a single empire, over which four gods, Ra, Shu, Sibou, and Osiris, reigned in turn. Osiris was treacherously killed by his brother, Set; his son, Horus, rose against the assassin, and the war raged until the day on which Sibou made an amicable division of the country between the two rivals. Set received the valley, Horus the Delta, with Memphis as its capital, and each of these two halves henceforth possessed a different king and its own emblems. The protecting goddess of the Delta is a serpent, Uatchit; that of Said a vulture, Nekhelbit. The crown of the North is red, that of the South is white. The papyrus was the symbolical plant of the North, the lotus that of the South. This separation into two states was not prolonged beyond the divine dynasties; since Menes, 'the half belonging to Horus and the half belonging to Set' have always been, at least theoretically, governed by the same sovereign.

In truth, the union is purely personal, and the two Egypts have only one king, without ceasing on that account to be two distinct Egypts. The sovereign is the king of the South and the king of the North, the master of the Southern vulture and of the protecting uræus. His crown, the pschent, is a composite arrangement of the red and white diadems. The lower sides of his throne are decorated with the lotus and papyrus bound together, or by two figures of the Nile god, who binds the two symbolical plants together by a great effort of the legs and arms. But, instead of the unity of the king at last producing the unity of the country, the dualism of the country produced an absolute duplication of the king, of all the objects that belonged to him, and of all the departments of the State. The palace is formed of two palaces joined together. It is therefore called *Piráoui*, the 'double great house,' and from this word the name of Pharaoh, so often heard on the lips of the people, is also derived. The Egyptian calls his master 'The double great house,' as others call their sovereign the 'Sublime Porte.' The royal treasury is the double house of silver and gold. Each of the granaries, in which the tax-receivers place the taxes in cereals, is the double granary. The corn, even when gathered in the same field, becomes the corn of the North and of the South. During a ceremony Pharaoh wears the crown of the South, and all that he offers to the gods is from the South, even to the wine and the incense; a few minutes later he places the crown of the North upon his brow, and offers incense and wine from the North. Still, his usual insignia are those of the gods, his parents. Like them, he bears the animal-headed sceptres, the hook, the scourge, the feathered head-dress, the two flaming horns, the emblem of light. The serpent which erects itself upon his forehead, the uræus of gold or gilded bronze always attached to his head-dress, is impregnated with mysterious life, which renders it the instrument of the royal anger and the executioner of secret designs. It is said, that it vomits flames and destroys in battle any one who dares to attack the king. It communicates supernatural virtues to the white and red crowns, and changes them into magicians or fairies (*oirithaqaou*), whom no one can resist.

Man by his body, god by his soul and by his attributes, through his double essence Pharaoh holds the privilege of being the constant intermediary between heaven and earth. He alone has naturally the position which enables him to transmit to the gods, his brothers, the prayers of men. When any one wishes to influence the invisibles in favour of a living or of a dead man, he does not address himself directly to Osiris, Ptah, or Mentu, for the request would not reach them; he takes Pharaoh for his mediator, and offers the sacrifice through his hands. His personal intervention is usually a devout fiction, and the ritual does not exact it, but the ceremony commences with the proclamation that *the King gives the offering—Souton di hotpou*—to Osiris, to Ptah, to Mentu, in order that these gods should grant the wishes of such-and-such an individual, and this declaration replaces the fact. Whenever a favour is requested from a god, or an *ex voto* is dedicated to him, the suppliant or thanksgiver shelters himself by using the king's invocation; there are probably not two funeral inscriptions out of a hundred which do not commence with the formula, *Souton di hotpou*, or which do not contain it. The gods, on their side, are in perpetual and direct communication with Pharaoh, by all the means at their disposal. They appear to him in dreams, to counsel him to make war against various peoples, to forbid him to take part in a battle, to command him to restore a monument which is falling into ruins. Whilst Thothmes IV. was still only prince royal, he frequently hunted the lion and gazelle in that part of the desert which lies to the west of Memphis, attended by only one servant. One day, when accident had led him to the neighbourhood of the Great Pyramid, he placed himself for the midday siesta beneath the shadow of the great Sphinx, the image of the powerful Khepera, the god towards whom all the houses of Memphis and all the cities of the neighbourhood raise their hands in adoration and make their offerings. The Sphinx was at that time more than half buried, and its head only issued from the sand (Fig. 30). When the prince was asleep, the god spoke to him as a father to his son: 'Look at me, contemplate me, O my son Thothmes, for I am thy father, Harmarchis Khepera Tmu, who promises the sovereignty to thee, for thou shalt wear the two crowns,

Fig. 30.—The Great Sphinx buried in the Sand.

the white and the red, upon the throne of Seb, the sovereign of the gods.* The sand of the mountain is covering me; recompense me for all my blessings by fulfilling my wishes. I know that thou art my son, my defender: come near, I am with thee, I am thy beloved father.' The prince, when he awoke, understood that the god had foretold his future royalty, and had requested as the thank-offering for his accession the promise that his statue should be excavated. As soon

* Seb is the Earth-god, the husband of Nut, the goddess of Heaven.

as he ascended the throne Thothmes remembered his dream, and ordered the sand to be cleared away from the great image. The *stèle* which he placed between its feet is still visible, and relates the vision to all who pass by.

The prophetic dream is not, however, the method usually employed by the gods in manifesting themselves to Pharaoh; their statues in the temples serve as their interpreters. Since they are animated by one of their doubles, they can speak when they like. Amen raised his voice in the shadow of the sanctuary and commanded the queen, Hatshepset, to send a fleet to the land of Punt, to fetch incense for the sacrifices. As a rule, the statues do not speak; they content themselves with gestures. When questioned upon any subject, if no movement is given their answer is negative; if, on the other hand, they decidedly bow the head twice, the affair is good and they approve of it. When Pharaoh is at Memphis he consults Ptah; at Thebes he consults Amen, and the animated statue of Amen decides the most important questions. Rameses, upon reaching the Governor's house, stops for a moment, and sends a message by one of the chamberlains who accompany him: 'Let Psarou come, without delay, to deliberate with his Majesty upon Syrian affairs.' Psarou bows low, in token of obedience, gets into his chariot, which happens to be already harnessed, and quickly joins the procession on its way to the temple (Fig. 31). Two runners, at full speed, clear the road with voice and gesture, and oblige the crowd to stand back against the wall, so as to leave a passage for the sovereign. Behind them, in groups with their officers, march some thirty soldiers of different regiments of the guard, standard-bearer and fan-bearer, mace-bearers carrying the long scourge of war, lancers armed with spear, axe, and shield, auxiliary barbarians, easily recognised by their costume and complexion. Pharaoh follows them alone in his chariot, a little in advance

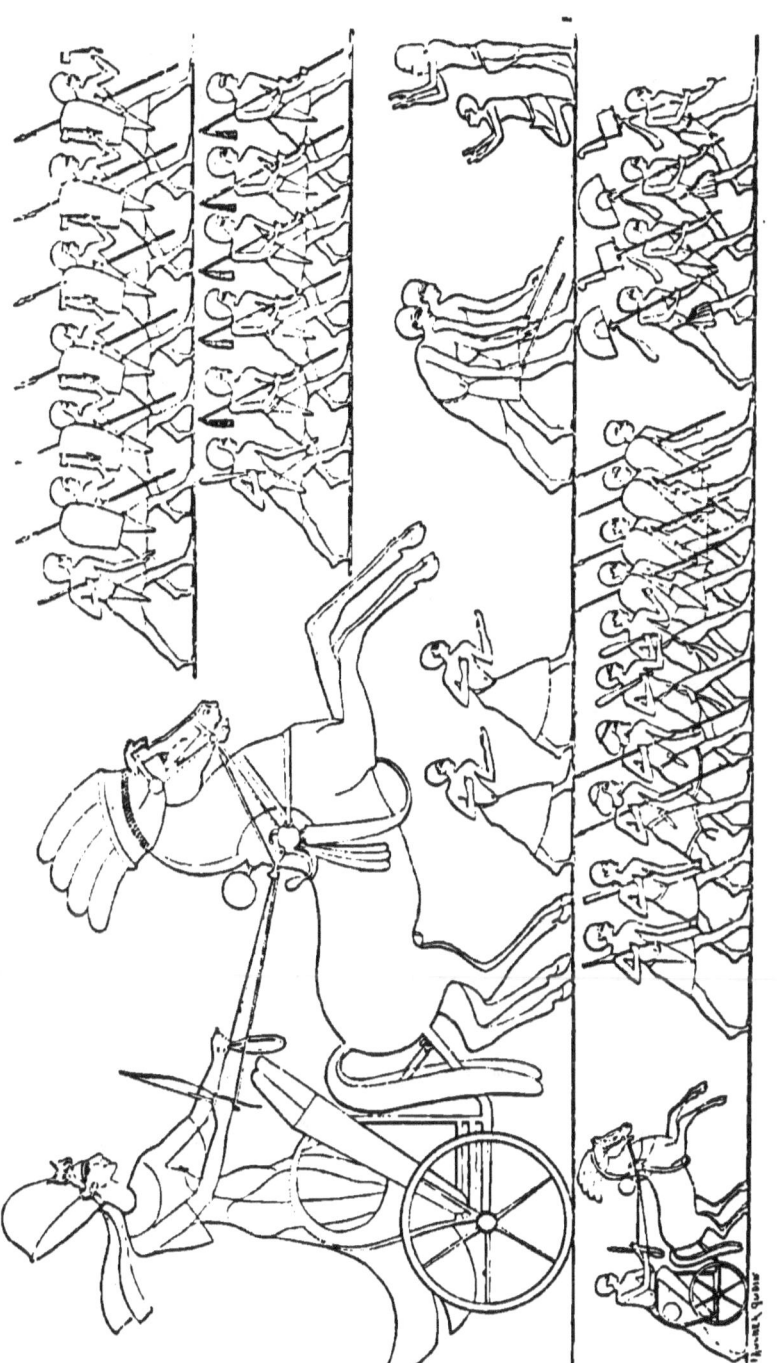

Fig. 31.—Pharaoh (Amenophis IV.) and his Escort.

of the queen, Nefertari (Fig. 32). She is still a young woman, with delicate, regular features, already faded and wrinkled under her powder. Like her husband, she wears a long robe, its folds, through the rapid motion, floating behind her. A large escort of princes and great dignitaries follow the royal pair, their number being continually augmented by fresh arrivals. Every one carries a fan, and stands in a chariot driven by a groom. The crowd cheers

Fig. 32.—The Queen in her Chariot behind Pharaoh.

Pharaoh as he passes, and tries to guess the reason of his morning's drive. 'He is going to offer sacrifice to Mut!' 'He is going to inaugurate the chapel of Chensu!' 'A messenger has arrived from Syria!' 'A post has arrived from Ethiopia!' Pharaoh, however, pursues his way, careless of the emotion he excites. In a few minutes he turns to the right, enters an avenue bordered with sphinxes of sandstone, and the temple of Amen rises before him, dwarfing the surrounding houses by its size.

# CHAPTER IV.

### AMEN, THE GREAT GOD OF THEBES.

*The temple is the house of god — History of the temple of Amen at Thebes — The king in the hypostyle hall — Amen the judge as the last resort — Thothmes the head of the granary-keepers and the patrimony of the god — Pillage of the god's granaries — Solemn council held in the temple — Amen gives judgment — A messenger from Syria and a dispatch in cuneiform writing: war is declared — The sacrifice of the bull — The ritual of the sacrifice and the Khri-habi — Amen promises victory to the king.*

THE temple is the house of the god, in which he dwells body and soul. At first, like the house of men, it consisted of a single narrow, gloomy room, but instead of a terrace, it was covered with a slightly convex roof, which slanted backwards; two great masts framed the opening, to which streamers were fastened, so as to attract the attention of the faithful at a distance, and an enclosure guarded with palisades extended before the façade. In the interior were found mats, low tables of stone, wood, and metal, some vessels to receive the blood, wine, and water, the liquids which were daily brought to the god. When the offerings for sacrifice increased, the number of rooms increased also, and chambers reserved for the flowers, stuffs, precious vases, and food were grouped round the original building, so that the primitive temple became only the sanctuary of the temple, the mysterious tabernacle of the sovereign god.

It is not more than two thousand years since

Thebes rose from obscurity.* Its first great kings, the Amenemhats and Usertsens, built there, in honour of Amen, a rather shabby edifice of white calcareous stone and sandstone with granite doors; pillars with sixteen sides decorated the interior. At that time Amen was only a poor provincial god, less esteemed and less popular than his neighbours, Mentu of Hermonthis or Minou of Coptos. A small temple sufficed for his worship, and a small estate provided for his sacrifices. His authority increased during the long centuries that followed, and when the Pharaohs of the eighteenth dynasty drove out the Hyksos, and reigned over the world without a rival, Amen acquired the sovereignty over the gods of the other cities, Egyptian or foreign, and his former house became too small for his new position. So many ancient souvenirs were attached to it, that it was carefully preserved from destruction, and was surrounded by a circle of new temples, which render this monument the largest we yet know. In front of the original façade, Thothmes I. built two chambers preceded by a court and flanked by isolated chapels; then arranged in proportion, one behind the other, three of those monumental gateways accompanied by towers, that are called pylons. Thothmes III. constructed immense halls towards the west. Amenophis III. added a fourth pylon of enormous height and width to those of Thothmes I. Lastly, Rameses I. and Seti I. employed their reigns in building the hall of columns, which joins the pylon of Amenophis III. It measures fifty metres long, by one hundred wide (Fig. 33). In the centre stands an avenue of twelve columns with bell-shaped capitals, the highest ever used in the interior of a building; in the lower sides, one hundred and twenty-two columns with

---

* It must be remembered that this narrative is placed at the commencement of the reign of Rameses II., in the middle of the fourteenth century before our era. The accession of the twelfth dynasty took place between 3200 and 3400 B.C., and that of the first Theban dynasty about the eleventh, two centuries earlier.

Fig. 33.—Entrance to the Hypostyle Hall of the Temple of Amen at Karnak.

lotiform capitals are arranged in nine rows of quincunx. The ceiling of the central hall is twenty-three metres above the ground, and the cornice of the two towers dominates this ceiling by about fifteen metres. Seti died when the decoration of the walls was scarcely half finished, and Rameses II. will not succeed in completing it unless he reigns long enough to be a centenarian.*

Pharaoh is received before the door by two priests with bare feet and shaven heads. They prostrate themselves whilst he alights from his chariot, then rise and silently await his commands. 'Is the high priest of Amen in the temple?' 'The high priest of Amen is in the temple.' 'Let him come here at once.' 'He cannot come at once. Amen, this morning, is giving his solemn judgment upon the business of the royal scribe, the overseer of the granaries, Thothmes, and the high priest is now before the sanctuary of the god.' Pharaoh throws a preoccupied glance through the door, and perceives the central triforium of the hypostyle hall half filled with a motionless crowd. At the extreme end of it, above the heads of the people, three sacred arks are visible in a ray of sunlight, which falls obliquely from the ceiling. The eldest of the priests adds that the ceremony is nearly over; the first prophet will be free in half an hour at the latest. Pharaoh enters the temple and proceeds to the left aisle of the hall. The temple slaves at once bring him a large gilt throne, lined with various fancy cushions, raised upon feet, and provided with a footstool (Fig. 34). He seats himself with Nefertari at his side. The majority of the escort, soldiers and messengers, remain outside the temple and guard the chariots. The princes and dignitaries follow the king, and group themselves behind him, standing amongst the columns in the order prescribed by etiquette. The

* In fact, Rameses died nearly a centenarian, in the sixty-seventh year of his reign.

solemn silence, broken for a moment by the arrival of the procession, reigns once more. Pharaoh, lost in the angle of the hall, separated from the crowd by the close rows of columns, might believe himself alone in the house of his father, Amen, if echo did not from time to time bring him some fragment of religious melody or the light rustle of a fly-flap.

The gods have sometimes to judge a lawsuit in which religion only is concerned. It happens that a theologian, through constant meditation upon the nature of the divinities, forms opinions that are opposed to the dogmas; if he ventures to express them, above all, if he has the misfortune to make a few proselytes, the sacerdotal college to which he belongs summons him to appear before the statue of the god, who excommunicates him, and if necessary condemns him to die by fire. The case of the scribe Thothmes does not refer to heresy; no point of doctrine is in question, and the accused has never intimated any wish to deviate from the regular observances of the ritual. Since he is a priest, and even of high rank, we must believe that he is versed in theology; but he is also the *Overseer of the granaries of Amen*, and it is in this capacity that he is now called upon to give an account of his conduct.

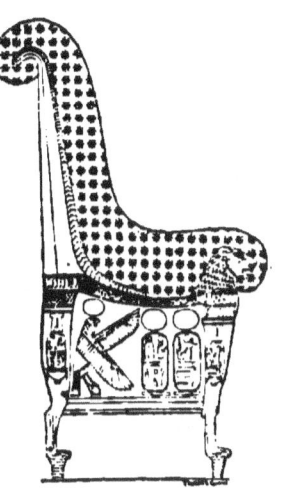

Fig. 34.—The royal Throne.

In fact, the gods are great nobles, who possess property, and maintain a large number of servants to manage it. Their temples must be enlarged, repaired, preserved in good order, like the palace of a prince. Their statues require furniture, clothes, and jewels; the doubles that dwell in them cannot live without daily food; they have also their servants, the priests, whose living and comfort, if not wealth, must be assured. These things are all provided for at the foundation of each temple by gifts of land, cattle, slaves, and divers revenues, which form their personal patrimony, and which they repay by prayers or by perpetual sacrifices to the memory of the donor. This patrimony, once given, remains inalienable by law, and is continually augmented by legacies and new donations. Houses are added to houses, fields to fields, revenues to revenues, and inheritance by mortmain— what is called the offerings of the god, *Hotpou noutir*— would at last absorb the whole territory and personal property of Egypt if the king or the feudal nobles did not confiscate a portion of it from time to time, under cover of a civil war or of a foreign invasion. Since the accession of the eighteenth dynasty, Amen has profited more than any other god, perhaps even more than Pharaoh himself, by the Egyptian victories over the peoples of Syria and Ethiopia. Each success has brought him a considerable share of the spoil collected upon the battle-fields, indemnities levied from the enemy, prisoners carried into slavery. He possesses lands and gardens by the hundred in Thebes and the rest of Egypt, fields and meadows, woods, hunting-grounds, and fisheries; he has colonies in Ethiopia or in the oases of the Libyan desert, and at the extremity of the land of Canaan there are cities under vassalage to him, for Pharaoh allows him to receive the tribute from them. The administration of these vast properties requires as many officials and departments as that of a kingdom. It includes innumerable bailiffs for the agriculture, overseers for the cattle and poultry, treasurers of twenty kinds for the gold, silver, and copper, the vases and valuable stuffs; foremen for the workshops and manufactures, engineers, architects, boatmen; a fleet and an army which often fight by the side of Pharaoh's fleet and army. It is really a State within the State.

Thothmes is one of the most important of these stewards. He manages the double granaries of Amen at Thebes, and all the wheat, barley, dhoura, and other grains, which the god cultivates himself or which he levies as a tax from his subjects, necessarily pass through his hands. The granaries in which he stores them are large brick buildings, containing high, narrow, vaulted rooms, placed side by side, but without any means of inter-communication (Fig. 35). They have but two openings, one at the top, by which the grain is put in, the other on the level of the

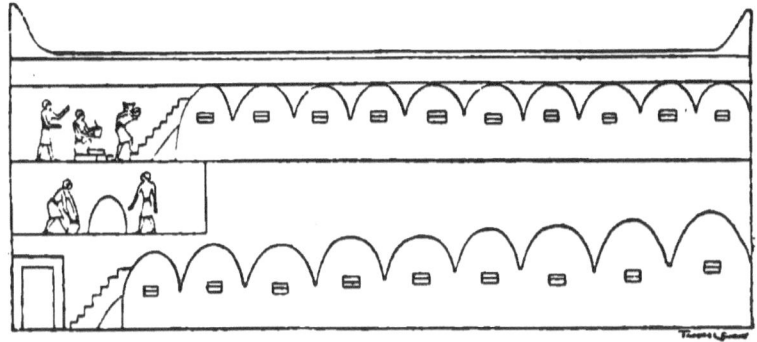

Fig. 35.—The Granaries: Registering and Storing the Grain.

ground, by which it is taken out. The corn, placed in heaps in the entrance court, is measured by sworn coopers, under the superintendence of a guardian; a crier announces each bushel, and a scribe registers it. As soon as one heap is finished, some labourers carry it away in rush baskets and store it under the direction of a warehouseman. Sometimes a movable ladder enables the workmen to reach the upper hole in each cell, sometimes the cells are surmounted by a terrace which is rendered accessible by a brick staircase. Thothmes knows the amount that each granary contains, the quantity of corn that has been deposited in it, and how much is daily taken from it; what the present year's harvest produced, and the amount left in the granaries from the crop of the preceding years. Dishonest or negligent, he could purloin or allow the god to lose an enormous portion of his revenue, without any chance of immediate detection.

Until lately the honesty of Thothmes had never been even questioned, and his life had been unstained; but last year a rumour spread that strange irregularities had been and were being committed in his department. Allusions were made to frauds in the reception and distribution of the corn, of falsified measures, of incorrect accounts in the registers, of thefts from the storehouses, committed with so much impudence that the unknown culprits must have felt sure of the tacit complicity, if not of the active co-operation, of the official guardians.

A certain granary, which contained two thousand bushels of dhoura when it was closed, had only twelve hundred bushels in it when it was opened three months later, and no one could account for the deficiency. The workmen had seen nothing amiss, and they pretended not to understand what was going on. They threw the responsibility from one to the other, and without positively accusing any one, they insinuated that the culprits must be searched for amongst their superiors if there were any real wish to discover them. Suspicion was soon directed towards Thothmes, and although vague at first, it speedily acquired so much strength that the chief prophet resolved to try the case before the judgment-seat of Amen.

The prophetic statues of the gods are usually concealed in the depths of the sanctuary. When they are brought out upon the solemn festivals, to be carried in state round the temple and sometimes through the city, their permission is first humbly requested. If the statue approve of the excursion, it acquiesces by a sign of the head; the ark upon which it rests is lifted up, and the procession starts. If it remain passive, the priests conclude that it is unwilling to show itself, and an inquiry is made as to the motive which induces it to deprive the people of its presence. On the day of the festival of Thebes the statue of Amen refused to go out. Its displeasure was attributed to the malpractices of which it had been the victim, and Thothmes was summoned for trial. If he were found guilty, he would be probably beheaded, or at least he would suffer imprisonment and confiscation. The inquiry, although strictly made, proved that he was innocent. Twenty of the warehouse-keepers and scribes had combined, first, to abstract a few measures of corn, which they divided between them; then, emboldened by success, they half emptied the granaries to which they were attached. Drawn too far by their cupidity, and feeling that discovery was imminent, they had endeavoured to save themselves by throwing suspicion upon their chief. The innocence of Thothmes was proved, and the god who had instigated the trial fixed a day upon which his decision would be publicly given.

This morning, therefore, the chief prophet, Baknikhonsou, his feet bare, his head shaven, a white scarf across his shoulders, penetrated into the sanctuary with Thothmes, and paused upon the *silver soil* opposite the ark of Amen. The Egyptian divinities regulate their lives according to the nature of the country they inhabit. Their ark is always a boat, a real boat, raised at each end, built with sufficient strength for navigation. It is launched upon the sacred lake of the temple several times a year, when certain mysterious rites, known only to the priests, are celebrated. That of Amen bears a ram's head in front and behind, surmounted by the solar disk and ornamented by a large round collar (Fig. 36). It is placed upon a litter, which rests upon a square, richly decorated pedestal. A cabin called a *naos* rises in the centre, and serves as the usual dwelling-place of the prophetic statue; a long white drapery, fastened at the back, falls over the sides of the *naos*, and half conceals it. A human-headed sphinx, upright upon a stand, guards the prow; a man's figure, standing at the stern, moves the large oar-helms; and statuettes, standing or kneeling in different postures, represent the king in adoration before his divine father.

Baknikhonsou respectfully opens the door of the *naos*, and the statue is visible; it is gilded, but the hair and the beard are black, the enamelled eyes

Fig. 36.—The Ark of Amen, borne by his Priests.

glitter in the shadow. The priest burns a few grains of incense, takes two rolls of sealed paper, places them upon the hands of the idol, and says in a clear voice, ' Amen-ra, my good master, here are two books before thee. One of them says that Thothmes the scribe must be prosecuted, that he is guilty; the other says that Thothmes the scribe must not be prosecuted, for he is innocent. Thou canst distinguish right from wrong; choose according to the right.' The god makes a sign that he consents, and seizes the roll which says: ' Thothmes, son of Souâamon, should not be prosecuted, for he is innocent.' The chief prophet continues, 'The scribe Thothmes has then found favour before Amen-ra, my master. My good lord god, grant that he be not executed by the sword, that he be not thrown into prison, that he be not punished by the confiscation of his property'—and the god approves; 'grant that he be reinstated in his dignities, and that he resume his position as *chief steward of the granaries.*' Again the god signifies his approval. Instantly fifteen priests raise the ark, and placing it upon their shoulders, carry it through the chambers and courts of the temple to the entrance of the hypostyle hall, where the ark of the goddess Mut and that of the child-god Chonsu join them. The ceremony recommences in the presence of the crowd. The god, again consulted, once more proclaims the innocence of Thothmes and his reinstalment in his functions. 'If any one, whoever he may be, say to Thothmes, son of Souâamon, " Thou wrongfully occupiest a post near to Amen-ra," the chief prophet of Amen-ra, the king of the gods, the great god, who existed before all things, will make this individual appear before the god, for it is the god himself who has established Thothmes in his dignity when he was solemnly enthroned in the temple.' Henceforth Thothmes is safe from all persecution; whoever would throw the past in his face will be exposed to the anger of the god.* The three shrines move slowly away and return to their gloomy chambers, the crowd retires noiselessly, and Baknikhonsou hastens to prostrate himself before Pharaoh. His life has been entirely passed in the temple, where he now commands as master: a priest at sixteen, a *divine father* at twenty,†

* The long inscription in which this lawsuit is related is so much mutilated in some places that the meaning is not always clear. I have abridged some of the details, and have endeavoured to restrict my narrative to almost certain facts.

† The title of *divine father* marked, as we see, one of the inferior grades of the sacerdotal hierarchy in the temple of Amen. No one knows what offices belonged to it.

third prophet at twenty-two, second prophet at forty-seven. Rameses promoted him to be first prophet a few months after his accession. The pontificate of Amen is by universal consent the most important of the three high religious dignities of Egypt. Those of Ra at Heliopolis and of Ptah at Memphis were superior for a long time; but now the priest of Amen takes the lead, and exercises almost unlimited power over the whole country. Rameses raises Baknikhonsou and tells him the object of his visit. He has not finished speaking when an officer, breathless with the speed he has made, hurries into the temple; the post from Syria has arrived, and is waiting at the door for his Majesty's orders Scarcely introduced into the royal presence, before he has time to fall down before Pharaoh, in accordance with etiquette, the sovereign addresses him, 'Who art thou?' 'I belong to the Prince of Megiddo, and come from him with a message to your Majesty.' The message is written on a thick tablet of baked clay, covered on both sides with letters. Pharaoh, like the majority of well-born Egyptians, has understood the Aramean tongue from his childhood, but he cannot easily read the cuneiform characters. The Syrian interpreter belonging to the royal escort comes forward, takes the tablet from the messenger and reads it aloud. 'To the king, my master, my sun, I, Abdadad, thy servant, I speak thus: Khitasir, the vanquished chief of the vile Khita, has broken the peace and the friendship which his fathers had made with thy fathers. He has forgotten the power of the gods, thy masters, and has assembled his generals, his infantry, his chariot soldiers; he has marched against the prefects and the kings that thou hast established in every land to pay tribute to thee and to render homage to thy Majesty. He has advanced against them, he has killed their warriors, he has taken their flocks, and has led away their wives and children into captivity. I have, therefore, sent spies into his camp, saying, "Go and see what the vile Khita is doing." And see, they found him established by the side of Kadesh, the city of the vanquished chief of Amaorou, with his impious allies. And know, my lord the king, my sun, that the chiefs of Girgashou, of Moushanit and of Aradou; the chiefs of Ilion, of Pedasos, of the Mysians, and of the Lycians, are with him, as well as the whole of the Naharanna. I pray my lord the king, my sun, to send as quickly as possible his archers and his chariots of war, for if he delay I shall be utterly destroyed.'* It is too late to consult the god as to whether he wishes for war or not; war is declared, and Pharaoh must leave at once and rejoin the army. He calls Psarou, commands him to take the necessary measures for placing the contingent from Thebes and Said in the field, dispatches messengers to the King of Ethiopia to inform him of his departure, then rises and goes into the centre of the temple, where everything is ready for the sacrifice.

Fig. 37.—Offering Red Water to the god Amen.

The preliminaries are rapidly accomplished in the usual order. The statue is placed upright in front of the sanctuary, the

* The letter from the Prince of Megiddo has been composed from the models of letters discovered at Tell-el-Amarna.

face turned towards the outside. Pharaoh dresses it, perfumes it, and presents to it successively five grains of incense from the south, five grains of alum from the north, four vases of red water, four vases of ordinary water (Fig. 37). There is a reason for the number four predominating in the ceremonies. The world is divided into four regions, or rather, to use the technical term, into four houses, which respond to our cardinal points, and are placed under the protection of different divinities. The king pays equal homage to them all, and each time consecrates one of the four parts of which the offering is composed, one for each house, or for each point of the horizon.

The water poured out, Pharaoh promptly returns to the court, in front of the old edifice of Amenemhat, and receives from the hands of a priest a lasso of plaited leather: his eldest son, Amenhikhopshouf, stands behind him. Originally the sacrifice was a repast which the celebrant—king, prince, or simple citizen—was obliged to prepare and serve to the god with his own hands. He then went to the fields, lassoed the half-wild bull, bound it, killed it, burnt one portion before the idol, and distributed the remainder amongst those present with a profusion of cakes, fruits, vegetables, and wine: the god was present, both in his body and in his double; he allowed himself to be dressed and scented, ate and drank of the best of all that was served upon the table. The use of the incense and of the water had prepared the prophetic statue for the banquet, as a guest is prepared by giving him water for washing, and by anointing him with perfumed ointments. The king is now ready for the chase.

Time has gradually softened the roughness of the primitive rite; it has transformed, the originally genuine hunt and feast into a similitude of pursuit and of feasting. Rameses is not free from the necessity of catching the beast himself, but he is no longer required to go and seek it in its pasturage, at the risk of seeing it escape or of receiving a dangerous blow. The high sacrifice which is celebrated on solemn occasions originally comprised four victims; the spirit of economy usually reduces the number to two, or even to one only, which is then called the *Bull from the South*. The servants of the temple lead it with a halter to the appointed place, and then attach the right horn to the right hind leg, throwing the head slightly back by passing the cord over the left shoulder, so as to hamper the animal's movements, and to almost paralyse the neck if it endeavours to use its horns. This done, it is pricked, and as soon as it starts, the prince royal seizes it by the tail with both hands, and Rameses throws the lasso over its horns (Fig. 38). As it stops, startled by this attack, and unable to understand what

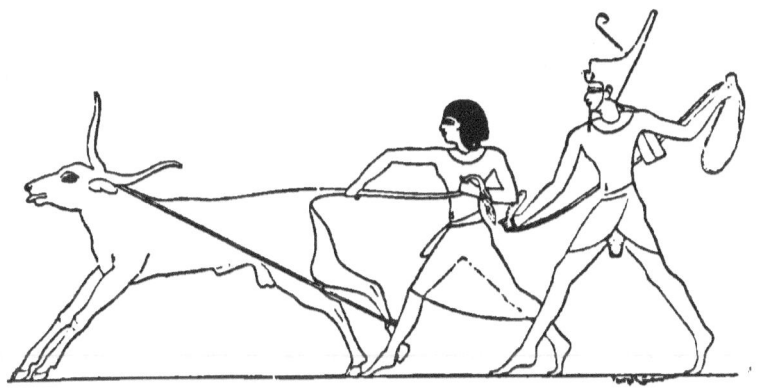

Fig. 38.—The King lassoes the sacrificial Bull.

has happened, the priests rush upon it, throw it down, and tie the four legs together (Fig. 39). Now Pharaoh has armed himself with a long, straight, plain stick, without any ornaments, and with a light club, tipped with white stone, a memorial of the club with which his ancestors struck down their prey. As soon as the victim is ready, he extends the club over it, as though about to strike (Fig. 40). The sacred butcher at once opens its throat from one ear to the other; one of the assistants receives the blood in a copper basin and places it, still warm, in front of the statue; others, with a few blows from the knife, cut off the sacramental portions—the heart, the liver, the spleen, and

Fig. 39.—The Priests throw down the Bull after the King has lassoed it.

the leg (Fig. 41). Lastly, the pieces are hurriedly brought to the king (Fig. 42). Rameses offers them as they arrive, then heaps them upon the ground with loaves, cakes, fruits, and vegetables of all kinds. Amen has but to choose the dishes which he prefers from the food placed before him.

These are only the outlines of the ceremony; each act in it is accompanied by movements, gestures, and words, which the gods have condescended to regulate in detail. Before all else they exact material cleanliness. The celebrant, whoever he may be, must carefully wash—*ouâbou*—his face, mouth, hands, and body, and this purification is considered so necessary, that the priest derives from it his name of *ouîbou*—the washed, the clean. The costume and head-dress vary according to the nature of the rite that is being celebrated; frequently, even, it is modified several times in the course of a single service. A certain sacrifice, or a certain moment in a

Fig. 40.—The King gives the Death Signal.

sacrifice, requires sandals with raised points, a panther's skin over the shoulder, and the thick tress falling over the right ear; in another the celebrant must be girded with cotton drawers and wear a jackal's tail, whilst he must take off his shoes before he commences the service, or sometimes put on an artificial beard. The nature, the hair, the age of the victim, the method of leading it, then of binding its limbs, the way of killing it, the order to be followed in opening and cutting up the body, are minutely and definitely prescribed, and are unalterable.

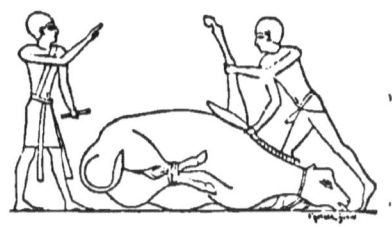

Fig. 41.—Cutting up the Victim.

Yet these are but the least exactions of the god, and the easiest to satisfy. The formulas which accompany each of the sacerdotal manipulations include a fixed number of words, which must not be modified in either sequence or harmony, even by the god himself, or they would lose their efficacy. They are recited in a certain rhythm, to a melody in which each tone has some special virtue, accompanied by movements which confirm the meaning and exercise an irresistible influence over the god; a false note, a discord between the succession of the gestures and the utterance of the sacramental words, any hesitation or blunder in the accomplishment of a single detail, and the whole sacrifice is nullified. The worship, therefore, resembles a judicial action, in the course of which the god alienates a portion of his liberty in exchange for certain compensations in kind, of which

Fig. 42.—The Priests bring the pieces of the Victim.

the value and the character are determined by law. Rameses solemnly transfers to his father Amen the cakes, the bread, the pieces of beef, the fruits, by which he hopes to gain his attention and render him more favourable to his petition. If the king scrupulously observes the innumerable conditions by which the offering is surrounded, Amen cannot avoid the obligation of fulfilling his prayer and of granting him the victory over the Khita; if he omits the most insignificant of them all, the offering remains the perquisite of the temple, but Amen is not in any way bound towards him.

The celebrant, king or private individual, has therefore a formidable responsibility towards his family; a defect of memory, or an involuntary impurity, renders him a bad priest, injurious to those who entrust him with the care of their interests before the gods. Since ritualistic perfection cannot be expected from a sovereign perpetually distracted by the business of the State, the errors he might commit, and which would annul the sacrifice, are averted by providing him with a master of the ceremonies—a prompter (*khri-habi*)—who watches over the regulated evolutions round the statue and the victim; points out the order of the gestures and of the changes of costume; if necessary, whispers to Pharaoh the words of each invocation from a book which he holds in his hand, and recites the majority of the prayers for him. When the king officiates, it is usually the eldest of his children who fulfils the duty of master of the ceremonies; by his side Amenhikhopshouf, the panther's skin on one shoulder, the tress of hair hanging correctly over his temple, the right arm held out in front, declaims the *Souton di hotpou* over the pile of offerings arranged before Amen, whilst Rameses burns the incense and pours out a farewell libation. Amen graciously accepts the homage of his son. 'Go in peace, good god, master of the two Egypts, Ousirmarisotpounrî, for thou shalt be stronger than any foreign country, and shalt spread terror in the hearts of the barbarians.' The wars are not only between king and king, or people and people, but between god and god. When Pharaoh starts for the army, he knows that he cannot triumph unless Amen enters the field with him; if Amen does not assist him personally, the foreign gods will easily overcome him and the Egyptians will be defeated. Amen is present upon the battle-fields; his hand shelters the king, turns the arrows away from him, and guides the chariot into the midst of the fight, to scatter and decimate the battalions of the enemy. 'I am here, O my son, and I grant thy prayer. Thou shalt crush the princes of Zahi. I throw them under thy feet throughout their countries. I will cause them to see thy Majesty as a lord of light, when thou shinest over their heads like my image, the sun.—I am here, I promise that thou shalt crush the barbarians of Asia, and shalt lead the chiefs of the people of Ruten into captivity. They shall see thy Majesty adorned with thy panoply of war, when thou seizest thy weapons above the chariot.—I am here, I grant that thou shalt crush the land of the East; the Phœnicians and Cyprus tremble before thee. They shall see thy Majesty like a young bull, strong of heart, armed with his horns, that nothing can resist.—I am come, I grant that thou shalt crush the peoples that dwell in their ports, and the regions of Mitani tremble for fear of thee. They shall see thy Majesty like the hippopotamus, lord of terror, upon the waters that no one may approach.— I am come, I grant that thou shalt crush the peoples who dwell in their islands, and those who live on the bosom of the sea are fascinated by thy roaring. They shall see thy Majesty like an avenger who stands on the back of his victim.—I am come, I grant that thou shalt crush the Tahonou, and the isles of the Danaens are in the power of thy friends. They shall see thy Majesty like a furious lion, that crouches over their corpses in the valley.—I am come, thou shalt crush the maritime countries, and all that surrounds the stream Ocean is bound to thy wrist. They shall see thy Majesty like the master of the wing, the hawk, that sees at a glance all that pleases him.—I am here, thou shalt crush the peoples of the marshes; thou shalt bind the Bedouins, masters of the sands, as captives. They shall see thy Majesty like a jackal of the south, lord of speed, the runner that roams over the two regions.—I am come, thou shalt crush the barbarians of Nubia, and even to the people of Punt; all is in thy hand. They shall see thy Majesty like thy two brothers, Horus and Set, whose two arms I have united to secure thy power.' *

* This song of triumph appears to have been composed for Thothmes III., but it has become a kind of common property of all the Egyptian conquerors, and fragments of it are found applied to Seti I. or to Rameses III. For this reason I could apply it here to Rameses II. without any improbability.

# CHAPTER V.

### THE RECRUITMENT OF THE ARMY.

The barony of Apu and its lord Nakhtminou—The city, the *Great Castle*—The administrative services of the barony—The little love felt by the Egyptians for a military career—The recruitment—Hereditary soldiers and their fiefs—The Egyptian horse—The Egyptian war-chariots—Arming the soldiers—The distribution of provisions for the campaign—The Egyptian army and its composition: the Shairetana—Opinion of learned men upon military life.

PSAROU is not only count of the nome of Thebes, but chief governor of the *Land of the South*, that is to say, of almost the whole of Upper Egypt, of the neighbourhood of Siout as far as the first cataract. He started the next day after receiving Pharaoh's commands to prepare everthing for the war, and levied his men and his provisions in one part of the nomes of his district, from Kousit and Coptos, from Denderah, the city of Hathor, and Tinis, where the Egyptian monarchy first took birth 4000 years ago. Since this morning his boat is moored in Apu,* the capital of the Panopoliti, where he is staying with the hereditary prince, Nakhtminou.

In the olden times the great feudal families that divide the land of Egypt were almost independent, forming a number of secondary dynasties under the sometimes nominal suzerainty of Pharaoh. Since the

* Apu, named by the Greeks Khemmis or Panopolis, is now Omun-el-Khemim, commonly called Ekhmem.

power has fallen into the energetic hands of the Theban kings, the chief barons have been obliged to restore the almost sovereign power which they had usurped, and they are now only the hereditary governors of their fiefs, rich and respected for their nobility, but carefully watched by the king's officers and threatened with deposition, if not with death, at the least suspicion. Most of them cherish the secret hope that they will soon witness a revival of the old state of things; a long minority, a succession of incapable kings, a revolution in the palace, an invasion by the maritime nations, or simply an unlucky war which would destroy the prestige of the dynasty, and enable them to reconquer their authority. In the meantime, some of them have taken office, and fill positions in the court near the person of Rameses; other, like Nakhtminou, live peacefully upon their estates, dividing their time unequally between their pleasures and the duties of an administration which the jealousy of the suzerain renders lighter every day.

Apu is celebrated for its spinning mills.* Seen from the stream it produces an illusion of life and activity. Some thirty boats are scattered along the bank, about one hundred porters are loading or unloading them, singing as they work; higher up, the royal warehouses—*the double white house*—in which the corn, flax, fruits, stuffs, and cattle are stored, crown the bank with their crenellated walls. An old city, indolent and silent, sleeps behind this foreground; narrow alleys, scarcely animated by the murmur of a few looms, are guarded at intervals by troops of emaciated dogs; there is a small market, clean and quiet, where some twenty contemplative merchants wait from morning until evening for customers who never seem to come. To the east the temple of Minou raises its imposing mass.

---

* The spinning mills of Ekhmem still exist; their chief manufacture is a material with little blue and white checks of which the fellah women make their outer garment, the *mélayah*.

Towards the north-east beautiful bushy gardens, separated by deep moats which serve as canals during the summer, as roadways during the winter, produce a rampart of verdure between the houses and the country. The walls of the enclosures are garnished with wild brambles, of which the branches fall into the road, greatly endangering the faces of travellers.

The usual residence of the prince, the *Great Castle*, is in the centre, a short distance from the river. It is built of masonry, rectangular, or nearly so, surrounded by a wall of unbaked bricks, high and thick, crenellated, with rounded merlons. An oblong court occupies the centre, closed to the west by the palace, bordered on the three other sides by arsenals, storehouses for the forage and provisions, as well as by smaller houses, in which the different officers of the various administrative departments of the principality and their respective chiefs are installed. It is really a fortress, capable of resisting a regular siege, in which the old lords of Apu have often held out against their rebellious subjects or against troops of Maaziou* Bedouins unexpectedly appearing from the desert; even against the disciplined bands of Pharaoh. They have been sometimes reduced by famine, never by force. Nakhtminou, peaceful through necessity, if not by temperament, was engaged with his Overseer of Granaries when the arrival of Psarou was announced to him. Each of the baronies, like Egypt itself, has its complete system of government, of which the prince is the natural head, and which he manages uncontrolled, except that he must perform all the obligations of a vassal towards his suzerain—personal service, annual contributions in metals and in kind, and a military contingent, of which the importance

---

* The Maaziou were Bedouins of Libyan origin. Their name, identified by a pun with the Arab word *meâzah* (kid), is preserved in that of the Meâzeh Bedouins, who are still found in Middle Egypt on both sides of the Nile.

varies according to the extent of the fief and its population. We find then in the nome of Apu: a manager of the cattle, an overseer of agriculture, a steward of the granaries, a director of the warehouses, a director of the spinning mills, a military governor, an overseer of the bakeries, a state council in miniature where the notables of the province meet; even a herald, who solemnly transmits the decrees of the noble lord to his subjects. Nakhtminou, who had known for some time, through a special messenger, of Psarou's business with him, had immediately taken all the measures which experience dictated to secure the execution of the royal orders, particularly of those relating to the militia.

The Egyptian of pure race does not like the military profession, and the miseries endured by soldiers furnish literary men with inexhaustible subjects for their satire. They delight in describing him, ragged, hungry, and thirsty, ill-treated by his officers for the most trifling faults, and only escaping the arrows of the enemy to succumb to the fatigue of the long marches; then, as a contrast to this unpleasant picture, they depict the scribe—rich, respected, and in safety. Consequently, at the first rumour of war, at least half of the men, whose age renders them liable to serve, hasten to take refuge in the mountains, out of reach of the recruiting agents. They remain in hiding until the operations are over and the conscripts on their way; they then return to their village, when a few well-placed gifts stop the indiscreet questions which might be asked as to their absence at such a critical moment. Nakhtminou has not given them time to resort to their traditional manœuvre: upon the same day that the royal decree reached him, he sent orders that the levy of the contingent should be made. The heads of the villages, who are answerable for the zeal of their officials and whose property is security for their conduct, at once seized all who were likely to fly, and for some weeks all the young men of Apu who could serve have been waiting in prison until it pleases Psarou to choose the tallest and strongest of them to send into Syria.

Nakhtminou hastens to meet his guest, salutes him, and conducts him into the council hall. The usual ceremonies are not yet completed, and the notable men of the district are already arriving, one after the other, all clad in white robes. The day is passed in paying compliments, the evening in feasting, and all serious business is deferred until the morrow. Early in the morning Psarou and Nakhtminou instal themselves at the back of the court under an open portico, where the sun will not annoy them. The military governor and his lieutenant are placed beside them; the scribes, who register the recruits, bring their books and desks and squat down behind them, the *kalam* behind their ears; a dozen *chaouiches*, half bailiffs, half executioners, stand on each side, stick in hand, ready to strike at the first sign. The country people have been assembled at the gates of the castle since daybreak, grouped by villages under the command of their mayors. At a gesture from Nakhtminou, the crier of the nome tells the door-keepers to let them in, and the first group appears. The mayor marches at their head, a kind of standard in one hand. When he reaches the prince and the emissary of Pharaoh, he bows and kneels down, whilst his people stand a few steps behind him, the spine bent, the arms swinging. One of the scribes indicates from the registers the population of the village, announces the number of able-bodied young men that it contains, and that of the recruits it should furnish; then reads the names one after the other. Each man raises his hand as his name is called. If any one is missing, the governor questions the mayor: Is the absent man ill? refractory? has he any occupation that exempts him from service, or any infirmity? The mayor does his best to answer the questions, trembling in every limb, for a *chaouiche* stands by his side, and he is certain to be bastinadoed if Pharaoh's representatives do not accept his excuses (Fig. 43). Selection made, the future soldiers are separated from their companions and shut into one of the storehouses of the castle; the others hasten back to their homes, rejoicing to be once more free with only a fright.

The same formalities are repeated for every village in the barony of Apu. In spite of the zeal with which the scribes try to hasten the sad work, it lasts several days. There is nothing but marching past, roll-calls, and bastinadoes from morning till night. The rela-

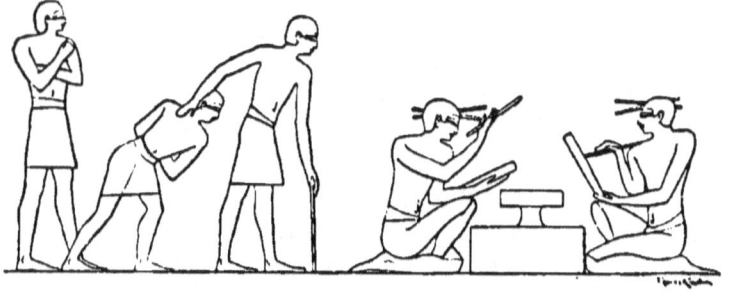

Fig. 43.—Before the Scribes.

tions gather round the doors to await the result of the trial. The army never restores the men that it leads into the distant countries of Syria or Ethiopia. Those that it absorbs are mourned by their families as if they were dead. As soon as a group of villagers go out, the women hasten forward and try to distinguish which of their relations are amongst them; those whose husband, brother, or son does not reappear burst into sobs, throw dust upon their hair and face, and lament as they are accustomed to do at a funeral. At last, on the fifth day, Psarou inspects the conscripts himself, and releases those that he deems the least strong until the total contingent is reduced to the number of six hundred infantry, which the principality is bound to furnish to the king.

This is the delicate point of the operation; the rest is easily, almost mechanically, accomplished. In fact there are in each nome, by the side of the fellahs for whom military service is the result of chance, families of a higher class for whom it is an hereditary duty. Each of them holds a fief—either from the sovereign or from the lord of the manor—an estate of about eight acres, free of taxes, transmissible in a direct or collateral line, but always under the condition of military service. All the men are inscribed upon special registers, which are deposited with the commandant of the nome. In times of peace only a small number of them are annually called out to form the guard of the princes or of Pharaoh, but in time of war they all go unless they can find some legitimate excuse—infirmity, old age, or temporary illness. If the father be too old to go himself, he is replaced by his son or by his nearest relation. The levy of the army is usually made very rapidly, for if courage fail, interest ensures promptitude. If the vassals neglect to respond punctually to the lightest summons, their fief is forfeited, seized by order of the officials, and their family is reduced to poverty.

The men are there; they must now be equipped. In common life the Egyptian never carries arms; only the shepherd who leads his, flocks to lonely spots at the foot of the mountains has an iron-tipped stick or a javelin, a bow and arrows, a knife or a dagger, with which to defend himself against wild beasts or the Bedouins he may encounter. The material of war is guarded under seals in the State depôts, that of the infantry in the *house of weapons*, that of the cavalry in the breeding studs. It is only recently that the horse has been known in Egypt; the shepherds introduced it into the land, and they perhaps owe the incredible rapidity of their success to the terror which their steeds inspired in the first encounters with the Egyptians. The horses are usually strong and of good height. The forehead is convex, which gives a slightly curved and sheepish profile to the head. The neck is tapered, the croup thin and rather narrow, the thigh lean, the leg spare, the tail long and full. They resemble in all respects the horses always seen amongst Asiatic peoples, but it is only with great trouble that they can be prevented from becoming weak and degenerate. The climate enervates them, the season of the inundation does not agree with them, and the race has to be continually recruited with stallions and mares bought or taken from Syria. Thebes, Memphis, Hermopolis, most of the great cities of Middle Egypt, contain breeding studs. The possession of many chariots is the chief luxury of the nobles. Pharaoh encourages it as much as possible by rewarding the owners of well-kept stables, and reprimanding or even punishing those who do not take sufficient care of their animals. Apu has not more than fifty which are fit to enter the field. Its geographical position and the limited extent of its territory prevent it from furnishing a larger number. The chariots, like the horses, are of foreign origin; the first were imported from Asia, but the Egyptian workmen soon learnt to make them more elegant, if not stronger, than their models. Lightness is their distinguishing quality; one man can carry a chariot upon his shoulders without feeling tired by it. Only leather and wood are used in their construction; a very small quantity of metal, gold or silver, iron or bronze, is admitted in the ornamentation (Fig. 44). Sometimes the wheels have four

Fig. 44.—The Manufacture of the Chariots.

or eight spokes, but the usual number is six. The axle is a thick, strong piece of acacia wood. Two pieces joined one above the other indicate the general form of the body, a half-circle, or rather a half-ellipsis, closed by a straight bar; upon this framework is fixed a floor of sycamore wood, or a bottom of thongs of crossed leather. Light panels fill up the centre of the ellipsis, full in front, hollowed at the sides, and provided with two curved supporting bars. The pole, which is all of one size, is connected with it at about one-fifth of its length. The large end is fixed in the centre of the axle, and the body is fixed upon it, like a gigantic T; the back flat upon the axle, the front set, so to speak, in the curve of the pole; a double thong of leather secures the solidity of the whole. A yoke, shaped like a bow, is attached to the free end of the pole, and serves to harness the horses. There are

Fig. 45.—The Wrestling Match.

generally three Asiatics in the same chariot; but there are never more than two Egyptians—the warrior who fights and the coachman who drives the horses or holds the shield during the battle.

The distribution of the weapons is a festival, which is made as brilliant as possible. When Pharaoh is present he remains from the beginning to the end; everywhere else the royal officials or the nobles are proud to preside over it. All the men included in the levy from Apu assemble in the court of the castle, and arrange themselves in companies: the country recruits, the hereditary soldiers, and the chariot soldiers. They first go through all the marches and counter-marches usual in the army, races in groups, jumps in line, the sudden halt; then the ranks are broken and the men engage in wrestling (Fig. 45).

After one or two hours of this exercise, they resume their original positions; the Director of the *House of Weapons* opens his storehouses and the distribution commences (Fig. 46). Only the kings, the princes, and a few foreign soldiers wear a helmet of iron or

Fig. 46.—Distribution of Weapons to the Recruits.

bronze and a leathern shirt, covered with bronze scales (Fig. 47). The Egyptians wear a striped handkerchief or a felt cap upon their heads; a kind of oval apron, fastened to the waist-belt and formed of bands of

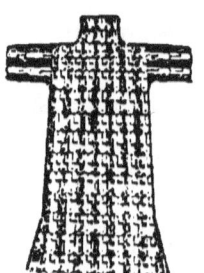

Fig. 47.—Royal Cuirass.

Fig. 48.—Shield.

leather sewn together, sometimes covers their stomach and hips. The shield (Fig. 48) consists of a framework of light wood, square at the base, rounded at the top, covered with an ox-hide, and provided towards the centre with a metal plate about eight inches wide. It has only one handle, and forms a kind of movable rampart, which is held up with the left hand, and which requires great skill to render it of any use. The soldier, sheltering himself behind it, sees the enemy's arrow or javelin coming towards him, and tries to receive it on the metal point; if he succeeds, it falls; if he fails, it pierces the hide and perhaps his chest too. For the attack he has a spear, six feet long, a javelin, axe, club, bow and arrow, a dagger, short sword, and sometimes a knife, with a wide curved blade, the favourite weapon of the kings, which is called the *khopshou*. Each man receives from the hands of the storekeepers the equipment of the regiment to which he belongs, and the horsemen re-

Fig. 49.—War-dance of the Archers.

ceive from the *Director of the Horse* a chariot and two horses: the coachman harnesses them quickly and attaches to the sides of the chariot two bow-cases, as well as two large quivers for the arrows and javelins. The distribution over, the manœuvres recommence, but in a new direction. Twenty archers first execute the war-dance of the Maaziou Bedouins. They place themselves in line, give a sudden spring as they utter their war-cry, turn round, brandishing their weapons above their heads, lay their bows upon the ground and pick them up again with eccentric contortions—alternately advance and retreat; their comrades marking their movements by clapping their hands or by striking two boomerangs together (Fig. 49). When this wild scene has lasted long enough the march past commences. The chariots lead the way, then follow the light troops, bareheaded, without apron or shield, a bow in the left hand, the axe or the boomerang in the right hand, the standard-bearer on

Fig. 50.—The Light Troops Marching Past.

the left, closing the ranks (Fig. 50). The heavy infantry follow to the sound of the trumpet, wearing the leather apron, the shield and spear on the left shoulder, the axe in the right hand; the officers do not carry any weapons, and merely hold a commander's

Fig 51.—The Line Infantry Marching Past.

bâton (Fig. 51). When all have passed, the officers and the standard-bearers leave their ranks and come forward to salute the prince kneeling (Fig. 52): the festival is over. Early on the following morning the men come in search of their provisions for the march. The director of the stud has prepared rations of forage and grain for the horses. The chief baker has not wasted his time, but has cooked the amount of bread necessary for feeding the whole troop during a fortnight. It is scarcely bread, but a kind of round, flat, black cake, made of a very close paste, which dries rapidly, and becomes as hard as a stone; it must be softened by soaking in water before it can be eaten. The soldiers arrive in squads; each carries a small linen bag, in which he places the allotted ration (Fig. 53). A flotilla of large boats is awaiting them; they crowd upon the bridge, amongst the horses, whilst the chariots and luggage are piled upon the roofs of the cabins.

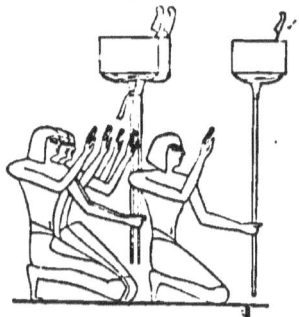

Fig. 52.—Saluting the Prince.

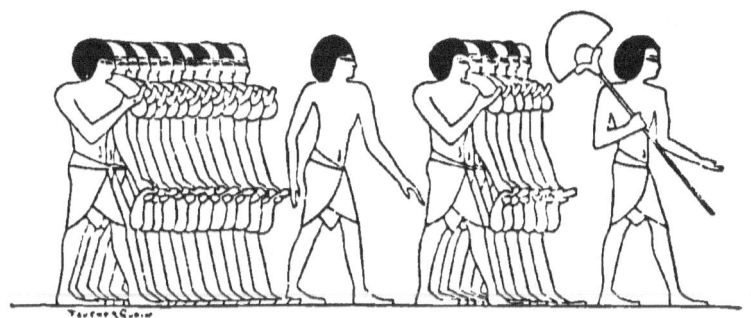

Fig. 53.—The Soldiers fetching their Rations for the Campaign.

In about a fortnight they will have rejoined the main army which Pharaoh has assembled at Zalu,* upon the eastern frontier of the Delta.

It is composed of unequal numbers of Egyptians and foreigners: the latter are attached to the person of Rameses. Like most kings, Pharaoh likes to surround himself with a guard of barbarians, whose wild

* Zalu, the *Sellé* of the geographers of the Roman epoch, is now a mass of ruins at some distance to the west of the Suez Canal, near the station of El-Kantarah.

physiognomy, strange weapons and costume, strike the imagination of his subjects, and heighten his prestige in their eyes. He recruits them from the Libyan tribes of the desert, and from amongst the pirates, who from time to time are drawn by greed of gain or the spirit of adventure as far as the coasts of Egypt, from distant Greece, the islands, and Asia Minor. One of these pillaging bands, belonging to the warlike nation of the Shairetana of Lydia, had been surprised and entirely carried off during the last year of Seti I. Rameses kept it beside him, added to its numbers all the prisoners of the same race taken during his early wars, and thus formed a small select corps devoted to himself. The Shairetana (Fig. 54) are clothed in the long Egyptian skirt and a close-fitting jerkin of thick stuff, with black and white stripes, opened at the side, and held in place by two braces. They are armed with a long double-edged sword, and a large leathern shield, sewn with disks of gilded metal. They wear a round helmet on the head, without any protection for the neck, frequently surmounted by a large ball and two pointed horns. They are the only foreigners that accompany Rameses this time; the Libyan auxiliaries, Bedouins, and negroes remain in Egypt, at the disposal of the queen and of the officers entrusted with the regency.

Fig. 54.—A Shairetana of the Guard.

The soldiers of native race are divided into four legions, each named after one of the great gods, the legion of Amen, the legion of Ra, the legion of Ptah, the legion of Sutekh. The contingents of the various nomes are distributed amongst them; when that of

Apu arrives it is joined to the legion of Amen. The war-chariots form a special corps, commanded by the king and his son in person. Foreigners, Egyptian infantry, chariot soldiers, are all jealous of each other. The Egyptians grudge the Shairetana the favour shown them by Pharaoh, and the post of honour which he gives them in the battles. The cavalry, which contains the young men of noble family, despise the legions in which the mass of fellahs and the common soldiers serve. This rivalry between the services might become dangerous under an ordinary general; Rameses takes advantage of it to stimulate the ardour of his soldiers. The Egyptian lacks fire and passion, but he is patient, endures fatigue for a long time, and fears neither pain nor death; he forms the nucleus of a strong resisting army. The Shairetana and the other foreign mercenaries are there to communicate to him the offensive qualities in which he is deficient—impulse and vigour.\*
They resemble yeast that is introduced into a heavy paste to lighten and improve it.

Nakhtminou's youngest son is scarcely ten years old. He is a fine child, slender, tall for his age, skilful in all bodily exercises, intelligent, and very lively. The sight of the weapons and the tumult of the last few days have filled him with a warlike ardour which continually displays itself, much to the annoyance of his family. He neglects his lessons, writes his exercises anyhow, and, when reprimanded by his father, only replies that he wishes to be an officer, and need not study so much. Psarou, amused by his enthusiasm, delights in talking to him on this subject whenever he

---

\* I have borrowed this description, changing the actual names, from the accounts of the campaigns of Mohammed Ali and Ibrahim Pacha. The fellah of to-day so absolutely resembles the fellah of antiquity, that I have not hesitated to apply to the armies of the Pharaohs the same remarks that are true of the modern armies. The Shairetana and other mercenaries must have filled the same *rôle* under Rameses that the Arnaoots and Europeans filled under Mahommed Ali.

meets him. 'Ask my old Ennana,' he says to the boy one day, 'what he thinks of the fine profession you are so fond of. He is a good adviser, and you will do well to listen to him as though he were the god Thoth.' Ennana is a scribe of the Double White House, who accompanies Psarou in all his journeys. He is unrivalled as a book-keeper, and no one is quicker in discovering an error of a sack of corn in twenty registers. He is also a poet at times, and whenever he has a moment's leisure he writes, in verses or in prose, upon every subject that offers itself, sacred or profane.

The departure of the infantry and of the chariot soldiers has inspired him, as we might suppose. When Nakhtminou's son asks his opinion, his answer is already written in rhythmical words that please the ear. 'Why, then, dost thou assert that an infantry officer is better off than a scribe? Come here, and I will tell thee the fate of an infantry officer, the extent of his sufferings. He is taken when quite a child, the tress still hanging over the ear,* and is imprisoned in a barrack. He is beaten, and his stomach is covered with wounds; he is beaten, and his head is broken by a wound; he is laid down and beaten like a papyrus,† and he is bruised all over by the stick. Come, now, whilst I tell you about his march into Syria, his journeys to distant lands. His provisions and his water are upon his shoulder like the burden of an ass, and weigh upon his neck like that of an ass, until the joints of his spine are displaced. He drinks foul water—still perpetually mounting guard. When he reaches the enemy?—he is only a trembling bird. If he return to Egypt?—he is no better than old, worm-eaten wood. He is ill, and must lie down, he is carried home upon an ass, whilst robbers steal his clothes and his servants run away.

* The hair of young children was gathered in a thick plait, which fell over the left ear. See Fig. 8, p. 14.

† The stems of the papyrus were vigorously beaten in order to weld the fibres together, and thus make leaves upon which the scribes could write.

Therefore, O my child! change the opinion thou hast formed upon the scribe and the officer.'

The son of Nakhtminou is a little disappointed by the sceptical, mocking tones of the lines he has just heard; the sound of the trumpets and the brilliancy of the weapons had prevented him from thinking of these discomforts. However, he consoles himself by saying that the cavalry officers have nothing to fear from all these annoyances. 'The chariot soldiers?' replied Ennana, gently. 'Now, let me tell you the fatiguing duties of the chariot soldier. He hastens to choose his horses from his Majesty's breeding studs; when he has chosen two fine horses he rejoices loudly, he returns to his village, and drives at a gallop—for he is pleased to gallop fast upon a chariot—but he does not yet know the fate that awaits him. He gives up his possessions to his grandfather; then he takes his chariot —a chariot of which the pole has cost three *outnou* of copper and the body five *outnou*\*—and gallops away in it. But he entangles himself in his reins, and falls to the ground amongst the thorns; a scorpion stings his foot and his heel is pierced by the bite. When his accoutrements are examined his misery is at its height; he is stretched upon the ground and receives one hundred blows from a stick.'

The son of Nakhtminou still persists in dreaming of chariots and battles; a love of struggle and noise is a weakness of all children. Age and reflection calm this youthful ardour; in a few years he will marry—'make a wife,' as they say here—take a lucrative post upon his father's estate or in Pharaoh's court, and never be more than a peaceful scribe. The Egyptians in the time of Thothmes III. and of Amenophis II. were more faithful to their childish impressions; they willingly served during their whole lives, and the profession of soldier seemed to them quite as good as the career of a

\* See p. 20, Note, the weight of the *outnou*, and the means of calculating the value in modern coin.

scribe. This deterioration of the military spirit is somewhat injurious to the greatness of the country. Seti I. and Rameses, good generals as they are, have not won so many victories as their predecessors of the eighteenth dynasty, and these victories have been less decisive. Amenophis III. still levied tribute from the Khita; Seti was obliged to treat with their king as an equal; the gods alone foresee the end of the campaign now about to commence. The mercenaries form only a portion of the army at present. If the aversion which the natives feel for military life increases, and everything leads us to believe that this will be the case, the number of barbarian soldiers must be enormously augmented, and then—every one knows what the result always is; the former slaves rapidly become the masters, and the day is not perhaps far distant when the foreign bands will place one of their own leaders upon the throne of Pharaoh.*

* This really happened about a hundred years later, after Seti II., when the foreigners gave the crown of Egypt to the Syrian Her-Heru.

# CHAPTER VI.

### LIFE IN THE CASTLE.

Aspect of the country of Apu—Passage of the ford—The incantations against the crocodiles—The villa of Nakhtminou—The garden and the fruit-trees of foreign origin—The ponds—The vines and the winepress—Irrigation—The shepherds—The fishpond: fishing and fowling in the marshes—Netting fish: salting fish—Netting birds: preserving game—Hunting in the desert in olden times—The gamekeeper's department—The valley of Apu—The written rock—Hunting in the desert—The monsters—Return to Thebes: the pillow and the god Bisou.

THE inspection of the registers of the taxes followed the levy and the departure of the troops. Psarou has taken part of the stuffs which the city pays into the treasury on account of its manufactures, and a portion of the arrears of the ordinary tax in grain stored in the royal granaries. He has embarked it all, and would be already on the road to Thebes if Nakhtminou had not requested the honour of retaining him as a guest for two or three days longer, and of giving him the pleasure of a chase in the desert. His favourite villa is situated on the north-east of the city, near the entrance of a wild valley, which leads straight to one of the districts of the mountain where game is most plentiful. The party leaves Apu early in the morning, and goes across the fields to avoid the long turns of the road; the beans are in flower at this season, and the stems are so tall that men and beasts are almost hidden in the perfumed verdure. Beyond the beans the way lies through fields of dhoura and corn; then, after passing a few groups of palm-trees, the riders cross the road, and a canal about fifteen yards wide lies before them, its stagnant water confined between two crumbling banks of clay.

The ford is not far away, but a herd of cattle, walking slowly along, reaches it first and stops the way for a moment (Fig. 55). The chief shepherd pauses, examines the water with a glance, and rapidly utters a few words: 'Halt, crocodile, son of Set! Do not wave thy tail; do not move thine arms; do not open thy mouth: but may the water become like a rampart of burning fire before thee! Halt, crocodile, son of Set!' The crocodile is always hidden near the fords. The

Fig. 55.—Cattle crossing the Ford.

incantation which the shepherd has just recited will infallibly blind it or stupefy it, so that it will not see either man or beast, or, if it see them, it cannot attack them. The water is not deep; it scarcely reaches the bodies of the oxen. Still, one of the calves is too small to cross on foot, and a herdsman is obliged to carry it over on his back. The unlucky calf does not appreciate this mode of travelling, and turns lowing towards its mother. The latter, equally uneasy, replies, but the herdsman who follows consoles her rather ironically: 'Oh, good mother, is the rascal carrying off thy calf?' A village formed of poor, low huts lies in front of the travellers, but the left bank of the canal is guarded by the crenellated brick wall which usually distinguishes the house of an important man; behind it stands the villa of Nakhtminou.

The garden is entered through a monumental brick gateway (Fig. 56). The opening is framed by doorposts and lintels of white stucco, covered with hieroglyphics; a dedicatory inscription, ornamented with the cartouches

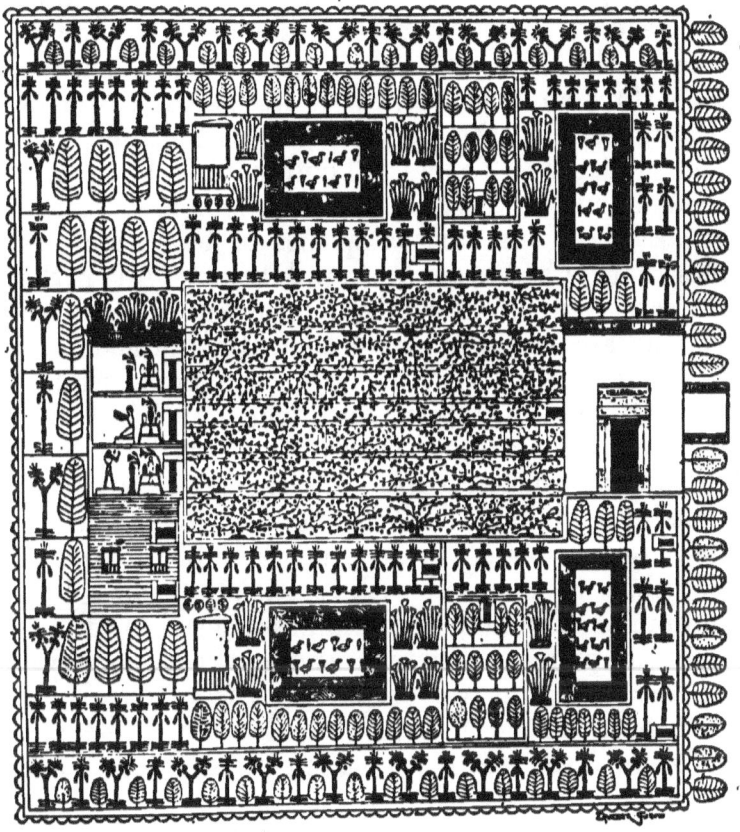

Fig. 56.—An Egyptian Villa.

of Seti I., states that it was constructed by Nakhtminou's father, nearly thirty years ago. The swingdoors are of massive cedar wood, strengthened by heavy bronze hinges. They are only opened upon grand occasions for the nobleman and his guests, the usual entrance to the enclosure being through two posterns to the left of the gateway. The garden forms a perfect square of about one hundred yards each way, divided into portions of unequal size by walls of dry stone, scarcely two feet high; rustic gates of painted wood lead from one to the other. They are planted partly with fruit-trees and partly with ornamental trees, some of foreign origin.

In fact, the Egyptians are very fond of new flowers and essences; they transport as many as possible to the banks of the Nile, and try to acclimatise them there. Queen Hatshepset sent a fleet of five ships to the land of Punt,\* to fetch the scented fig-trees that she placed in her orchards at Thebes. Thothmes III. had pictures placed in one of the chapels of the temple of Amen at Karnak of all the various species of beasts and vegetables that he had brought from his campaigns in Syria and from the regions of the Upper Nile. Private individuals are not less active than the Pharaohs. For the last four centuries the Egyptian flora, which is naturally poor, has been continually enriched by at least twenty useful or decorative plants, the apple, almond, and pomegranate, besides some new varieties of raisins and figs. Nakhtminou has found means of collecting specimens of nearly all these plants, and now shows them to his guest with legitimate pride. In his own opinion, his most valuable possession is a very rare species of palm-tree, which is found occasionally, at long intervals, in two or three parts of the Nubian desert, between the Nile and the Red Sea. The poets, who know it by hearsay, compare it to Thoth, the god of wisdom, because of its fine size and marvellous properties. Its fruit, before reaching maturity, contains a kind of sweet milk, of which the barbarians are very fond. This tree has a unique history. The father of Nakhtminou brought it from the land of Akiti, when he went to dig the wells upon the road to the gold mines in the time of Seti I. There is not

---

\* The land of Punt responds to the southern coasts of Arabia and the land of the Somali.

another specimen for thirty leagues round the country —Pharaoh himself has only two or three in his parks at Thebes. Four oblong pools, bordered by a stone kerb, ornamented by great bunches of lotus, and crowded with ducks, are symmetrically placed in the midst of the trees. A screen of common dates and of cassia-trees alternating with dom palms* runs along the inside of the wall, and shelters the villa from the dusty wind of the desert. Thousands of birds—lapwings, sparrows, green-robed siskins, grey doves with black collars—nest in the bower and enliven it with their

Fig. 57.—A Vine: Gathering the Fruit.

quarrels. Shade and fresh, cool air prevail in the grounds. The contrast is delightful after the barrenness and heat of the surrounding plain. As soon as the threshold is crossed one comprehends why the pious Egyptian hopes that his soul, as its supreme felicity, will return to sit under the trees he has planted, by the side of the pools he has dug, there to enjoy the refreshing breeze from the north. A large trellis planted with vines extends from the gate to the dwelling

* The dom is a kind of palm-tree, of which the trunk is divided into two branches, and each branch into two new ones. It bears rather large fruit, which the old Egyptians seem to have greatly appreciated. The dom palm is not found before Siout in ascending the Nile. The tree is gradually disappearing from Egypt proper.

(Fig. 57). It is supported by several rows of painted wooden columns with lotus capitals. The vines, placed in a line between them, grow high above the heads of the pedestrians beneath. Every year Nakhtminou amuses himself with the vintage. He watches the slaves gathering the grapes, placing them in baskets, and pressing them in long bags of coarse linen (Fig. 58). He thus obtains a thick, sweet wine, which easily turns sour, unless mixed with resin. Two small open

Fig. 58.—Pressing the Grapes.

kiosks are placed to the right and left of the house, each facing one of the basins. The master delights to come here in the afternoon to play at draughts or indolently watch the gambols of his ducks. The storehouses, stables, all the materials for agricultural labour, are placed in a second enclosure at some distance from the first.

The land, which extends outside as far as the desert, has been adapted, with some little trouble, to the establishment of a market garden. It is watered from the canal by means of a series of balances placed at intervals along the banks (Fig. 59). Imagine a beam forming a lever and suspended about one-third of its length between two vertical posts; the shortest arm bears a counterweight in clay; a basket of palm-leaves is suspended to the longest. From sunrise to sunset a fellah fills the basket, raises it to about the middle of his body, losing half its contents in the process, and empties the remainder into a trench, which conducts the water towards a given part of the estate, which is

Fig. 59.—The Balance for drawing Water: the *Shadouf*.

divided by small embankments into squares of various sizes, called *houses*, in which the vegetables are planted. The water passes from house to house until it reaches the other end of the field. The overflow is carefully collected into pools, which serve for both cattle and men to drink from. In this way the prince procures all the vegetables he requires for his table during every season of the year—onions, cucumbers, mad apples, lupins, gombos, and mallows of various kinds.

The land, which is not regularly watered, but only moistened by the infiltering of the canal, is not useless on that account. Wherever the water penetrates, the grass grows strong and close, and for a few weeks it is a carpet of verdure profusely sown with pink, violet, or yellow flowers; where moisture ceases, vegetation abruptly vanishes. Flocks and herds graze on these lands during the winter months. They remain six or seven days at a time, under the guidance of the shepherds, sleeping out of doors, drinking from the pools or the canal. When one spot is exhausted, they migrate to a fresh place, and do not return to the village until after they have traversed all the land that belongs to their master. The shepherds, accustomed to living together, form a special class, of rougher habits and more savage character than the usual population. They allow their hair and beard to grow; many of them even have red hair, which is held in horror by the devout. It is, in fact, believed that red-haired men or beasts are the agents of Set, who assassinated Osiris, and who is execrated as the spirit of evil. The shepherds occupy their leisure hours in weaving mats, cooking, and preparing the balls with which they fatten their stock. They often find some difficulty in protecting themselves against the marauding Bedouins or the wild beasts. Nevertheless they are gay, fond of singing, and full of contempt for sedentary occupations.

A little to the north of the village the canal widens into a large marshy pool, in which papyri, water-lilies, the blue lotus, and twenty species of aquatic plants grow well and thickly. The plants are so bushy that they resemble a number of islands, amongst which small canals wind capriciously, with scarcely width enough to allow a boat to pass through. Each of them forms a miniature world, where thousands of insects and birds live peaceably: pelicans, geese, and ducks by the side of the heron, bittern, white ibis, and teal. Sometimes, however, an ichneumon, a marten, or simply a cat from the neighbourhood, will slyly get in, and make great havoc amongst the half-fledged nestlings. The waters are as well stocked as the plants: eels, pike, lampreys, mormyrus, all fresh-water fish abound there. The crocodile frequents them, and sometimes even a hippopotamus that has lost its way will take refuge in one of the pools after the inundation has subsided. The depth and extent of the pool are not too great for it to be easily drained and cultivated; moreover, each year the Nile raises the bottom by a fresh deposit of mud, thus rendering the task easier. The princes of Apu have never cared to undertake it. Arable land is not lacking upon their estates, and they prefer to leave preserves for fishing and hunting near their towns.

The morning after their arrival, Nakhtminou, his wife, and children, lead their guest to the pool, where they all embark. The boats they use consist of an oblong wooden case, placed in the middle of a bundle of rushes, and secured by strings of papyrus. The two extremities are tightly tied, and are sometimes elongated into a point, sometimes carried straight out of the water, or sometimes ornamented with a large lotus blossom. The whole bark is so light that one or two men, according to the length, easily carry it from one pool to the other upon their shoulders. It frequently capsizes, but no one troubles about that, for all Egyptians swim from infancy, and the simplicity of their costume prevents any great dread of an unexpected bath. Nakhtminou only takes with him a long, double-pointed harpoon (Fig. 60). He rapidly pushes into the thicket of plants with his wife and two children, who manage the skiff. Standing with his body bent slightly forward, he scrutinises the water. Suddenly he plunges one arm down with a rapid movement and catches two fine perch at a stroke. Psarou, who prefers fowling, is accompanied by the two daughters of his host. They take a tame goose, which serves as a decoy for the game, and a cat trained to retrieve. Psarou carries neither bow nor javelin, only about twenty boomerangs. The boomerang is a curved stick, slightly rounded on one side, flat upon the other, sometimes unornamented, sometimes shaped like a serpent. It is held in one hand, then thrown into the air; any bird hit upon the neck falls, half dead. Psarou is unusually skilful in this sport, and every boomerang that he launches hits its mark. The cat springs forward and picks up the game, not without

Fig. 60.—Fishing with a Double Harpoon.

swallowing some eggs or nestlings that it passes on the way (Fig. 61).

Fowling and fishing of this kind are amusements reserved for the rich and noble. Professional fowlers and fishermen use appliances of more certain effect, particularly nets (Fig. 62). The fishing-net is a long sweep-net with large meshes. Its upper part is supported on the surface by wooden floats, whilst the lower part is furnished with leaden balls, which sink it to the bottom and give the necessary tension. It is thrown either from the bank or from a boat, then upon a signal from the leader half-a-dozen men take the cords and haul it to land. The largest fish are carried in the arms, the smaller ones in baskets, to a neigh-

Fig. 61.—Fowling with a Boomerang upon the Pond.

bouring shed, where salters open and cleanse them; then, after rubbing them with salt, hang them in the

Fig. 62.—Fishing with Nets.

open air to dry. This method is not particularly efficacious. The fish thus prepared have always a disagreeable taste and a strong smell; they also spoil very quickly. The working classes do not seem to mind these defects; to them it is a feast unobtainable every day, and the rich themselves eat it occasionally.

Large nets are used for fowling (Fig. 63). They are stretched upon an hexagonal frame of wood, which opens with hinges. The favourite spot for putting them out is a piece of almost clear water between two tufts of reeds. The net is opened and then fastened by a

Fig. 63.—Fowling with a Net.

rather short cord to a stake driven into the mud; three or four men hold a second very long cord, which is so arranged as to shut the net when it is drawn. The head fowler throws down the bait, a few handfuls of grain or some crumbled bread, and, concealing himself as much as possible, he watches the movements of the birds. As soon as he considers them in a good position, he issues his instructions in a low voice, 'Attention, walk well, the game is ready!' He then rises suddenly, unfolding a linen band, the men draw the cord, and the two sides close with a loud noise. Half-a-dozen geese that were outside fly away, about thirty remain prisoners. The fowlers quickly cage the young ones that they hope to tame, and tie the others by the feet, three or four together. One wrings their necks and plucks them, a second cuts off the heads and draws them, a third pots them with salt without smoking them (Fig. 64). Not only geese and ducks are treated in this way, but small birds, like quails and partridges. The game thus preserved is soaked in cold water for some hours before it is used, and when sufficiently freed from salt, the birds are eaten raw, or arranged in a stew; well prepared, they form a dish which, if not delicate, is at least preferable to the fish.

# LIFE IN THE CASTLE. 105

Hunting in the desert was originally not only a pleasure but a necessity. It had two equally important objects, the reinforcement of the herds and the destruction of wild beasts. Most of the animals now seen on the farms were not at that time entirely subject to man. Sheep, goats, and perhaps asses, were domesticated, but the pig was still half wild in the sloughs of the Delta, and the ox itself could be captured only with the lasso. The unclaimed lands, which laid between the last canals of the Nile and the foot of the mountains, formed the best hunting-grounds; there the gazelle, oryx, mouflon, and ibex, which came down to water in the plain, were easily attacked and pursued into the gorges or over the desert table-lands where they lived. Mixed packs, in which the jackal and hyena-dog figured by the side of the wolf-dog and the greyhound, scented and retrieved for the master the

Fig. 64.—Preserving Game in Salt.

prey which he shot with his arrows. Sometimes a young animal followed the hunter who had just killed its mother, and was carrying the body home. Sometimes a gazelle but slightly wounded was taken to the village and cured there. These prisoners were tamed by daily contact with man, and formed round his dwelling a kind of incongruous herd, which was kept partly for amusement, but chiefly for the profit it yielded. It was, in case of need, a provision of meat on the spot. Frequent hunts kept up the numbers, and some of the herds included hundreds of stock. Time gradually taught their keepers to distinguish between the species which could be rendered profitable, and those which by nature were incapable of domestication; now we occasionally find a few tame gazelles in the houses of the rich, the delight of the women and children, but herds of them are no longer reared, and hunting is now an amusement, not a duty.

Most of the principalities or nomes have their regular gamekeepers, under the command of a head keeper. Accustomed to wander over the mountain perpetually, they at last know every yard of it. There is no path that they have not followed, spring or well which they have not discovered, ravine which they have not explored from one end to the other; they are the vanguard of Egypt, who keep watch against the Bedouins, and their vigilance has more than once saved the richest cantons and cities in the valley from the incursions of the Tahonou, the Anou, the Qahaq, and other half-barbarous tribes that roam to the east and west. Nakhtminou has charged Bakourro, the present head gamekeeper, to make the necessary preparations for a battue of two or three days' duration in the direction of the Lake of Gazelles; the general meet is to take place at the entrance of the Valley of Apu, under the Written Rock, between nine and ten in the morning. A few minutes' walk along the canal, then an abrupt turn to the east, and the entrance of the valley is reached. It is the bed of a dried-up torrent, with a bottom of fine sand strewn with fallen stones. The walls are perpendicular, but the action of the sun has destroyed the ridge and the upper strata, and the loosened rock has crumbled into long banks of rubbish (Fig. 65). At every rainy season this rubbish is displaced; the waters undermine the banks during the winter wherever the current strikes them, then carries them away block by block, throwing them further down towards the plain. The gorge, which is fairly wide at first, soon narrows. It is divided in six places by beds of hard, compact stone, which the water has not yet worn away; they form six successive steps, from which fall six cascades in the rainy season. In passing from one to the other, the pedestrian must

Fig. 65.—The Valley of Apu.

climb the wall by steep, narrow paths, full of rolling stones. The interval between the fourth and fifth steps forms a level plain about two hundred yards square, divided in the centre by a narrow gorge. The waters continue there in miniature the work that they have executed on a larger scale in forming the valley. They have hollowed out a trench from six to eight yards deep, and three or four yards wide, obstructed by pebbles and enormous blocks of stone, which are displaced and carried a little further down every year.

A strong vegetation develops and flourishes in the shade of the rocks long after the summer heat has dried up everything around. One variety of caper-bush with a violet flower, a rich plant with round, fleshy leaves, and a species of small tamarisk, climb and grow in the crevices wherever they find a handful of vegetable earth. A few puddles, the last traces of the winter rains, sparkle here and there; in one spot, more enclosed than the others, a thin line of water, still running and leaping from one stone to another, gives itself the airs of a cascade.

The cavalcade painfully advances up this ravine. An enormous rock, detached from the mountain many centuries ago—perhaps before Egypt itself existed—stands next the waterfall on the right side of the valley. This is the *Written Rock*. It is larger at the summit than at the base, and forms a kind of tent, which can easily shelter five or six men from the sun. From time immemorial the gazelle-hunters have made their siesta beneath its shade, and many of them have written their names upon it, or drawn hunting scenes with their knives—a gazelle, an ostrich, or a goose, which is one of the symbols of the god Minou, the protector of the desert; lastly, the image of Minou himself, his arms raised, wearing feathers upon his head. Bakourro and his men had arrived the previous evening. Some of them carry the nets and the stakes to stretch them with, others hold the large greyhounds with strange names—Abaïkaro, Pouhtes, Togrou—in a leash. The two parties join and ascend the valley together as far as the well of the spring. Here the water slowly collects at the bottom of a narrow funnel, where it is always cool. A rock overhangs it, in which a grotto, or, rather, a niche has been hewn; it is shallow, but high enough for a man to stand upright in; it is dedicated to Minou. A halt is made in this spot for lunch, and for the party to wait in the shade until the hours of noon are passed. About three o'clock the hunters proceed at a more rapid pace, for the way is long and laborious. The valley ends in a blind gully, about six or eight hundred yards from the well. It is first a narrow gorge, half barred by enormous stones, then a valley in which a few inferior herbs and a group of palm-trees are found; then a new spring, which filters drop by drop from the base of the mountain; then an immense circle filled with scattered rocks. A winding path leads to the higher table-land, which extends beyond the range of sight in gentle undulations. At nightfall the caravan reaches the bank of a hollow,

Fig. 66.—Hunting in the Desert.

filled with water, which receives from the natives the pompous name of the Lake of Gazelles. During the night the hunters bar the entrance to an abrupt ravine which opens near the lake with nets extended over stakes. They then make a wide circuit, and post themselves at the other extremity with a dozen dogs. At dawn, the animals from the neighbourhood, which pass this way as they go down to drink, enter the gorge as usual; as soon as about a hundred have passed, the ravine is closed with other nets and they are taken in a trap. The dogs are loosed, and (Fig. 66) drive them along to where Psarou and Nakhtminou, posted behind the improvised fold, can without fatigue shoot with their arrows all that come within range—hares, oryx, antelopes, ostriches, jackals, lynx, even striped or spotted hyenas; in less than two hours all are taken, wounded, or killed. Formerly this pastime, apparently so inoffensive, was attended by some danger. The lions and great felines, such as the leopard or the tiger, were fairly numerous, and the sportsman who started in search of a wild goat sometimes met them face to face on his road; then the hunter would become the game. Now, however, lions have almost disappeared. The Pharaohs pursue them continually, and destroy as many as possible. Amenophis III. killed

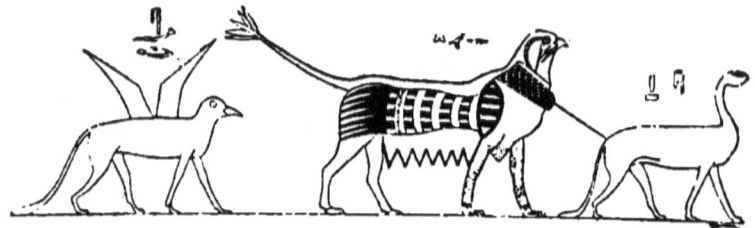

Fig. 67.—The Monsters that live in the Desert.

one hundred and twelve in the first ten years of his reign, and if Rameses II. has not yet attained the same number, it is because his predecessors have nearly destroyed the race.

According to the tribes that inhabit the desert, it formerly contained animals still more terrible, though fortunately rarer, than the lion: sphinxes with human heads; griffins with jackals' bodies, eagles' heads, and hawks' wings; tigers with serpents' heads (Fig. 67). No one could ever boast of having killed one of these monsters. They avoid man, whom they could easily kill, and are only seen far away, on the furthest limits of the horizon. Many people, Psarou amongst them, do not believe in their existence, but, on the other hand, the hunters and the leaders of caravans tell a thousand tales of their marvellous strength and curious characteristics. Every one knows that an oryx can turn a man into stone with a glance, and that the lion fascinates its victim with its eyes; once stupefied he loses all his will, the lion forces him to follow it as long as it pleases, and then kills and eats him at its leisure, when it is next hungry. The monsters not only possess the same power, but exert a malignant influence which no one can define over all that they meet. These creatures form the theme of conversation round the camp-fires in the evening, and many wonderful anecdotes are told about them, but none of them are seen during the two days that the party remain near the Lake of Gazelles. Perhaps in order to meet them one should penetrate further into the desert, to the vicinity of the peak of Bakhou and the mysterious regions where the sun first appears every morning at break of day.

Psarou, who is no longer young, returns delighted but exhausted from this excursion into the desert. For some days his head has felt heavy, and he has found some trouble in working, or even in thinking. Perhaps this is only a passing ailment, but, anyhow, he prefers returning home and being ill at Thebes if really indisposed. He bids Nakhtminou farewell, collects the boats which carry the corn for the taxes as he passes, and invites the stewards of the granaries to go with him. Their zeal deserves some reward, and he wishes to present them himself to Pharaoh for the decoration of the Golden Collar. At last, one week after leaving Apu, he reaches home; his wife Khâit and her children, who were impatiently awaiting his arrival, keep him talking for a good part of the night, and he is too pleased to see them again to think of his indisposition. At last he retires, but, tired as he is, Psarou cannot sleep for some time. The events of the last few days continually recur to his memory, and this recollection possesses him so completely that it produces a species of delirium, of which he is vaguely conscious. The Egyptians rest the head upon a pillow of curved wood mounted upon a foot (Fig. 68). The grotesque figure of the god Bisou (Fig. 69) is often carved upon it, a dwarf with short legs, large stomach, and ugly mask, but of a pleasant disposition, who guards the sleeper from the spirits and

Fig. 68.—A Pillow.

Fig. 69.—The god Bisou.

demons that roam about during the night. Now, either Bisou is busy elsewhere, or he is careless in performing his office, for Psarou feels that he is surrounded and, as it were, invaded by a malevolent force against which he struggles in vain. At last, towards morning, he falls asleep, but his repose is troubled by disquieting dreams, and he obtains no rest.

# CHAPTER VII.

### ILLNESS AND DEATH.

*Pharaoh's palace—Psarou's audience—The distribution of golden collars—The Egyptian doctor: sorcerers and doctors—Treatises upon medicine—The exorcist: incantation against the spirits in possession of the patient—Death and the first mourning—Duration of the soul—Osiris, the first mummy—Embalmment—Preparation of the funeral furniture—The coffin and the amulets—The mummy.*

Two sharp knocks at the door suddenly awaken him; a herald is there, to take him to the palace by Pharaoh's command. No invitation could be less welcome, for his indisposition, instead of passing off as he hoped, had increased during the night. His head feels heavy and burning, his tongue dry and bitter; he aches all over, and strange starts shake him from time to time. But no matter: when Pharaoh speaks, all must obey. He rises, rouges his cheeks and lips to conceal their pallor, puts on the long, curled wig, which has never felt so heavy before, and the white linen robe, and painfully enters his chariot. The Egyptian palaces are not built for eternity like the temples. They are light constructions of wood, brick, or undressed freestone, but rarely blended with granite except for the decoration of the great doorways. They recall the villa of Nakhtminou on a large scale: isolated pavilions for the harem, storehouses for the provisions, barracks and quarters for the royal guard and for the personages attached to the household; large courts planted with trees, gardens with kiosks and pools, where the women can amuse themselves. A strong crenellated wall gives the dwelling the appearance of a fortress or of an entrenched camp, and at times, in case of riots or conspiracies, the *royal god* has owed his safety to the solidity of his doors and the height of his walls. Without dismounting, Psarou crosses a yard, where the Shairetana\* are on duty with a few Egyptian archers; and after making himself known to their officer, he enters the court of honour, followed by his band of collectors and rural officials.

The gallery, where the king sits during the audience, is placed exactly opposite the entrance-gate, projecting from the wall of the façade, and communicating directly with the private apartments. It is raised four or five yards above the ground, ornamented breast-high with a cushion of stuff embroidered with red and blue, and sheltered by a canopy of curiously carved planks, supported by two slender wooden pillars painted in bright colours and ornamented at the top by many-coloured streamers. As Psarou leaves his chariot and prostrates himself between the two columns, Rameses appears in the front of the box with Nefertari and addresses some affable words to him, which he is careful not to answer. Etiquette forbids any subject to present himself before Pharaoh without being apparently stupefied and overwhelmed; his tongue fails, his limbs sink beneath him, his heart ceases to beat, he does not know whether he is alive or dead.

He does not recover himself until he hears Pharaoh say to one of the *Friends*† who stand at the foot of the tribune, 'Raise him, that he may speak to me.' Then Psarou officially returns to life and stands. 'Thou art then returned in peace,' continues Pharaoh, 'and thy business has been well done. But are not those who

---

\* See page 88, what is said of the Shairetana.

† The word *Friend* is one of the titles given to the highest positions in the household of the king.

stand behind thee the stewards of the granaries and their scribes?' 'They are, Sovereign, our Master. They have done more for thee than has ever been

Fig. 70.—The King (Amenophis IV.) and his Family throwing Golden Collars to the People.

done since the time of the god Ra, for they have collected more wheat in this one season than has been harvested during the last thirty years.' 'That is well,' replied Pharaoh; then turning towards the queen, 'Here is Psarou, who has returned to us from the fields. Does it not seem to you that he has acquired something of the appearance and manners of a rustic?' This jest, which is a proof of unusual satisfaction, delights all present. The laughter passes from the king to the queen, from thence to the *friends*, and then on by precedence to the groups scattered in the court. Pharaoh then calls one of his chamberlains. 'Let gold, much gold, be given to the praiseworthy nomarch, the Count of Thebes, Psarou, whose age is advanced and happy, and who has never committed a fault.' Some attendants bring him upon a stand a pile of collars and bracelets in gold and silver gilt, of weight and size proportioned to the value of the services rendered (Fig. 70). He takes one and throws it from the box, the queen follows his example, and three little princesses, running up as to a new game, soon throw down the remainder.

The friends pass the largest collar round Psarou's neck, and fasten the smaller ones to it, so that they fall upon his chest like a golden breastplate. Standing upright, with raised arms, he chants a hymn of thanks. 'Beautiful is thy rising, good prince, beloved of Amen, thou who art eternally equal to thy father, Ra, and who sharest his immortality. Oh, prince! who art Horus amongst men, thou who hast given me life, me and my double, we are joyful in thy presence, happy are those who obey thee; I am humble, but thou hast made me great by all that thou hast done for me, and I have reached a happy old age without being once found criminal.' Officials issuing from the two doors which flank the tribune now enter the yard laden with collars and bracelets, with which they decorate the stewards of the granaries. Full of gratitude, the latter salute Pharaoh with raised hands and straight bodies, then kneeling, prostrate themselves till their faces touch the ground, rising with bowed spine and drooping arms, finally standing upright, in the successive postures of adoration (Fig. 71). A busy scribe rapidly registers the number of the jewels distributed,

Fig. 71.—Postures of Adoration before Pnaraoh.

and the names of the recipients (Fig. 72); the soldiers come from their quarters and join their shouts to those of the fortunate officials; slaves bending beneath the weight of large amphoræ come forward and pour out wine and beer for the crowd assembled outside (Fig. 73).

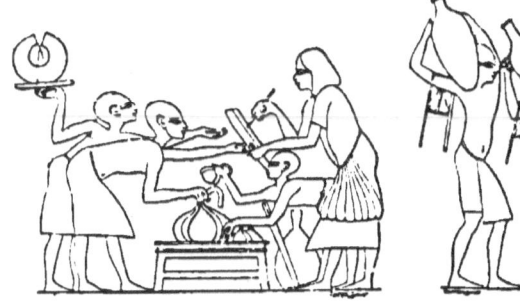 

Fig. 72.—The Scribe registering the Golden Collars.

Fig. 73.—The Slaves bearing the Jars of Wine.

For a few minutes the whole scene is full of confusion and of noisy delight, which appear to give much satisfaction to the royal family. Psarou at length retires; as soon as he has crossed the threshold his friends, slaves, all the members of his family and household, rush to him, and overwhelm him with caresses, kissing his hands, feet, and clothes, and congratulating him in broken phrases (Fig. 74). If he has worked hard, at all events his reward is great, and one hour like this in a man's life suffices to redeem many years of trial.

Psarou, sustained by pride and emotion, has never faltered for an instant during this long ceremony; but pain resumes its ascendancy even before he leaves the palace, and when he reaches home he falls rather than alights from his chariot, and sinks into the arms of his wife, who has come to meet and welcome him. The attendants quickly remove the mass of gold that weighs upon his chest, he is undressed and laid upon a bed, but he only regains partial consciousness, and remains plunged in a kind of painful stupor; it is no longer a passing indisposition, but a serious illness, and no one can tell how it will end. The Egyptians are not yet resigned to think that illness and death are natural and inevitable. They think that life, once commenced, should be indefinitely prolonged; if no accident intervened, what reason could there be for its ceasing?

Fig. 74.—Psarou congratulated by his Family.

In Egypt, therefore, man does not die, but some one or something assassinates him. The murderer often belongs to our world, and can be easily pointed out: another man, an animal, an inanimate object, a stone detached from the mountain, a tree falling upon a traveller and crushing him. Often, though, it belongs to the invisible world, and only reveals itself by the malignity of its attacks: it is a god, a spirit, the soul of a dead man, that has cunningly entered a living person, or that throws itself upon him with irresistible violence. Once in possession of the body, the evil influence breaks the bones, sucks out the marrow, drinks the blood, gnaws the intestines and the heart, and devours the flesh. The invalid perishes according to the progress of this destructive work; and death speedily ensues, unless the evil genius can be driven out before it has committed irreparable damage. Whoever treats a sick person has therefore two equally important duties to perform. He must first discover the nature of the spirit in possession, and, if necessary, its name, and then attack it, drive it out, or even destroy it. He can only succeed by powerful magic, so he must be an expert in reciting incantations, and skilful in making amulets. He must then use medicine to contend with the disorders which the presence of the strange being has produced in the body; this is done by a finely graduated *régime* and various remedies. The cure-workers are therefore divided into several categories. Some incline towards sorcery, and have faith in formulas and talismen only; they think they have done enough if they have driven out the spirit. Others extol the use of drugs; they study the qualities of plants and minerals, describe the diseases to which each of the substances provided by nature is suitable, and settle the exact time when they must be procured and applied: certain herbs have no power unless they are gathered during the night at the full moon, others are efficacious in summer only, another acts equally well in winter or summer. The best doctors carefully avoid binding themselves exclusively to either method, they carefully distinguish between those cases in which magic is sovereign and those in which natural methods suffice, whilst their treatment is a mixture of remedies and exorcisms which vary from patient to patient.

They are usually priests, and derive their knowledge from the source of all science—the works that Thoth and Imhotpou* composed upon this subject soon after the creation. Deposited in the sanctuaries, these works were for a long time unknown to all, but they have been restored to us one after the other by special revelation in the centuries which followed the accession of Menes. The *Treatise upon the Destruction of Pustules upon the Limbs of Man* was found in this way 'beneath the feet of the god Anubis at Letopolis, and brought to the king Housaphaïti' of the second dynasty. Another 'was found in the great hall of the temple of Coptos by a priest belonging to the temple. Whilst the whole earth was plunged in darkness, the moon suddenly rising shone upon the book and lighted it by her beams. It was then brought to King Kheops as a miraculous discovery.' To these divine works physicians have now added prescriptions borrowed from celebrated foreign doctors, Phœnician or Syrian, and have also enriched them with all the observations they have made in the course of their own practice. Every doctor who has tried one of the remedies recommended by the author notes the case in the margin or between the lines of his copy, and briefly states the result obtained—which formula is good, which is uncertain, and which is ineffectual or produces fatal results; by this means the experience gained is not lost, and the treasure of science increases from generation to generation.

Khâit summons an exorcist to see her husband. Nibamon is unequalled in Thebes for his skill in curing the most violent headaches. He arrives towards evening, accompanied by two servants; one carries his black book, the other a casket, filled with the necessary ingredients for manufacturing every variety of talisman on the spot—clay for modelling, plants, dried or freshly

---

* Imhotpou was the god of medicine, whom the Greeks afterwards identified with their Esculapius; he was a Memphite god, the son of Ptah.

culled, consecrated linen, black or red ink, small figures in wax or baked earth. One glance at the patient tells him the cause of the illness; a dead man visits Psarou every night, and is slowly devouring him. After a few moments' reflection, he takes a little clay, mixes some blades of grass with it, and kneads the whole into a rather large ball, over which he recites, in a low tone, one of the most powerful incantations contained in his book.

The best way of driving away the rebellious spirits is to persuade them that their victims are placed under the immediate protection of one or of several divinities; in tormenting him it is the gods themselves that they unconsciously provoke, and if they persevere in their evil designs they risk annihilation from the person whom they expected to destroy with impunity. Nibamon's incantation commences by announcing that 'The magic virtues of Psarou, son of the Lady Tentnoubit, are the virtues of Osiris-Atmu, the father of the gods,' and then, since this too general proposition would not suffice to alarm the ghost, the magician enumerates the portions which compose the head of Psarou, and proves that they are all armed with divine charms. 'The magic virtues of his left temple are the virtues of the temple of Tmu; the virtues of his right eye are the virtues of that eye of Tmu which pierces the darkness with its rays. The virtues of his left eye are the virtues of that eye of Horus which destroys.' When the litany is ended, if the evil one does not yield, he is told that each of Psarou's limbs is, so to speak, a distinct god. 'His upper lip is Isis, his lower lip is Nephthys, his neck is the goddess, his teeth are swords, his flesh is Osiris, his hands are divine souls; his fingers are blue serpents, the adders, the sons of the goddess Selk; his loins are the two feathers of Amen, his back is the spine of Sibou, his stomach is Nou,' and so on to the soles of his feet: in short, he is a god, and one of the most formidable of the gods, that one to whom nothing in Heliopolis is closed. This is an ingenious method of insinuating that Psarou is an incarnation of Ra, without, however, directly making the assertion. Four times Nibamon repeats his formula, and then glides the ball under the sick man's head. To-night when the dead man appears he will not have sufficient strength to do any harm, and he will remain powerless so long as the ball remains in its place.

Khâit, half reassured, rapidly slips a few golden rings into the hand of the holy man, and invites him to return to-morrow to see the success of his remedy. Psarou, after dreaming all night, has bled from the nose during the following morning and has been seized with foetid diarrhœa. These incidents distress Nibamon but do not surprise him. The evil spirits are always unwilling to leave their prey, and always endeavour to dispute it, inch by inch, with the magician who opposes them. The ghost, driven from the head, now attacks the stomach, and he will only yield to a new spell. Tradition relates that Ra was one day seized with horrible pains; Horus at once modelled a statue of Isis as a child, and by their magic the gods of Heliopolis transferred to it the pain endured by the Sun. Nibamon unhesitatingly applies the same remedy to Psarou. He takes a doll from his casket which resembles the one used by Horus, and murmurs over it an incantation, in which the history of the cure is briefly related. 'Horus is there with Ra, who is suffering in the stomach. Cry aloud to the chiefs of Heliopolis: "Come quickly with your writings! for Ra is suffering, and if he is allowed to suffer for an instant, it will be all over with the living god." Cry aloud to the guardian of the west, the chief of the desert, that he may come and relieve this suffering body that it may be cured.' These words, intentionally obscure, may lead the gods of Heliopolis to suppose that their king is ill once more; they will hurry with their books of magic, and will save Psarou in believing they are saving Ra.

The malady will pass into the image of Isis, who will henceforth retain it and the spirit that produces it.

The second incantation succeeds no better than the first, and days pass by bringing no improvement: the headache diminishes, but round, pink spots appear upon the body; the strength diminishes, the stupor increases, and Psarou seems no longer conscious of what passes around him. The exorcist has failed; it is time to call in a doctor. Pshadou has studied in the temple of Heliopolis, he is chief physician to Pharaoh, and has often succeeded in curing cases that others had despaired of. His first impression is unfavourable, but he does not express it, for fear of alarming the family; he inquires into the symptoms, the treatment adopted, then methodically examines the patient from head to foot. It is unmistakably one of those formidable internal maladies minutely described in the books of Thoth. The illness has been left to itself so long that no human aid can now arrest its course; Pshadou prescribes a remedy more to satisfy his own conscience than in any hope of relieving his patient.

At nightfall a severe pain in the stomach rouses Psarou from his stupor; he is seized with shivering fits and sickness; death will soon follow. Khâit remains by her husband, and the children sitting about the room sorrowfully await the end. Sometimes one of the women interrupts the silence by a short exclamation, 'Oh, my master!' 'Oh, my father!' 'Oh, my beloved!' which the others repeat in a louder tone, prolong for a moment, and then abruptly cease. Towards morning a sudden burst of lamentations and cries wakens the neighbours and tells them that all is over. Wife, children, relations, slaves— the whole family appear smitten with sudden madness. They throw themselves upon the corpse, embrace it, literally inundate it with tears; they beat their chests and tear their clothes. After a few moments the women leave the chamber of death; then, with nude bosoms, head sullied with dust, the hair dishevelled, and feet bare, they rush from the house into the still, deserted streets. Everywhere, as they pass, their acquaintances, friends, and clients arrive, but half clothed, and join the procession, crying aloud. Soon the whole neighbourhood re-echoes with wild clamour, to which even the indifferent respond from their houses. In the meantime the slaves who remain with the corpse hastily wash it and carry it to the embalmers. Two hours later, when the women, tired of running about, return to the house, they find the doors open, the fires out, the rooms empty. Psarou has left his dwelling 'above the earth,' and the place where yesterday he was master already knows him no more.

The soul does not die at the same time that the breath expires upon the lips of man; it survives, but with a precarious life, of which the duration depends upon that of the corpse, and is measured by it. Whilst it decays, the soul perishes at the same time; it loses consciousness, and gradually loses substance too, until nothing but an unconscious, empty form remains, which is finally effaced, when no traces of the skeleton are left. Such an existence is agony uselessly prolonged, and to deliver the double from it, the flesh must be rendered incorruptible. This is attained by embalming it as a mummy. Like every art that is useful to man, this one is of divine origin. It was unknown in the ages that followed the creation, and the firstborn of men died twice, first in the body and then in the double. But Typhon having assassinated Osiris, Horus collected the pieces of his father, perfumed them with the help of Isis and Nephthys, of Thoth and Anubis, saturated them with preserving fluids, and enveloped them in bands, pronouncing all the time certain formulas, which rendered his work eternal (Fig. 75). Osiris was therefore the first mummy, and from it the others were all copied.

When the embalmers receive a corpse, they show

the relations three models in wood of natural size from which they ask them to choose the preparation they wish for. In the first the body is treated exactly in the same way as Horus treated Osiris: perfumes, drugs, stuffs, amulets, prayers, are all repeated, even to the smallest details, so as to secure for the man the

Fig. 75.—Anubis and the Mummy of Osiris.

immortality attained by the god. This method is admirable in its effect, but it is so long and so costly that only princes and the great men of this world are wealthy enough to pay for it. The second, which does not involve such complicated operations, requires less time and money, and is reserved for people of average fortune. The third, which is performed for a very small sum, is applied to the poor, that is, to four-fifths of the Egyptian population. The three methods are based upon the same principle

—to extract from the body those parts which easily decay, then saturate the remainder in salts and aromatics to prevent any change taking place in it. The drugs used are more or less valuable, the work more or less carefully done, the appearance of the mummy more or less luxurious, according to the price given; but the result is the same in all cases—the body lasts instead of perishing, and its perpetuity guarantees that of its double.

Psarou is of too high rank for any hesitation to be possible even for a minute; the first class of embalmment is ordered for him. Besides, Pharaoh has informed the family that he will defray all the expenses of it in consideration of the services of the deceased. The corpse is undressed, washed, stretched upon the ground, the head to the south, under the direction of a master of the ceremonies. A prayer is said, and a surgeon passes a curved instrument up the left nostril, with which he breaks the divisions of the skull and withdraws the brain piece by piece. Another prayer, and a scribe tracks a line in ink about four inches long upon the left side of the stomach above the groin, at the exact spot where Horus opened the body of Osiris. Another prayer, and an eviscerator makes the incision with an Ethiopian stone knife. It is considered sacrilege to open a human body, so as soon as the operator has accomplished his task the assistants attack him, hustle and abuse him, and drive him from the room with sticks and stones. One of the embalmers thrusts his hand into the wound with every mark of profound respect, and rapidly removes the intestines, heart, lungs—all the vital organs—washes the cavities with palm wine, and fills them with crushed aromatics. One last prayer, and the funeral workmen carry the mutilated remains of what was Psarou, to plunge them into the bath of liquid natron in which they must soak for seventy days.

Whilst they are being slowly impregnated with immortality, twenty workshops of different trades are busy preparing a trousseau and furniture for the double, worthy of the rank he occupied in this world and that he hopes to regain in the next. It is really a house that is being prepared for him, with equal, if not superior, luxury to that he had enjoyed during his life. Sculptors are engaged in forming statuettes by the dozen, seated, standing, squatting. Engravers are preparing beautiful *stèles* upon which posterity may read his name, functions, and titles, the eulogy of his virtues, the assurance of his perfect felicity. Potters are baking figurines of blue and green enamel; goldsmiths are working at rings, finger-rings, and collars; hairdressers are preparing wigs of every shape—high, low, with or without curls, black or blue. He has already in reserve a storehouse full of armchairs, stools, beds, tables, linen and perfume chests, to which is now added the new furniture for which he has just been measured—the coffins. He must have two at least, exactly fitting each other, the outline following the general lines of a human body, or rather mummy. The feet and legs are joined together. The curves of the knee, calf of the leg, thigh, and stomach, are vaguely modelled in the wood. The head reproduces the features of Psarou, a little idealised (Fig. 76); the cheeks are full, the mouth smiling, and large enamel eyes fastened into bronze eyelids give to the physiognomy a strikingly life-like expression.

Fig. 76.—A Mummy's Head in the Coffin.

The dead man in his coffins resembles a statue of himself, which can stand upon its feet as upon a base when necessary. Then there are some requisite but less important objects to be made, useful for his comfort and pleasure—chariots for travelling upon the earth, small boats for crossing the water or for transporting his harvests, weapons for war and for hunting, games of different kinds, particularly draughts with many-coloured pieces, the instruments required for his work as a scribe, palettes, kalams, cups, pastilles of colour and of dry ink; even a small library, traced upon pieces of calcareous stone, containing extracts of novels, pieces of poetry, and religious hymns. The dead, to be quite happy in his *eternal home*, must find in it the equivalent of all that he has liked upon earth. Meanwhile his family pass the long days of waiting in tears and sadness. They take no baths, and scarcely wash themselves. They abstain from wine, meat, and wheaten bread, living on black bread and water. The men allow the hair and beard to grow. The women abstain from dressing their hair, rouging their eyes and face, or dyeing their hands with henna. Twice a-day they meet in the mortuary chamber to weep together. The master's death has suspended the whole course of the ordinary life of the house.

The body taken from the brine is but a skeleton, covered with a yellowish, parchment-like skin; but the head has retained nearly all its purity of form. The cheeks are slightly hollowed, the lips are thinner, the nostrils are finer, more drawn than during life, but the face is not changed; but for the immobility of the features and the brown colour of the skin, beneath which the blood no longer flows, one might say that Psarou still lives and will soon awake (Fig. 77). The embalmers take advantage of the suppleness which the *natron* has preserved in the limbs to place the feet closely together and to cross the arms. They wad the stomach and chest with linen and saw-

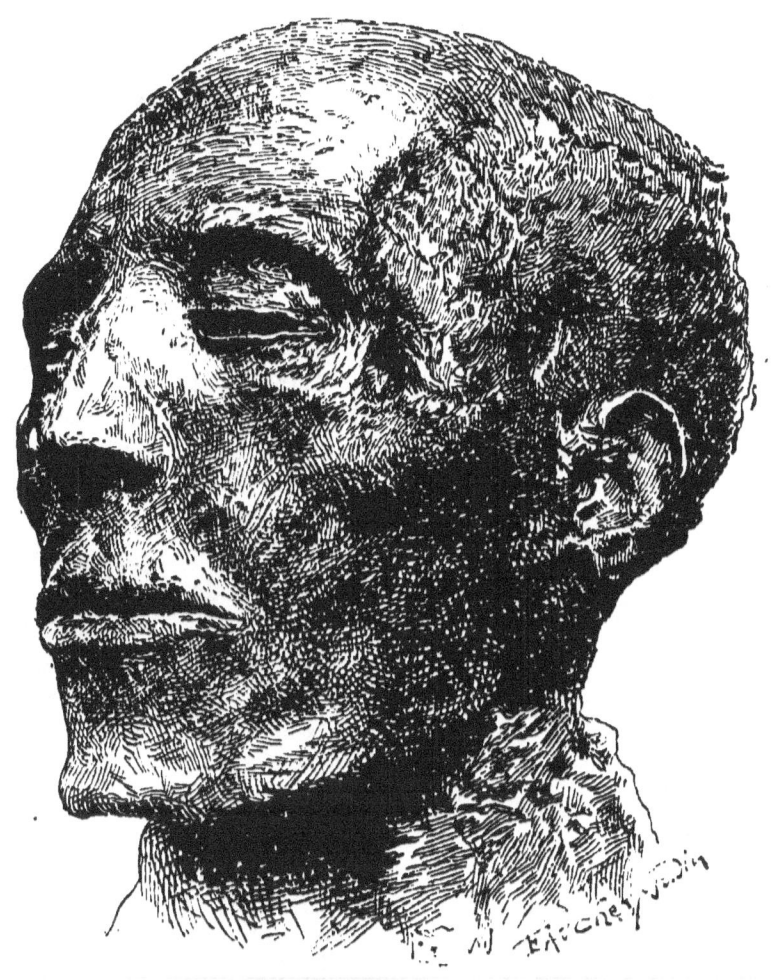

Fig. 77.—A Mummy's Head: the King Seti I. from a Photograph taken from the Corpse preserved in the Museum at Boulak.

K

dust mixed with aromatic powders, then commence the wrapping of the body. Their profession obliges them to be priests and expert magicians as well as skilful surgeons. They fulfil towards the corpse those duties which Anubis and the children of Horus accomplished for Osiris in the fabrication of the first mummy, like incarnate forms of these divinities. The funeral swathe becomes in their hands a lacing of mystic bands, each with its own signification, destined to guard the body from all the dangers and all the enemies which threaten it—gods and men as well as insects and decay; in it they place amulets, figurines, dry flowers, blades of grass, plates covered with hieroglyphics, which form a kind of magic armour for the dead. The master of the ceremonies fastens at the dead man's throat a scarabæus of green jasper bearing an inscription, which forbids his heart, 'the heart which came to him from his mother, the heart which accompanied him upon the earth, to rise up and witness against him before the tribunal of Osiris.' Rings of gold and of blue or green enamel are placed upon his fingers as amulets, which give him a correct voice and enable him to recite prayers with the intonation which renders them irresistible. The head disappears beneath a lawn mask and a network of gummed bands, which almost double its size. The limbs and trunk are wrapped in a first layer of supple, soft stuff, warm to the touch (Fig. 78). Pieces of half-pulverised *natron* are thrown here and there as relays of preservative materials. Packets placed in the interstices of the legs, between the arms and hips, in the hollow of the stomach and

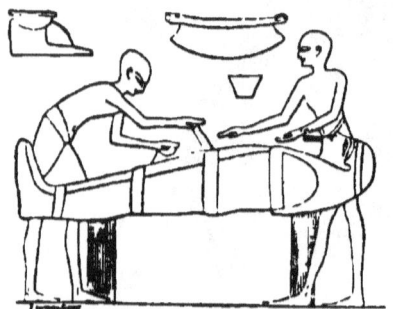

Fig. 78.—Wrapping up the Mummy.

round the neck, enclose the heart, spleen, dried fragments of the brain, the hair, and parings of the beard or nails. In magic the hair plays an important *rôle*: by burning it with certain incantations almost unlimited power is acquired over the person to whom it has belonged. The embalmers therefore conceal with the mummy all the hair they have been forced to

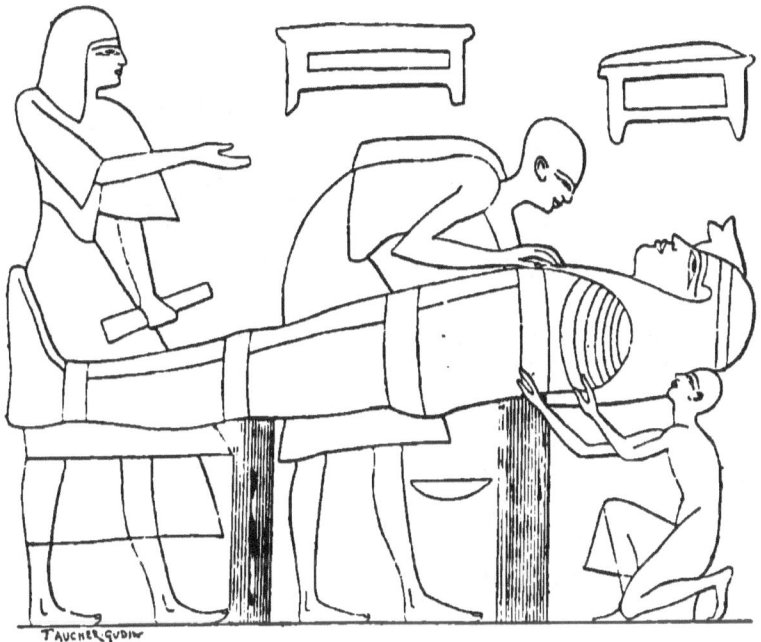

Fig. 79.—The Master of the Ceremonies reciting Prayers during the Swathing of the Mummy.

cut from it, this being the surest method of preserving it from the malignant uses which sorcerers would put it to. Over this first garment a long piece of linen is wound, upon which a caligraphic scribe has copied a selection of the text or the vignettes of the chapters contained in the *Book for Going Out during the Day*. If Psarou read them he will recover his senses, he can leave his tomb or return to it as he will, he will gain the favour of the gods he is likely to meet in the paths of the other life, he can embark upon the boat of the sun or rest in the fields of the blessed, under the paternal sceptre of Osiris. A few turns with the bandages, then another layer of stuff, then new bandages, finally a last shroud of coarse canvas and a red linen sheet sewn at the back and held by bands arranged parallelly from the head to the feet (Fig. 79). As every piece is placed the master of the ceremonies re-

Fig. 80.—The Mummy finished.

cites a prayer defining its nature and efficacy (Fig. 80); at intervals he bends over the corpse and murmurs mysterious instructions in a low voice, which no living person may hear without sin. The wrapping ended, Psarou knows the use of everything that has been given to him, and the advantages which he will derive from it in the other world: mummy and double, he is ready for the tomb.

# CHAPTER VIII.

### THE FUNERAL AND THE TOMB.

The cemetery at Thebes — Violations of the sepulchres — Leaving the mortuary house — The procession — The mourners and their songs — Crossing the Nile — The arrival at the tomb — The offerings and the farewells before the gates — The tomb: its arrangement, furniture, revenue — The ceremonies of the *opening of the mouth* — The funeral meal, the dances, the harpist and his song — The future of the double after death — Its travels — The sycamore of Nut — The tribunal of Osiris.

THE cemetery of Thebes is situated upon the left bank of the Nile, in a detached chain of the Libyan mountains, which ends exactly opposite the great temple of Amen.* The principal height is hewn perpendicularly, and is pierced by deep valleys in every direction; it is preceded by a range of sandy hills, separated from each other by ravines. When Thebes was still a small city the inhabitants buried their dead in the small mound nearest to the stream. As it became more populous the necropolis increased in size, and, growing towards the west, filled the valley of Dayr-el-Bahari. Since then it has been perpetually enlarged towards the south-west, and every height, every turn of the land, has been gradually invaded by the hypogea. Now it is really a city of the dead, that extends some distance from the Nile, as a pendant to that of the living, and that, like it, has its rich quarters, its districts for the

\* Not knowing the ancient names of these localities, I have been forced in this chapter to use the modern Arab names. Dayr-el-Bahari, Drah-abou'l-Neggah, Gournah, El Assassif, Medinet-Abou are all anachronisms that I have been unable to avoid.

poor, its palaces and chapels. Some fifteen small pyramids still standing upon the ridge of Drah-abou'l-Neggah mark the spot where the Pharaohs of the eleventh and twelfth dynasties repose, surrounded by the highest officials of their court. Amenophis I. and his mother, Nefertari, are placed at the entrance of El Assassif, and there receive a solemn worship which renders them the protecting divinities of the canton. Thothmes II., Thothmes III., and their sister, Hatshepset, sleep beneath the terraces of Dayr-el-Bahari. The less-known Pharaohs, princes who have not reigned, princesses of the blood royal, the great officials of the crown, statesmen, generals, and administrators of the past divide the interval, almost grouped by epochs. The traveller, carefully visiting the whole district, sees the history of Theban Egypt gradually unrolled before him, illustrated by the tombs of those who made it.

Groups of mud huts, scattered in the hollows of the ravines, shelter the police-soldiers, the watchmen and their families, the workmen who hew out the funeral galleries and those who decorate them, the lower clergy attached to the funeral and commemorative services, and the sellers of offerings. There is not one amongst these poor people that does not know the quantity of gold and jewels buried daily with the mummies, and these riches, heaped round them a few feet below the earth, are a perpetual temptation, which they never resist. Violations of the sepulchres are common occurrences with them, and form their surest method of enriching themselves. The timid amongst them trust no one, and work alone, touching only the old monuments belonging to extinct families, and therefore seldom entered. The others combine together, pay a high price for the complicity of the local police, and boldly spoil the recent sepulchres, sometimes even the royal ones. Not content with taking the furniture placed in the tombs, they open the coffins, unpack or break the bodies to steal the jewels, then rearrange the fragments and fabricate false mummies, so skilfully arranged that they cannot outwardly be distinguished from the true ones; the first bandages must be removed before the fraud can be discovered. From time to time some of the criminals are captured or denounce their companions. The count-nomarch and the chief prophet of Amen, who have the jurisdiction over this portion of the nome, order an inquiry. A commission examines the damage that has been done and seeks for the guilty parties. The tribunal condemns half-a-dozen to be impaled, and twenty to be beaten. Two months later, the impression produced by this severity has faded away, and the depredations recommence.

Psarou has returned to his dwelling once more. He has been placed upon a state bed; four large alabaster vases, the Canopic jars containing the viscera, being placed beneath it. Each bears a cover of different shape; one has the head of a man, another that of a jackal, the third of a hawk, the fourth of a cynophelus. They represent the gods of the four quarters of the world, the sons of Horus, Hâpi and Amset, Tuamautef and Kebhsenuf; they watch the dead, and prevent the internal organs, the most fragile and yet the most necessary to life, from being stolen or destroyed. And now his tomb is waiting for him, his furniture is ready, his parents and friends have been summoned to escort him, the morning has risen for him 'to go and hide his head in the funeral valley,' and to 'reunite himself to the earth.' At this supreme moment his wife and servants make a last effort to prevent his departure. They cling to the mummy and throw themselves howling upon the men who have come to fetch it; at last they yield, and Psarou crosses the threshold of his home for ever.

A group of slaves and vassals bearing offerings lead the procession (Fig. 80*). The first six carry cakes, flowers, jars of water, bottles of liqueur, and vials of perfume. One holds before him three large birds upon a light saddle; another leads the calf for sacrifice; six carry painted boxes, destined to contain part of the food provided and part of the funeral figurines; lastly, two carry between them a low table, upon which are heaped pots full of fruit and branches

Fig. 80*.—The Funeral Procession: Slaves bearing Offerings.

of palm. This is the provision of food. The following group is entrusted with the usual furniture—chests of linen, folding stools, armchairs, a state bed; two grooms bend beneath the weight of a chariot, with its yoke and quiver; an equerry leads another chariot, drawn by a pair of horses (Fig. 81). The furniture

Fig. 81.—The Funeral Procession: Carriage and passage of the Chariots.

for the funeral chambers is in the hands of a third detachment, more numerous than the two others put together. First, the flagons for the libations; then a case, painted in red and white squares, intended to hold the Canoptic jars; then the jars themselves; then, upon square trays, a mask in gilded cardboard relieved with blue (Fig. 82), weapons, sceptres, bâtons of command, collars, scarabæi, hawks standing with their wings extended in a circle, to be worn on the breast upon festival days, chains, figurines, a human-headed hawk, the image of the soul (Fig. 83). Many of these objects are of massive gold, others are only gilded, some are of wood covered with gold. On all sides the

Fig. 82.—The Funeral Procession: the Furniture.

precious metal shines with a profusion which excites the admiration and envy of the crowd assembled to watch the procession. It is surely too great a defiance of human cupidity to openly display all this wealth,

Fig. 83.—The Funeral Procession: the Weapons and Jewels.

and the watchmen attached to Psarou's hypogeum will have much to do if they wish to preserve it from thieves.

More offerings, then a noisy group of mourners, a slave, who from time to time throws a few drops of milk upon the ground as though to allay the dust; a master of the ceremonies, who, with a panther's skin over one shoulder, sprinkles the crowd with scented water with a large golden spoon (Fig. 84); behind him the catafalque at last appears (Fig. 85). It is, as usual, shaped like a boat mounted upon a sledge, drawn by a double team of oxen and fellahs; the bark of Osiris, with its two mourners, Isis and Nephthys, and its closed cabin, which conceals the mummy from the

Fig. 84.—The Funeral Procession : the Mourners and the Priests.

crowd. Khâit and her children walk anywhere, in front, behind, or at the sides of the coffin; then follow the friends of the family, cane in hand, wrapped in their long festival cloaks, and lastly, the crowd of

Fig. 85.—The Funeral Procession : the Catafalque followed by the Friends.

sightseers. The procession passes through the winding streets at the slow pace of the oxen, stopping all traffic and circulation, stopping itself upon the smallest pretext: one might say that Psarou, regretting his departure from the world, endeavours to prolong his sojourn here, if but for a few hours. Funerals at Thebes are not silent processions, in which grief is scarcely betrayed, save by a few furtive tears. The dead require a noise, sobs, and extravagant gestures. The family not only hire mourners, whose trade is to cry aloud, to tear their hair, to sing their lamentations, and conscientiously to portray the utmost despair, but the relations and friends of the deceased do not hesitate to make a spectacle of themselves, and to disturb, by their sorrow, the indifference of passers-by. Sometimes one of the groups, sometimes the other, utters some brief sentence suitable to the occasion. 'To the West, the dwelling of Osiris; to the West, thou who wert the best of men, who always detested duplicity.' And the hired mourners reply in chorus: 'Oh, chief, as thou goest to the West, the gods themselves lament, as thou goest to the West!' The ox-driver, goading on his oxen, says, to encourage them, 'To the West, oh, bulls that draw the catafalque, to the West! Your master is behind you.' 'To the West!' repeat the friends; 'the excellent man who loved truth and hated falsehood lives no more.' The lamentations die away at intervals, and for a few minutes the procession wends its way in silence. But soon one of the hired mourners recommences, the others join her, and the tumult begins again, louder and more lugubrious than ever. The lament is not remarkable for either originality of thought or deep feeling. Grief is expressed by regular forms which never vary; the habit of attending funerals, and of joining in these manifestations, soon leads each person to compose a rather monotonous repertory of exclamations and condolences. The wish 'To the West' is the foundation of them all; a few commonplace epithets are added to it, and all is said. The near relations only sometimes find sincere accents and touching images to express their sorrow. With inarticulate cries, appeals, and formulas, they mingle praise of their dead with eulogies of his virtues, allusions to his tastes and actions, to the position he has filled, the honours he has obtained, reflections upon the uncertainty of human life, and counsels against the dangers of the life beyond the tomb: a melancholy refrain which each generation repeats over the preceding one, until, in their turn, the following generation chants it over them.

On the banks of the Nile the procession embarks. The bearers of offerings, friends and slaves crowd into three hired barges. The professional mourners and the members of the family enter two of Psarou's boats, which have been dismasted; the outside of the cabin has been covered with striped drapery, in embroidered stuff or cut leather, to represent a monumental *socle*,

Fig. 86.—The Funeral Procession: the Mourners' Bark.

in which the passengers stand, their faces turned towards the funeral bark (Fig. 86). The latter s built in exact imitation of the mysterious skiff used f r the obsequies of Osiris, and now adored in the small city of Abydos, under the name of Noshemit (Fig. 87). It is swift, light and long, decorated at each end by a lotus flower in metal, which bends gracefully as though drooping by its own weight. A chapel stands in the centre, adorned with flowers and green palms. Khâit and her daughters crouch lamenting at the sides; two priestesses, dressed like the goddesses Isis and Nephthys, stand behind so as to protect the body; the master of the ceremonies places himself in the front and burns some grains of incense. The mourners' boat takes this funeral bark in tow, and the whole flotilla starts under the efforts of some fifty rowers.

This is the solemn moment, when Psarou, leaving the city where he has lived, commences his journey beyond the tomb. The crowd assembled on the banks salute him with their good wishes: 'Mayest thou land in peace to the west of Thebes! In peace, in peace to-

Fig. 87.—The Funeral Procession : the Bark of the Dead.

wards Abydos! Descend in peace towards Abydos, towards the western sea!' In fact, this passage across the Nile is of great importance to the future of the dead. The voyage from this earth to the 'other land' is not accomplished with equal facility at every place: like most nations, the Egyptians know the exact spot from whence the souls depart for their entrance to the new world. It is a cleft in the mountain to the west of Abydos; no one can enter it without the aid of Osiris on his bark, and the transport of the mummy beyond the Nile is the emblem of the supernatural journey which the soul undertakes in order to reach the *mouth of the cleft.* The departure for the Thebes of the dead is, in fact, a departure for Abydos, and this is why the name of Abydos is mingled with that of Thebes in the shouts of the crowd. The voices of the dead man's friends are the most frequently heard and they are the most sorrowful: 'To the West, to the West—the land of the righteous! The place which thou lovedst mourns and laments!' And the hired mourners: 'In peace, in peace, to the West; oh, praiseworthy prince, go in peace! If it please god, when the eternal day cometh, we shall see thee again, for thou goest to the land where all men are equal!' Khâit, carried away by her grief, forgets the conventional formulas: 'Oh, my husband! oh, my brother! oh, my beloved! stay, live in thy place; do not leave this terrestrial spot where thou art! Alas! thou goest towards the ferry-boat to cross the river! Oh! sailors, do not hurry, leave him; you will return to your homes, but he is going to the eternal land! Oh! bark of Osiris, why art thou come to take him from me, that he should now abandon me!'

The sailors remain deaf to this appeal, and the pilot interrupts the dirges of the hired mourners: 'Steady, up there on the platform, for we are close to land.' The rebound of the shock which the boat receives in touching would make them lose their balance and throw them into the water, if no one warned them. Whilst the boat containing the friends manœuvres in order to draw up to the banks, its rudder strikes the side of a small sloop behind, and upsets some of the offerings which it contains (Fig. 88), but no one pays any attention to this accident, and the friends continue their dirge without disturbing themselves. 'He is happy, the great one, for destiny allows him to go and rest in the tomb that he has prepared for himself; he obtains the good-will of the Theban Chonsu and the god has granted that he shall depart for the West escorted by generations of his servants, all in tears.' The mummy is replaced upon the sledge, the groups rearrange themselves in their former order, and the procession goes towards the hill of Sheikh Abd-el-Gournah. It is here, upon the *Forehead of Thebes*,* in the neighbourhood of the cave where the serpent goddess Miritskro utters her oracles and accompilshes her miraculous cures, that Psarou has built his 'eternal house,' between the hypogea of Rekhmiri, of Mankhopirrisonbou, of Pahsoukhirou, and of the great statesmen who distinguished the reign of Thothmes III. or of his sons. The path which leads to it is too steep for the oxen to climb with the enormous weight which is dragging behind them. The friends take the catafalque upon their shoulders, and ascend, staggering beneath

Fig. 88.—The Funeral Procession: the Friends' Boat striking the Sloop.

the load, by the uncertain paths which wind amongst the tombs.

At last they pause, quite out of breath, nearly halfway up the ascent, upon a small platform cut in the flank of the hill; here is a piece of rock hewn straight down like a façade, with a low, narrow door opening in the centre. Having reached the end of its journey, the mummy is placed standing upon a heap of sand, its back to the wall, its face turned to the assembled

* The Forehead of Thebes (*ta tohnit*) appears to have been the name of the highest of the hills of Sheikh Abd-el-Gournah. The cave, which is well known to the fellahs, who avoid showing it to Europeans, is now consecrated to the Mussulman sheikh, who cured cases of rheumatism chiefly, like the goddess Miritskro had formerly done.

party, like the master of a new house, whose friends have accompanied him to the door, and who turns back for a moment upon the threshold to bid them farewell before entering. A sacrifice, an offering, a prayer, a fresh outburst of sorrow; the mourners redouble their lamentations, and roll upon the ground; the women of the family adorn the mummy with flowers, press it to their nude bosoms, and embrace its breast and knees.

'I am thy sister, thy wife Khâit! Oh, great one, do not leave me! Is it truly thy wish, my good father, that I should go from thee? If I leave thee, thou wilt be alone, and will any one be with thee to follow thee? Oh, thou who delightedst to jest with me, thou art silent, thou dost not speak!' An old servant, crouching behind her mistress, exclaims, 'Our guardian is then torn from us, and he leaves his slaves!' Then the mourners recommence their chorus. 'Cry aloud! cry aloud! Make your lamentations. Lament and cease not, cry as loudly as you can! Oh, excellent traveller, who art going to the land of eternity, thou hast been torn from us! Oh, thou who hadst so many around thee, thou art now in the land which imposes isolation. Thou, who lovedst to open thy legs and walk, art now chained, bound, swathed! Thou who hadst much fine stuff and who lovedst white linen, art now clothed in the garments of yesterday! She who weeps for thee is become like one bereaved of her mother; her bosom veiled, she laments and mourns, she rolls round thy funeral couch.' Indifferent, in the midst of this clamour, the priest offers the usual incense and libations, with the consecrated phrase: 'To thy double, Osiris, count-nomarch of Thebes, Psarou, whose voice is righteous before the great god' (Fig. 89). The mummy disappears in the tomb, borne in the arms of two men; the night of the other world has seized it, and will never release it.

Like all well-arranged dwellings, the tomb includes state apartments, a chapel—where the double receives the homage and presents of his relations upon festival days—and private apartments, which no one may enter but himself. Psarou's chapel is composed of two rooms: one, wider than it is long, runs parallel to the façade; the other, longer than it is wide, opens perpendicularly to the former, opposite the entrance door. Its walls are covered with paintings executed in fresco upon a coating of beaten, polished earth, which represent every imaginable scene of life. We there see depicted, one above the other from the floor to the ceiling, ploughing, sowing, reaping, harvesting the wheat,

Fig. 89.—The Funeral: the Farewells before the Door of the Hypogeum.

raising the cattle, fishing, hunting in the desert; the workshops of the carpenter, wheelwright, sculptor, goldsmith, glassworker, baker; the preparation of food, then a great dinner, with music and dances by the almahs. These form so many talismans, which have the virtue of securing the effective enjoyment of these objects. If the double be hungry it chooses one of the painted oxen, follows it through the series of pictures from the pasture to the butcher, the kitchen, and the banquet. Whilst it looks at them the actions represented become real; when it sees its portrait upon the wall take a roast joint from the hands of the servant, the joint is before it, gratifying its eyes and satisfying its appetite. Rich doubles of high rank are seldom

L

obliged to resort to this arrangement during the early period of their subterranean existence. The widow, children, or parents frequently bring or send them offerings through their sacrifices. They offer a bull, geese, wine, and cakes to their favourite god, Amen or Osiris, Ptah or Chonsu; the god retains a portion of the good things for himself and transmits the remainder to the souls commended to him. There are also contracts made with the priests of a temple, who, in exchange for an annual payment or a donation, undertake to celebrate commemorative services, to re-provision the tomb a certain number of times every year at fixed dates.

Yet, in spite of all the care taken to provide for the future, the day arrives when the offerings finally cease. The family becomes extinct, changes its home, forgets its old dead; the priests, no longer watched, neglect the terms of the contract; the double, deprived of everything, would die of hunger if it had not the means upon its walls of eternally satisfying its appetite. One last ceremony invests it with a new faculty which differs from any that it has hitherto possessed. The process of embalmment has transformed the man's body into an inert, powerless form, incapable of walking, eating, speaking, seeing, or accomplishing any of the functions of existence; these effects must be cancelled if he is to live again, and this end is attained by the *opening of the mouth* and its complicated rites. The master of the ceremonies and his assistants, the children of Horus, once more stand Psarou upright upon a heap of sand at the end of the chapel, and accomplish round him the same divine mysteries which Horus had celebrated round the mummy of Osiris. They purify him by common water and by red water, by incense from the south and by alum from the north, in the same way as the statues of the gods are purified at the commencement of a sacrifice; then they execute various rites which awaken the double from the sleep in which it is plunged, free it from its shroud, bring back the shadow which it lost at the time of death, and restore the power of movement. Then the sacred butchers kill the bull of the south and cut it up, the priest seizes the bloody leg and raises it towards the lips of the gilded mask, as though inviting it to eat, but the lips remain closed and refuse to perform their office; he then touches them with several instruments, with wooden hands and iron blades, which are supposed to open them. The double is henceforth free; it comes and goes at will, sees, hears, speaks, takes its share of the offerings, and at once uses its new power to invite all who accompany it to a banquet, the first given in Psarou's eternal home.

A passage, cut at the most distant corner of the second hall, leads to a kind of cell, naked, low, without paintings or ornaments of any kind: this is Psarou's room, the spot where his mummy will repose until the end of the centuries, if it please the gods to preserve it from thieves. The workmen of the necropolis lay the double coffin, with its wreaths, close to the west wall; the slaves bring in the Canoptic jars, the caskets, furniture, and provisions which have accompanied the procession during the day, and place them on the ground; the priest recites a last prayer and retires; the masons rapidly build a brick wall before the door. The sound of their trowels ceases at last, the noise of their steps dies away and is lost, the end of a torch they had left in the room burns itself out. However, in the upper room, upon the platform, and in the chapel the slaves have commenced to serve the banquet. The statue of the dead, sculptured in relief at the back of the second hall, presides over the festival, and receives the first portion of each dish. The objects have a soul, a double, like men or animals, and this double, once passed into the other world, enjoys the same properties which its body possessed in this one. The double of a chair or bed is really a chair or a bed for the double of a man. The double of Pharou, present at the festival, enjoys the double of the liqueurs and of the viands quite as fully as its still living guests can do the real liquids and the food. Whilst all present, visible or invisible, are eating, the almahs sing and execute their dances (Fig. 90). Sometimes they address themselves directly to the dead, sometimes to the living, but the same refrain is always heard in their songs: 'Make a good day; life only lasts for a moment. Make a good day; when you have entered your tombs you will rest there

Fig. 90.—The Dance of the Almahs.

for ever, all the hours of each day.' The repast is finished at last, all must now leave and break the last link which still hold the dead to his family. The sacred harpist plays a prelude, then standing before the statue, he chants the dirge first sung long ago at the funeral of the Pharaoh Antouf. 'The world,' he says, 'is but perpetual movement and change. It is an admirable decision of the great Osiris, a beautiful arrangement of destiny, that as one body is destroyed and disappears, others come after him ever since the most ancient times. The Pharaohs, those gods who have lived before us and who repose in their pyramids, their mummies and their doubles are also buried in their pyramids, but the castles that they have built they have no place therein —all is over for them. . . . . Do not, therefore, despair, but follow thy desire and thine happiness so long as thou art upon the earth, and do not wear out thine heart until the day comes for thee in which man prays, without Osiris, the god whose heart has ceased to beat, listening to the prayer. Not all the lamentations in the world will restore happiness to the man who is in the sepulchre; make, then, a good day, and do not be idle in enjoying thyself. Certainly no man can carry his wealth to the other world with him; certainly no man ever went there and came back again!'

Fig. 91.—The Harpist.

What becomes of the double after the funeral? The bulk of the population have very vague ideas upon this point. They are content to think that it inhabits the tomb, and there leads an uncertain existence, scarcely conscious of itself. It never comes out unless it has no food and is driven by hunger: it is then seen wandering in the villages at night, and eagerly throwing itself upon the remnants of food thrown into the streets. Misery then produces a feeling of hatred and vengeance against the living who have forsaken it; it attacks them, tortures them, and afflicts them with illness. Certain doubles do not wait for the moment when they are forgotten before they injure the living; they are instinctively bad, and take a certain pleasure in persecuting their nearest relations. The scribe Qeni was haunted for months by the spirit of his wife Onkhari. He had always treated her well while she was in the world, had given her an expensive funeral, and left her a considerable income; yet she was angry with him, and continually returned to disturb him. He could only free himself from the annoyance by threatening her with a legal action. He wrote to her asking the reason of her posthumous rage, and reminding her of all the affection that he had shown her. 'Since I became thy husband until this day what have I done against thee that I should hide? What wilt thou do when I am obliged to bear witness as to my treatment of thee when I appear with thee before the tribunal of Osiris to plead my own cause before the gods of the West, and thou wilt be judged according to this writing, which will contain my complaints against thee—what wilt thou do?' The roll of papyrus, attached to a wooden statuette of the woman and placed in the tomb, reached its address: Onkhari, fearing to be called in judgment before Osiris, ceased to torment the poor man.

Many of the faithful, to whom the prospect of such a gloomy seclusion is extremely repugnant, suppose that the soul leaves the funeral chamber after a longer or shorter sojourn there, and emigrates to 'another land.' In the regions to which the *mouth of the cleft* gives access there are kingdoms of the dead which are each placed under the sovereignty of a different god —Khontamentit, Phtah-Socharis, and Osiris. Here they welcome the souls of the Egyptians who have had a special devotion for the sovereign divinity and have declared themselves his vassals—*amakhou*. The kingdom of Osiris is the most populated amongst them. It is formed of several islands, of which the outlines are visible from our earth, in the north-east of heaven at the southern extremity of the Milky Way. It cannot be reached without a long and dangerous voyage. The soul, upon leaving its tomb, must turn its back to the valley and boldly enter the desert. It will soon encounter one of those sycamores which grow far from the Nile, and which the fellahs consider fairy trees. A goddess—Nut, Hathor, or Neith—will show herself partially through the foliage, and will hold out a dish covered with loaves and a vase full of water (Fig. 92). Whoever accepts these gifts becomes through them a guest of the goddess, and henceforth he cannot retrace his steps without special permission.

A frightful country extends beyond the sycamore, infested by serpents and savage animals, divided by torrents of boiling water, interspersed with marshes in which gigantic monkeys catch the doubles in a net. Many souls succumb to the dangers of the road and die; those only who are provided with amulets and powerful incantations at last reach the shores of an immense lake, the lake of Kha, from whence they can discern the happy islands afar off. Thoth, the ibis, lifts them upon his wings, or the divine ferryman takes them into his boat and conducts them to Osiris.

Fig. 92.—The Sycamore of Nut.

The god questions them before his forty-two assessors. Thoth weighs their heart in his scales. Maat, the goddess of Truth, whispers to them the negative confession, which in each article declares them to be innocent of a sin (Fig. 93); they are at last acknowledged to be worthy of entering the *Fields of Beans* with the blessed. The Fields of Beans (Sokhit-Ialou) are of inexhaustible fertility; the wheat is seven cubits high, two of the cubits being ear. The dead cultivate and harvest it, carrying in the grain by turns. They may be replaced if they like by small enamelled statues, which are placed in the tomb with them, and which are called the Ushabti or Answerers, because they

Fig. 93.—The Judgment of the Soul at the Tribunal of Osiris.

answer for their master each time that he is called for the work. The remainder of the time is spent in perpetual feasting, singing, long conversations, and games of every kind. Many people consider that this conception of the other world is too material to be true, and they try to imagine a higher destiny for the soul; the priests of Amen-ra hold secret doctrines upon this subject, which they do not like to reveal. These are speculations of the theologians in which the people do not meddle. Men can survive death, that is a fact; how they do so, only the gods can know with any certainty.

# CHAPTER IX.

### THE JOURNEY.

Rameses II. in Syria—Council of war—Baoukou sent to reconnoitre —From Gaza to Joppa: the Syrian fortresses—From Joppa to Megiddo: the forest—Megiddo: condition of the Syrian cities under the rule of Egypt—The sea: the navy and the maritime commerce of the Egyptians—Tyre: its position, its population— Egyptian and Phœnician vessels—Commerce between the Tyrians and the barbarians—Crossing Mount Lebanon—The Hittite army advances to attack Rameses.

PHARAOH had quitted his Theban palace long before the funeral of Psarou. He had reviewed the troops collected at Zalu, and had sent them slowly on towards Syria, through the desert and by the coasts of the Mediterranean, from Zalu to Magdilu, from Magdilu to Raphia and Gaza. Since Thothmes I. Gaza has become an Egyptian city. Rameses spends several days there, waiting for the rest of his army, receiving the reports of his officers and governors, consulting with his generals. All the southern part of the country is quiet to beyond Megiddo; the Sidonian Phœnicia has not stirred, and no movement has been reported from the side of the Orontes. It might be supposed that the peace was universal, and that the forces of the Khita have vanished without leaving any trace of their presence. The king is puzzled to know what this apparent inertia can mean. His eldest son, Amenhikhopshouf, states his opinion that the vile chief of the Khita, despairing of a successful struggle in the open country against the

Egyptian veterans, had scattered his soldiers amongst the fortresses, and was preparing for a defensive war. It would be necessary to take all the citadels of southern Syria one after the other (Fig. 94): Kadesh, Hamath, Khilibu, Nii, and Karchemish. The strongest armies become worn out in these thankless duties, and years pass by before the enemy is beaten. Rameses

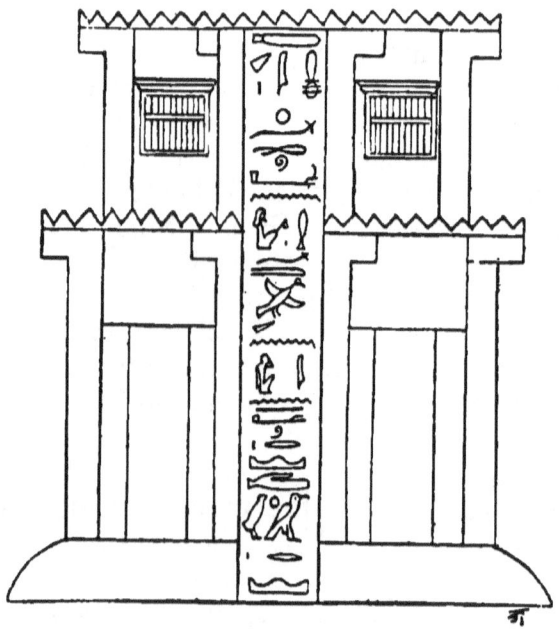

Fig. 94.—A Syrian Fortress.

rejects the conjectures of his son upon the ground that they are not based upon events that have occurred up to the present time.

In fact, Khitasir has called out all the allies that he has secured in Asia Minor: not only the Lycians, but the Mysians, the Dardanians, the peoples of Ilion and Pedasos who dwell upon the shores of the distant sea, have answered his appeal, and their contingents have been with him for several weeks already. They are warlike barbarians, greedy of gain, formidable in battle, but they would never consent to be long away from their own land. Khitasir knows their temperament, and would not have summoned them unless he contemplated some rapid movement. A battle must therefore be expected before long, and if the enemy do not appear, it is because their generals have concealed them in some corner of Lebanon, whence they will suddenly appear as soon as they see a favourable opportunity of surprising the Egyptians. Rameses sends orders to the governors and chiefs of the advanced guard to redouble their vigilance and to explore all the country round Kadesh, to ascertain something of the positions occupied by the Khita. He also dispatches single scouts in different directions: the captain of the mercenaries, Phrahiounamif, towards the east beyond the Jordan to ascertain the intentions of the Bedouins; Roi, the lieutenant of infantry, towards Damascus, although as a rule there is nothing to dread from the tribes that live in the Gaulan; lastly, Baoukou, one of his equerries, towards Tyre and Sidon, commanding him to cross the Lebanon by Gabouna to join the army to the south of Kadesh, and to collect as much information as he can upon the strength and composition of the Khita forces. He (Pharaoh) will follow cautiously by the usual route from Gaza to Megiddo, from Megiddo to Kadesh, and will only arrange a definite plan after receiving the reports of his messengers.

Baoukou, accompanied by one servant only, starts well armed in his chariot. He rapidly crosses the plain which separates Gaza from Joppa. The harvest has already commenced, but the country is deserted, and the villages that he passes are almost entirely abandoned. Although the Egyptian battalions are well disciplined, they do not include amongst their chief qualities any respect for the property of others, and all the localities through which they pass, even in a friendly country, are doomed to pillage. The inhabitants, hearing of the arrival of Rameses at Gaza, have collected all their valuables, jewels, furniture, and goods, and have taken refuge with their flocks in the fortified cities that, with their crenellated walls, crown the hills to the right and left of the road. Beyond Joppa the aspect of the country is changed. A reddish sandy soil succeeds the black soil; a few scattered oaks appear, which soon become grouped in clumps, then, growing closely, the forest commences. The trunks are knotty, twisted, badly grown; the tallest are about thirty feet high, but the majority are small, and do not exceed the height of the brushwood. Muddy rivers, infested by crocodiles, wind slowly amongst the thicket, and lose themselves at intervals in pestilential marshes. It is both a curious and disquieting spectacle for an Egyptian, accustomed to the woodless country on the banks of the Nile, and Baoukou enters the forest with instinctive repugnance. Without counting the Bedouins who haunt these parts, he may encounter wild and formidable animals—hyenas, savage boars, and bears. It is there, so they say, that Kazariti, king of Assur, formerly hunted, and the recollection of his exploits has become popular; but Kazariti was a great hunter before the Eternal, a legendary hero, and Baoukou is only a man—a brave one, no doubt, but still only a man. Alone, without guide or escort, he advances, a little uncertainly, upon badly defined paths, encumbered by stones and quagmires. All his attention is absorbed in driving his chariot over these obstacles, and his heart is in his hand. He perpetually watches the thicket, fearing to discover some ambuscade; if a branch strikes him, or a bramble unexpectedly catches him, he thinks himself attacked, and prepares for defence. Once in turning round he draws his reins too tightly, the horses take fright and plunge to one side, the chariot upsets, he is thrown out, and gets up bleeding and wounded. However, the road gradually rises, and high mountains appear on the horizon. The path winds in the ascent and passes between a wall of rocks and a deep precipice; this is the worst point in the journey. Baoukou advances cautiously, step by step, alighting at the smallest obstacle. He cannot prevent his chariot from violently striking an enormous block of stone and being damaged by the shock. The bolts break which fasten the pole to the body of the chariot. He repairs them as well as he can, just well enough for him to reach the next city with a great deal of management. Fortunately the gorge becomes wider, the slope begins to descend very gently, the mountain seems to open; through the gap he sees a fertile plain, and in the distance he descries the towers of Megiddo.

Megiddo is placed upon the top of a rather high hill. It is not easy to reach; a muddy stream, the Kanah, protects it on the east, and, after winding in the plain, joins the river Kishon through meadows and marshy lands. It is a small, poor town, sordid in appearance, but well fortified and important through its situation. The Syrian fortresses are not, like the Egyptian, rectangles or squares, surrounded by brick walls running straight from one end to the other, without projections or recesses; their walls are built in cut stone, and exactly follow the outlines of the land upon which they are erected; they are defended by high, square towers, which are heightened in war-time by the addition of rough wooden walls. The gates are always placed between two towers, built so near to each other that the defenders can harass by arrows and stones the flank of the enemy, who approach to break through with axes or the ram. Well-fortified towns are sometimes taken by assault, but usually by famine. Megiddo has been often besieged. As it commands the principal roads between northern and southern Syria, between Egypt and the land of Khita, the shores of the Nile and the Euphrates, many armies have met beneath its walls, and have fought there as in a closed field.

Here Thothmes III. defeated the Syrians, who had combined under the leadership of the Prince of Kadesh, and he reduced the city after a blockade of some weeks. From that time it has always remained in the power of the Pharaohs.

It is governed by an hereditary prince of native race, under the superintendence of an Egyptian garrison. As a rule, the Egyptians do not colonise the cities which they conquer, or place them under the direct authority of a governor nominated by Pharaoh. They generally leave the power and the royal titles to the sovereigns, great or small, whom they have vanquished, and content themselves with imposing a more or less heavy tribute upon them. Every year the royal envoys arrive from Thebes, receive the tax, and regulate any difficulties that may have arisen between the vassal and his sovereign. They, however, possess no authority enabling them to interfere in the internal affairs of the principality: the laws and customs are preserved, the priests of the local religions celebrate their own ritual without any constraint, and the hereditary succession to the throne continues according to the traditional practice of the country. It frequently happens, particularly upon the accession of a new Pharaoh, that the Syrians endeavour to throw off this light yoke; they refuse to pay the tribute, drive out or massacre the royal messengers, and, too feeble to resist if they were alone, some twenty or thirty princes combine in order to form a common army capable of taking the field and maintaining a campaign. Pharaoh hastens to the spot, defeats them, disperses their troops, and forces them to submit one after the other. Sometimes he forgives them and re-establishes things as they were before, sometimes he imprisons the rebel or puts him to death; but he establishes one of the prisoner's sons in his place, or if the sons are too much compromised by the paternal revolt, one of the relations who appears devoted to Egypt.

Two routes lead from Megiddo to Tyre. One, the longest, but the most frequented, descends to the sea, following the base of Mount Carmel, and passing by Accho, continues near the coast. The other is rather shorter, but it crosses a mountainous district, in which the inhabitants have a bad reputation. They are perpetually robbing isolated travellers or the rich caravans which pass from Tyre to Damascus; they pillage the bales, keep the beasts of burden, and sell the merchants as slaves. Baoukou, however, decides to take this dangerous way, for he hopes to receive information upon the movements of the Khita through these wandering bandits. He makes an arrangement with one of them, who undertakes to conduct him near to Tyre in consideration of a handsome reward. The journey is accomplished without a hitch, and Baoukou gains the first road, a little to the north of Achshaph, safe and well, but having learnt nothing. Either the barbarians have nothing to say or they will not speak, for they declare that they do not know what the Khita are doing. They have not met any parties of the enemy during their excursions, and do not believe that for the present the Khita are in the neighbourhood of Kadesh. Baoukou, leaving the ravines which divide Mount Ousirou,* is filled with astonishment. Born in the Theban nome he has rarely seen the sea, and whenever he sees it he deems it greater and more beautiful than ever. From the limits of the horizon almost to his feet extends an immense plain of water dotted with sails, bordered with white foam at the places where the waves dash themselves upon the rocks.

Most foreigners believe that the Egyptians consider the sea impure, and that they have a horror of it, so that none of them willingly venture upon it. This is an error. The Egyptians do not dislike the sea, but they are not acquainted with it. Their country has

* This is the Egyptian name of one part of the hills which the Jewish tribe of Ashur inhabited later on.

very little coast, and is chiefly bordered by sand-hills and marshes, which render it uninhabitable. Some islands situated towards Rakoti,* at the eastern extremity of the Delta, would make a good anchorage for merchant vessels or war galleys; but elsewhere the ships overtaken by a storm have no other resource but to take refuge in one of the mouths of the Nile, at the risk of stranding or even of being lost upon the sand and mud-banks which render it so difficult of access. The Egyptians have, therefore, until now preferred the land routes to the sea; however, when any accident forces them to face the Very-Green,† they have come out of their adventure with credit to themselves. The Nile has accustomed them to handle oars and sails from childhood; the experience acquired in navigation upon soft water enables them to dispense with a long apprenticeship upon the sea. The sailors of Thebes, transported by Queen Hatshepset to the Red Sea, knew how to take their five ships to Punt, and brought them back laden with incense and valuable produce. The galleys of Rameses II. ply regularly between Tanis or Pi-Ramisou and Tyre; yet the Syrian seas are rough, and the Phœnicians themselves, skilful as they claim to be, have immense trouble in avoiding the current which flows along their coasts, and carries to them the mud from the Nile.

As Baoukou pursues his journey his astonishment redoubles. The mountains press closely upon the shore, and the road sometimes descends upon the beach to avoid a peaked link of the mountain chain, sometimes rises and ascends in a zig-zag to cross a rocky spur which advances straight into the sea. In one spot it has been necessary to cut into the stone, and to hew out large steps, forming an immense ladder

* Rakoti was the name of the small Egyptian town upon the site where Alexandria afterwards stood.

† The *Very-Green* is the name that the Egyptians gave to the two seas with which they were acquainted, the Red Sea and the Mediterranean.

(Fig. 95). The waves dash with fury at the foot of the narrow cliff, and when a high wind rises each of

Fig. 95.—The Tyrian Ladders.

its breakers shakes the whole wall like a blow from a ram, and detaches a fragment of the rock. Baoukou, although emboldened by the desert and the perils he has escaped, at first ventures upon this path trembling as he advances step by step; but he soon realises that there is no serious danger and hastens his march. This is the last obstacle. Beyond these Tyrian Ladders the mountain retires inland, and leaves room for a fairly wide plain, bordered towards the north by a great cape. Cultivated fields, olive woods, shady orchards, then a city stretching along the sand on the edge of the water, and opposite another city girded with towers, which seems to have risen from the bottom of the sea by magic spells.

The first Phœnicians established themselves upon the continent more than twelve centuries ago and there founded the original Tyre, which was once prosperous. Their descendants afterwards settled upon the islands, which extended like a broken jetty parallel with the coast; the new Tyre, which they then built, gradually ruined the old one. The site was in a wild spot, continually beaten by the waves and wind. There was very little water, with the exception of a few brackish springs; even now the inhabitants have only the water collected in their cisterns, and dainty people send boats every day to fetch spring water from the continent. However, these are minor inconveniences, if we compare them to the advantages secured to the Island Tyre by her position. In case of war the arm of the sea which separates her from the coast becomes a moat : behind it she can defy all the threats of the enemy. Her fleet brings her provisions from a distance, and supplies her without the possibility of any human interference with as much food and as many mercenaries as she can wish for. She continues her trade with neutral or allied nations as in time of peace, and whilst uselessly blockaded, amasses in two or three campaigns as much as she requires to rebuild the old Tyre, reconstruct the villas, and restore the farms which have been burnt or pillaged during the war. The Tyrians might have refused the suzerainty of Pharaoh and have easily evaded the tribute, like their fellow-countrymen of Aradou, in Northern Phœnicia, had they wished to do so. This noble independence would have satisfied their vanity, but it would have injured their interests: besides the ravages to which their mainland would have been exposed, they would have been for ever excluded from Egypt; that is, from the market where, at present, the most business is carried on. They have established the balance between the small wound which prompt submission inflicted upon their vanity and the considerable damage which the hostility of Egypt could inflict upon their commerce, and have resigned themselves to paying a tribute, which they multiply one hundred-fold every year, whilst Pharaoh from that time has never owned more faithful vassals, or any that have given him less trouble.

Baoukou leaves his chariot and horses at Old Tyre, in the house of the royal messenger who comes annually to collect the tribute-money, and embarks with his servant for New Tyre. It is built upon three small islands, separated from each other by shallow canals strewn with half-submerged rocks. The city bears no resemblance to any of the towns which an Egyptian is accustomed to see on the banks of the Nile. Here the smallest inch of ground is valuable, and there are neither gardens nor squares, nor wide irregularly built streets. The latter are really alleys gliding between the houses, which are four or five stories high, and so close together that they resemble the cells of a hive. The temples—even that of Melkarth, the most ancient and most venerated of them all—have but just enough space left round them to allow for the worship and the passage of the processions. The dry docks, in which the ships are built and repaired, lay along the canals, especially on the north and the south-east, in what is called the Sidonian and Egyptian ports. The shops are low and narrow, and the rooms are very small in which the Tyrians manufacture those purple stuffs, glass-ware, gold and silver vases, amulets copied from the Egyptian amulets, which the merchant captains carry with them, and scatter in profusion over all the shores of the Mediterranean. Save in the quarters near the port, or in the vicinity of the temple of Astarte, where the crews of newly arrived vessels spend their share of the profits in feasting, the crowd which fills the street is entirely absorbed in its business.

Fig. 96.—A Phœnician.

The majority of the natives wear similar costumes (Fig. 96): nude bust, short many-coloured cotton drawers, fastened round the waist by a long sash, its ends falling in the front; the feet are either bare or protected by high boots reaching to the calf; the hair flowing in ringlets, sometimes to the waist, and ornamented in front by four rows of curls. From this original type twenty others may be distinguished — the Amorrean and the mountaineer from Lebanon, with his long red and blue robe, which forms a cape over the shoulders, and his hair massed in a bunch upon each side of his head and the nape of his neck, but held back in front by a head-band (Fig. 97); the Egyptian, with his white drawers and curled wig; the Toursha and the Sagalasha of Asia Minor, wearing a mariner's red woollen cap; the barbarous Acheans and Daneans, white of skin, with red or fair hair, clothed in an animal's skin or in a tunic; some negroes, even, and some tattooed savages from Hesperia and the silver

# THE JOURNEY.

and tin mines from beyond Gadir. Neither in Memphis, Thebes, or Tarsis had Baoukou ever seen such a mixture of foreign types and races, and could he but enter the houses his stupefaction would be redoubled. In fact, the Tyrians are the most skilful agents of the slave trade in the whole world. They sell most of the slaves that they import upon their vessels to Egyptian or Assyrian merchants, but a great many remain upon their hands, particularly women and young girls. It is not only the countries of Asia that furnish their contingent, Chaldea, Assyria, Elam, Ourati, but the coasts of the Archipelago and Euxine seas, and the Achean islands, Lybia, and the countries beyond; but with regard to the latter they are very secretive, and will neither disclose their situation nor even mention them before a stranger, fearing to rouse jealousy and perhaps excite competition.

Fig. 97.—A Syrian from the North.

A few Egyptian vessels are anchored in the port, loading with merchandise for Tanis or Memphis. They nearly resemble the boats on the Nile, and are in fact destined for navigation upon the river as well as the sea (Fig. 98). The hull, placed upon a rounded keel, is low and narrow, raised and sharpened at each end, decked all over. The prow is armed with a metal spur, held in place by strong cords, and projecting about three feet out of the water, then straightened and overhanging the front of the ship about one yard more. The poop, longer and higher than the prow, is surmounted by a long metal lotus-stalk with a fully opened flower bending inwards. Prow and poop have each a deck, provided with a wooden balustrade, and serving as the forecastle and quarter-deck. The hold is not deep, and can only contain the ballast, weapons, cargo, and provisions. The bulwarks are about half a yard higher than the bridge. The short, narrow benches for the rowers are placed close to the bulwarks, leaving an empty space in the centre, where a

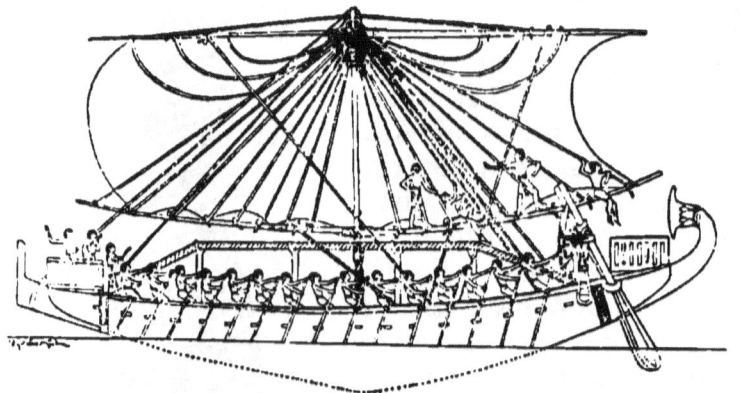

Fig. 98.—An Egyptian Ship, Sailing and Rowing.

boat, if there be one, may be put, or bales of merchandise, soldiers, slaves, or extra passengers may be stowed.

The rowers, all Egyptians, are fifteen in a band, and each handles one oar. The helm is formed of two thick oars, supported by an upright placed on either side of the poop, and each managed by a helmsman standing before it. A single mast about eight yards high, and secured by two stays in front and two behind, stands perpendicularly in the midst. One sail is stretched between the two yards about fifteen yards long, each formed of two solidly bound pieces. The crew includes thirty rowers, four topmen, two helmsmen, one pilot at the prow, who transmits to the helmsmen the necessary indications for steering, a captain, and one overseer for the galley slaves, which, with passengers or soldiers, make about fifty men on board each vessel. In battle the bulwarks are raised by a long mantlet, which shields the bodies of the rowers and leaves only their heads exposed. The soldiers are then distributed: two of them are placed upon the forecastle, a third is perched at the top of the mast in an improvised cross-trees; the remainder are posted upon the bridge and quarter-deck, from whence they endeavour to shoot the archers on the enemy's galley.

The Phœnician vessels differ from the Egyptian in details only. Built of excellent timber from Lebanon and Amanus, they are stronger and longer; they are more seaworthy, and can undertake more dangerous voyages. Their crews are also more daring and skilful than the Egyptian. These latter rarely venture beyond sight of the coast. They travel within range of the shore by day and stop at night, continuing their course in the morning. In this way they succeed in the most dangerous voyages, in gaining the *ladders of incense* in the land of Punt; for them it is but a question of time, and time does not count for much in Egypt. The Phœnicians have learnt to venture upon the open sea, and even to navigate during the night. They sail directly from Tyre or Sidon to the island of Asi,* from the isle of Asi to the promontories of Lycia and the distant Rhodes, then from island to island to the lands of the Acheans, the Daneans, and from thence towards Hesperia. They observe the position of the sun by day, and steer by the Great Bear at night. They have at many points stable establishments, which in some cases have developed into great cities; elsewhere they only appear at certain seasons of the year, and depart after trading with the natives. They all disembark, and display on the ground, or upon rapidly erected

* The island of Asi, Asia, is the island of Cyprus.

stalls, the produce which they know the inhabitants of the country consider valuable: sometimes jewels, bracelets, collars, amulets of glass or enamelled stone, of gold or silver; sometimes weapons, axes, swords damascened and chased; sometimes vases, or stuffs dyed purple or embroidered in brilliant colours. Most of these objects are of Egyptian manufacture, or fabricated in Phœnicia from Egyptian models more or less modified by the influence of the Chaldean types. We may thus see poignards from Egypt worn by the chiefs of Tyrinthe or Mycenea; on their fingers, rings decorated with lotus blossoms; on their necks, cylinders of Babylonian origin.

The exchange does not always take place without a quarrel, nor even without danger. Sometimes the natives, over-excited by the sight of so many beautiful things, try to obtain possession of them by craft or violence. They surprise the merchants that have landed, kill them, and even seize the vessels. But most frequently it is the Phœnicians who take advantage of the honesty or weakness of the natives. They fall upon the unarmed crowd, spoil and kill the old men, bind the young men, women, and children, and carry them into slavery; or they invent some pretext for inveigling the daughters of the chiefs upon their vessels. They pretend that they have some particularly valuable jewels and materials that they dare not land for fear of being robbed. Whilst the women are looking at the goods the anchor is gently raised, and as soon as the ship is well away from land their guests are seized and bound to prevent them from throwing themselves overboard and swimming to land. Greek or Lycian women are valuable in the Egyptian and Assyrian markets, and more than one amongst them has ended her life as a slave or favourite in the harems of Thebes or Nineveh.

At last Baoukou receives in Tyre some certain information about the Khita, and also upon the march of the Egyptian army. Rameses has penetrated into the valley of the Orontes, and is leisurely advancing towards Kadesh. As to the Khita, they have only parties of light troops on the plains, holding the main body of their forces concealed in the recesses of Lebanon to the north-west of the city. Baoukou, after hesitating a moment, decides to push on beyond Sidon, then to cross the mountain towards the point where the enemies are hidden, so that he may carry to Pharaoh precise information upon the positions which they occupy. There is no beaten route between Sidon and the valley of the Orontes, but travellers follow the faint tracks known to the goatherds and Bedouins only. The cyprus commences half-way up, mingled with firs and large centenarian cedars, which seem to ascend to heaven, their thick foliage almost impenetrable to the light. Not even between Joppa and Megiddo has Baoukou ever found himself in such gloomy masses of forest, so stifling, so dumb. The silence and isolation overwhelm him, as they are reported to overwhelm the souls in the voyage beyond the tomb in search of the paradise of Osiris; a religious horror of the great woods seizes him. Once more his chariot breaks down half-way up the hill, and the horses drag it laboriously; sometimes a lion roars in the distance, or the yelping laugh of a hyena is heard in the thicket.

Towards evening he reaches the summit of the mountain, and, tired out, he falls asleep, without eating, without even lighting a camp fire; when awakened by the cold of the morning, he is alone, no one is near him. The guide had tried to steal his horses, but they snorted at the touch of a strange hand, so he was forced to relinquish his intention; the thief has fallen back upon the luggage, and has carried off one portion of it. However, the servant, roused by the noise, caught sight of him and took care not to warn his master; the robber once gone, he laid hands upon the remainder of the goods and decamped in his turn. Baoukou is, therefore, alone upon the mountain, in the midst of a thick fog, which prevents him seeing twenty steps before him. One false movement will throw him off the road, into some ravine, where he may perhaps break both arms and legs; the best thing is to wait for the dawn. Soon the mist rises, the peaks slowly emerge above it, followed by the wooded slopes, and the vapours gradually retire to the valley, from whence the sun's rays quickly dislodge them. Baoukou sees at his feet the whole plain of Syria unrolled before him, like a chess-board, with its fields, its clumps of trees, its scattered villages, its rivers, their winding course traced out by double rows of trees, the Egyptian camp, and, beyond, the small lake of Kadesh shining in the sun. The path improves as he descends the hill and drives quickly towards the valley. Baoukou now abandons the fragments of his chariot, takes the two horses by the reins, and starts again, glad to have escaped so easily. Once at the foot of the mountain, he intends to mount one of the animals and lead the other as a second horse, while a gallop of two hours will take him to the Egyptian camp.*

But at a turn in the road a confused noise, as of a great multitude, suddenly strikes his ear. He cautiously advances, puts aside the branches of a bush and perceives below him, in a large valley, columns of men and horses arranged in good order and ready to start at the first signal. This is the army of the Prince of Khita, which its chief has concealed until now and which he had assembled in this spot on the previous day. As Baoukou watches, a movement commences and spreads through the mass. The aides-de-camp hurry to and fro, carrying orders, the soldiers cast a last glance over the harness of their horses, the wheels and poles, then mount their chariots and seize the

* The journey here ascribed to Baoukou is the journey described in some pages of the *Papyrus Anastasi*, No. 1, reversed.

reins. A shout of command is heard, then the cracking of many whips, and the chariots roll away, division after division. The Khita are at the head of the column; their chariots, heavier and larger than those of the Egyptians, each contain three men—a warrior, a coachman, and a shield-bearer, who protects his two comrades. They wear long striped robes of red and blue, red and white, or blue and white, and are armed with the bow, lance, and dagger. Their auxiliaries, the Dardenians and Mysians follow them, and the remainder of the contingents from Asia Minor and Syria close the rear. There are two thousand five hundred chariots, divided into four bands of almost equal force. Baoukou follows them with his eyes, and notices that, instead of hastening across the plain, they advance slowly, concealing themselves behind the trees and taking advantage of the least irregularity of the ground to hide their approach. A surprise is being prepared, and will perhaps entail disaster for the Egyptian army if Pharaoh be not warned in time. Baoukou hastens his steps, reaches the foot of the mountain, and gallops straight to the camp. At last the enemy catches sight of him as he reaches the open country: three or four chariots leave the first division, but, seeing that they cannot overtake him, return to the ranks, after shooting some arrows at him, which fall far short of their mark.

# CHAPTER X.

### THE BATTLE.

*The Egyptian camp before Kadesh—Incidents of camp life—The Khita spies—Departure: the order of the march—The Egyptian camp surprised by the Khita—Rameses charges the enemy—Speech of Rameses to his generals—The battle of Kadesh—After the victory—Khitasir sues for peace—Treaty between Rameses and the Khita.*

THE Egyptian camp has been established for some days upon the right bank of the Orontes, at some distance to the south of Kadesh. It is a rectangular enclosure, twice as long as it is wide (Fig. 99). The earth from the moat, thrown inwards and heaped together, forms a rampart of almost the same height as a man; large wicker-work shields, square at the base, rounded at the top, are placed on the outer side of this rudimentary wall and serve as a facing. A single door opens in one of the walls, and a plank serves as a bridge for entrance and exit. Two squads of infantry posted inside, half at each side of the gate, keep guard night and day, stick and bare sword in hand (Fig. 100). The inside area is divided lengthways into three compartments, traced out by light walls. The centre division belongs to the king, and contains his pavilion; in it Pharaoh finds all the comfort and luxury of his Egyptian palaces—a bedroom, an audience-hall, a dining-room, and even a chapel, where he offers water and incense every morning to his father, Amen-ra, lord of Thebes. The princes who accompany him, his equerries and

# THE BATTLE. 173

Fig. 99.—The Egyptian Camp before Kadesh: the persons kneeling in the king's tent are priests reciting a prayer. The Khita have forced the wall towards the upper corner to the right, and their chariots are entering the camp; a few of the infantry are hurrying up to meet them.

generals, are lodged near him; behind, in long lines, stand the horses and war-chariots, the luggage-cars, and the oxen that drag them. Before the oxen, a waggon covered with an awning serves to convey the strangest auxiliary that man ever dreamed of taking upon a field of battle. Rameses is always accompanied by an enormous lion, tamed and trained to attack the enemy. Usually the animal is fairly gentle, and displays all the friendliness of a large dog; but it becomes excited in battle, and returns to its natural ferocity. The two compartments to the right and left are abandoned to the soldiers. They contain neither tents nor temporary huts. The Egyptians are accustomed to live in the open air; they cook, eat, sleep, attend to all their business in public. Here one of them watches a saucepan whilst cleaning his weapons; another is drinking from a skin of wine that a slave assists him to hold; a third has dismounted his chariot and is replacing a worn piece of it; others sharpen their daggers or lances—exchange blows with fist or stick. The chariots are placed in the front of each squad, the luggage is piled upon the ground—linen, weapons, provisions. The war-horses and luggage-asses eat and rest at their ease; here and there a jovial donkey rolls upon the ground, braying with pleasure (Fig. 101).

Fig. 100.—The Guard at the Gate.

The officers who return from the outside bring news to those who have not left the camp. Nothing yet: the vile Khita persist in remaining invisible, and all the Asiatics whom they question either know nothing or will know nothing. A few young men are inclined to consider the action of the enemy a proof of

# THE BATTLE.

Fig. 101.—Scenes in the Egyptian Camp.

impotence and cowardice: Khitasir is hiding because he is afraid. The veterans shake their heads as they listen to these remarks; like Pharaoh, they think that the battle is near, and the less the enemy shows himself the more they distrust him. The vile Khita has good generals, a well-disciplined army, allies full of energy; if he does not move it is because he is preparing some surprise. If the eye could penetrate the ravines and woody mountains that surround the plain, perhaps the army so vainly sought for two months might be discovered. The storm usually gathers on the heights; woe to us on the day that it bursts over the plain. Meanwhile Pharaoh would do well to redouble his vigilance. A surprise is sudden in warfare, and a defeat under the walls of Kadesh would take the army back to Gaza more quickly than it had come.

Rameses is not less preoccupied than his old captains. All the reports that he received from the scouts agree that there is no inimical army for twenty leagues round, but how can they believe that Khitasir would consent to abandon the richest provinces of his kingdom to the Egyptians without striking a blow in their defence? The Bedouins that come before him assert that the Khita are still forty leagues away, near to Khilibu; their army is assembling but slowly, and perhaps it would be wise to attack them before it is completely organized. After a long hesitation, it is finally decided to act upon this information. Rameses summons his generals, describes his plan of campaign, and issues orders for a general departure at daybreak. He leaves Kadesh behind him and proposes going in search of the allies in the heart of their own country. The legion of Phra will form the left, and will cross the valley to the south of Shabtouna; the legion of Ptah will advance in the centre towards the village of Arnam; the legion of Sutekh will take up its position to the right and will follow the high road. The legion of Amen will remain in camp and only go out on the morrow with the king. Every preparation is made during the night, and at the first hour of dawn the three columns commence their march, each in the direction already indicated.

The enemy's scouts, who are watching the Egyptians from the top of the hills, signal their departure. Khitasir at once places his troops under arms, and prepares for any emergency. Does Rameses suspect the snare laid for him, and is this a manœuvre to draw the enemy into the plain? Is he really raising his camp and going towards Khilibu, deceived by the false reports sent to him through the Bedouins? Gradually the movement increases, the Egyptian columns disappear and are lost in the clouds of dust raised by the wheels of their chariots and the feet of their horses. Khitasir has recognised the standards and knows that two-thirds of the Egyptian army are already beyond Kadesh. Rameses is left with but a single legion and his household guard. It is true that they are the best soldiers of Egypt, but for how many hours could they sustain the shock of 2500 Asiatic chariots? There would be time to force the camp, whilst the divisions so imprudently launched towards the north would be still marching forward. The legion of Amen would be crushed, Pharaoh killed or taken prisoner before they could return, and they could be easily defeated in their turn, when once deprived of their leader. The morning advances, the sun is already high in the horizon, the Egyptian camp has returned to its usual state, and no one seems to suspect that anything is likely to happen. Khitasir gives the signal so long expected, and his army descends into the plain at a gallop.

Rameses, having witnessed the departure of his troops, re-enters his tent, and seats himself upon his golden throne. He is talking to his two eldest sons, when some of his scouts arrive, bringing with them two of the Khita spies, whom they lead before the King. His Majesty inquires, 'What nation do you belong to?' At first they refuse to answer, but a severe beating forces them to speak (Fig. 102). They own that they belong to the King of Khita, and have been sent to see where His Majesty is established. Rameses then asks, 'Where is the miserable Khita? for I have been told that he is near Khilibu.' The spies answer, 'Behold, the King of Khita, he and the nations he has brought with him in great numbers, all the peoples that dwell in the land of Khita, from the whole of Naharanna and Sidi.* Now he is powerful with many soldiers, with chariot soldiers with their harness, as many as the sand of the seashore, and they are ready to fight behind Kadesh.' This revelation fills the king with rage and anxiety. Is there yet time to recall the three legions, or must he abandon the camp and try to rejoin them before the enemy appears?

Fig. 102.—The Spies are beaten.

Pharaoh immediately summons the captain of the legion of Amen, the captain of the Shairetana, and the leaders of his chariot soldiers, to tell them the news that the stick has just wrested from the two spies of the Khita (Fig. 103). 'See what the chiefs of the scouts and the vassal princes of the lands of Pharaoh have done. They have said daily unto me, "The King of Khita is at Khilibu; he has fled before Pharaoh." They have asserted this as a certainty, and behold I have now learnt from the two spies that the King of Khita has come up with much people, with men and horses as many as the sand, and that he is behind Kadesh. Yet the scouts of the vassal princes of the land knew nothing of this.' The generals are quite

---

* Naharanna is the country between Orontes and Balikh; Sidi, the coast of Cilicia, the Ketis of the Greek geographers.

THE BATTLE. 179

as much disturbed as the king had been. 'The fault is great that the governors of the land and the vassal princes of Pharaoh have committed in neglecting to watch the movements of the Khita.' But there is no time for recriminations, the king must act quickly. He decides to send orders to the legions to return by forced marches, and the Council was about to separate, so that the camp might be prepared for defence, when Baoukou entered the tent and announced the

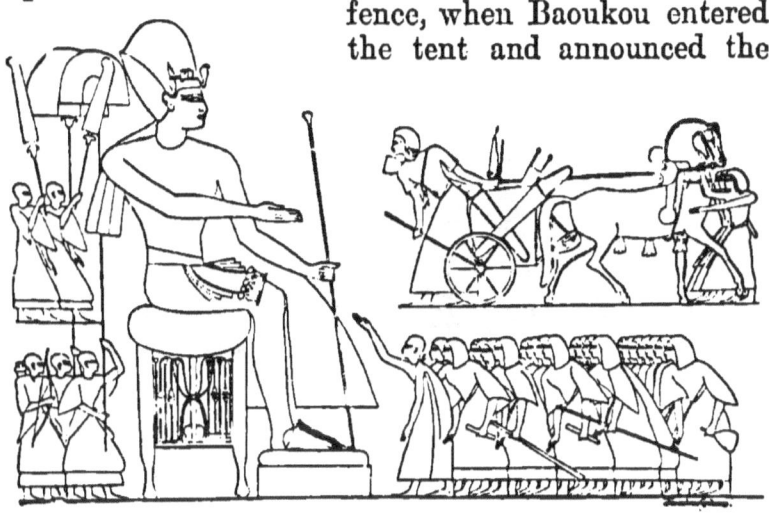

Fig. 103.—Rameses holds a Council of War.

coming of the enemy. Khitasir arrived almost immediately with his whole army: in a few minutes the moat was filled up, the earthwork thrown down in spite of the shields which covered it, and the Asiatics swarmed into the camp through the breach. The surprise was complete: a number of foot soldiers were killed before they could seize their weapons; a few squadrons rallied, and, supported by the Shairetana, for a short time succeeded in checking the enemy at the gates of the royal quarters. They were borne down by numbers, and were already breaking their ranks, when a war-cry was suddenly heard throughout the camp, blended with a loud roar

—Rameses II. and his lion at last appeared on the field of battle.

Pharaoh, when he first saw the Khita chariots, was beside himself with rage, like his father Menthu of Thebes. He put on his armour, seized his lance, ordered his lion to be loosened; then, entering his chariot, he rushed into the thickest part of the conflict (Fig. 104). The few chariots that followed him

Fig. 104.—Rameses II. in his Chariot: the King's Lion charges by the side of the Horses.

were quickly overthrown, their warriors killed or taken prisoners, and Pharaoh found himself alone with his equerry, Menni, separated from those of his troops that still resisted by a number of the enemy's chariots. When Menni saw himself surrounded his courage failed, a great terror seized him, and he said to Pharaoh: 'My lord, O generous king! Egypt's great protector in the day of battle! behold, we are alone in the midst of the enemy, for the archers and chariots have left us. Let us return, that our lives may be saved. Save us, O my lord, Rameses Miamun!' But Pharaoh answered: 'Take courage, strengthen thine heart, O mine equerry! I will go amongst them like the hawk pounces upon his prey; killing and massacring, I will lay them in the dust! What, therefore, are these wretches in thine eyes? Amen has delivered them into mine hand.' And raising his voice towards the god, he continued: 'I invoke thee, O my father Amen! behold me in the midst of a numerous and strange people; all the nations are united against me, and I am alone; no other is with me. My soldiers have abandoned me, not one of our horsemen have looked towards me, and when I called to them not one of them hearkened unto my voice. But I believe that Amen is stronger on my side than a million soldiers, than a hundred thousand horsemen, than a myriad of brothers or of young sons, were they all assembled here. The work of many men is as nothing; Amen will outweigh them all. I have done all things according to thy counsels, O Amen! and I have not disobeyed thy words. Behold, I render glory unto thee, even to the extremities of the earth!' He charged, and 'his hand devoured them in the space of an instant,' and they said one to the other, 'This is not a man in the midst of us, it is Sutekh, the great warrior; it is Baal himself. These are not the deeds of a man; alone, quite alone, he repulses hundreds of thousands, without captains or soldiers. Let us make haste and flee before him; let us save our lives that we may yet breathe upon earth.' Five times Pharaoh rushed upon them, and five times the scarcely broken ranks closed round him; at the sixth attack he succeeded in breaking the circle which surrounded him and in rejoining his army. Pharaoh does not usually engage in the battles which are fought in his presence. He watches rather than fights, and his generals never allow him to be in any serious danger. On this occasion Rameses II. fought without any precautions, like a private soldier. He encouraged his men by voice and gesture, himself led them to the attack, and covered their retreat when they were outnumbered. He loudly invoked Amen before each fresh charge, and it seemed as though Amen covered him with an invisible shield. Whilst all his faithful servants fell, one after the other, his chariot was intact, and he remained unwounded.

The unequal combat lasted for some hours, and the

Fig. 105.—The Legion of Ptah entering the Field.

Egyptians, decimated, dying of thirst and fatigue, now only thought of selling their lives as dearly as possible. Suddenly a loud tumult was heard at the rear of the enemy; the legion of Ptah was entering the field (Fig. 105). The officer dispatched in search of it had found it a little to the north-east of Kadesh; it hastened forward in good order, the chariots in front and in the rear, the foot soldiers in a deep column. The Khita and their allies, already discouraged by their struggle with the king's household, did not wait for the attack. They turned round, and retired in confusion towards Kadesh. A vigorous charge would doubtless have changed their retreat into a rout, but the Egyptian troops, having marched or fought all through the day, were quite exhausted, and retired to their camp. The legion of Sutekh arrived soon afterwards; that of Phra only joined them later in the evening. It had been surprised by a sudden attack from the Asiatic chariots, and had been partly overthrown. But the soldiers who composed it were mostly veterans from the Syrian wars, so that they quickly recovered from their dismay, and remained masters of the field after several hours of bloody conflict. Khitasir's plan, well arranged and well led though it had been, had failed before the indomitable valour of Rameses and the steadiness of his troops.

Pharaoh alights from his chariot, and his first thought is for the horses who have so gallantly carried him through the battle, *Victory-in-Thebes* and *Maut-is-satisfied*. Neither the horses nor the lion are wounded, but their caparison is sullied with blood and dust, the feathers that decorate their heads are in shreds, and their collars are half broken. Rameses caresses them, speaks to them, and promises them a place of honour in his stables, unlimited rations of forage, and superb decorations for the remainder of their lives. The faithful animals appear to understand him, and raise their heads at his voice, in spite of their fatigue. He then gives orders that all the chiefs of the army should be summoned. They hurry to his presence and greet him as usual as they approach him: 'Thou, O great warrior! hast saved thine army. Son of the god Atmu and the work of his hands, thou hast destroyed the people of Khita with thy powerful scimitar! Thou art the perfect warrior, and there is no king that fights like thee for his soldiers in the day of battle! Thou art the bravest of heroes, thou art foremost in the conflict, and dost not even inquire if the whole world be united against thee! Thou art the bravest of the brave before thine army and before the whole world! No one can deny it. Thou art the protector of Egypt and the chastisement of the nations! Thou hast broken the power of the Khita for ever!'

In spite of their flattery the generals are not quite sure that Pharaoh will not make them pay dearly for the negligence which so nearly cost him his life, and his first words are not calculated to disperse their fear. 'What a crime you have committed, oh, my generals, my foot soldiers, my chariot soldiers, in not joining in the fight! Is not a man honoured by his country when he has displayed his courage by the side of his lord, and won the fame of a warrior? Verily, verily, a man is valued for his bravery.'

He recalls the benefits he has showered upon them, which deserved some gratitude. 'Have I not shown kindness to you all, that you should leave me alone in the midst of the enemy? You were afraid and you are still alive; you still breathe, and I, through your fault, am left alone. Could you not say in your hearts that I am your rampart of iron? What will my father, Amen-ra of Thebes, say when he knows that you left me alone, unaided? That not one prince, not one officer of the chariots or the armies was ready to help me?' However, the recollection of their former exploits softens Pharaoh's anger, and secretly he is not annoyed at having had this opportunity of giving brilliant proof of his strength and valour. He consents to forget their crime, and to recall the names of those only who had come to his assistance in the hour of danger. 'I have fought, I have repulsed millions of nations with mine own hand. *Force-in-Thebes* and *Maut-is-satisfied* were my great horses, they were under my hand when I was alone in the midst of the trembling enemy. Henceforth their food shall be given them before me, each day, when I am in my palace; for I found them when I was in the midst of the enemy, with the chief, Menni, mine equerry, and with the officers of my household who accompany me, and who are my witnesses in the fight: they are all that I found. I have returned victorious from the battle, and with my sword have I smitten the assembled multitudes.'

It was a success, but dearly bought: the camp surprised and partly pillaged, one-half of the legion of Amen and of the foreign guard destroyed or dispersed. The enemy repulsed, but only repulsed with great difficulty, and ready to recommence the attack. Rameses makes his arrangements for the morrow. The legions of Phra, Ptah, and Sutekh will be placed in the same order as they started for the march that morning, to the left, the centre, and the right; the remnant of the legion of Amen and of the Shairetana will form the reserve. Khitasir, on his side, calls up the regiments that had not been present in the action, and draws them up in front of Kadesh (Fig. 106). The city originally occupied a curve which the river formed as it issued from a small lake: the running water protected it upon three sides; the east only was left uncovered by this natural moat, and remained exposed to a direct attack. One of the old kings, wishing to render the city invulnerable, pierced the strip of land that joined it to the plain by a double canal dug from the lake to the stream. The en-

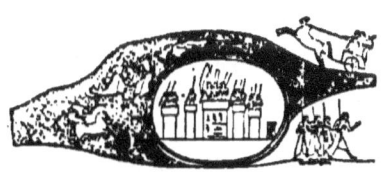

Fig. 106.—The City of Kadesh.

closure now forms an almost perfect circle. The wall, built of large stones, is garnished with towers; those which defend the door are higher than the others, and are more solidly constructed. Kadesh thus forms an island linked to the mainland by two bridges, which, thrown over the two moats, can be raised or lowered at will. Khitasir has still four thousand chariots, which he marshals at some little distance in front of the city, those to the right protected by the stream, those to the left extending over the plain; he leaves his infantry in the city with orders to remain there, unless he is defeated, when they must stop the pursuit by the Egyptians.

The battle commences early in the morning by a skirmish between the archers, but they have scarcely had time to exchange a few arrows when Rameses and Khitasir order them to scatter and to make way for the cavalry. If we could trust appearances, the forces appear unequal. The chariots of the Khita—high, heavy, containing three men each—should easily bear down the light Egyptian chariots and upset them by their weight alone. The two masses first started, then, quickening their speed, rushed upon each other at full gallop, with a heavy, rolling sound, like thunder. The Egyptians, trained by frequent drill to move together, advance with as much regularity as though they were still on parade in Thebes. No one chariot is in front of the others, and their galloping steeds form but one unbroken line upon the ground. The warrior has tied the reins together, and has passed them round his waist; then leaning upon them to right or left, loosening the pressure by bending forward or tightening it by a backward step, he turns, quickens, or stops his horse by a simple movement of the body. His bow is strung to its utmost extent, the arrow pointed ready for flight, whilst the coachman, holding to the chariot with one hand, with the other protects his comrade with the shield (Fig. 107). The Khita are less skilful, and do not keep their distances so well after the first few minutes' galloping; the line wavers and curves as they advance in spite of their efforts to keep it straight. Although they have bows like their adversaries, they do not use them; the majority prefer using the lance, and already hold it half-couched, ready to strike as soon as they close with the enemy.

Already the two lines are within two horse-lengths of each other; a short order, and all the Egyptian

Fig. 107.—Collision of the Chariots. The Egyptians are to the left, the Khita to the right.

arrows fly through the air with a loud whistle. Twenty of the Khita and Dardanians fall, as many horses are thrown down; the disabled chariots fall back upon their neighbours and upset. A second discharge brings the disorder to its height; the first line of the allies is broken, the injured chariots are dispersed. The warriors thrown out of the broken chariots seize a horse, cut the traces that attach it to the pole, mount it with a spring, and hurry off. Khitasir launches a second division, which renews the fight, and at last, closing with the Egyptians, inflicts heavy losses upon them and penetrates their centre, driving the remnant of the force before them. At this moment Rameses places himself at the head of his right wing and rushes upon the Khita, who, taken in the rear by the king, are gradually pressed back into the river, into which many of them fall. The conflict rages around them. Khitasir sees his most devoted servants fall one after the other: Tarakennas, leader of his cavalry; Agama, captain of the infantry; his historiographer, Khirapusar; Zaouazas, prince of Tonisa; his own brother, Matsurama. Pressed from all sides, the king urges his chariot towards the water, so that he may cross the lake and take refuge beneath the walls of Kadesh. A great many of his soldiers who follow his example are drawn into the current and drowned, whilst he himself is landed half dead at the foot of the ramparts. Some of the inhabitants pick him up, and hold him upside down to make him disgorge the water he has swallowed. However, his infantry now issue from the town and fall upon the Egyptians in a solid mass of eight thousand men. This intervention, which comes too late to change the fate of the day, arrests the progress of the conquerors and saves the remnant of the cavalry. The struggle of yesterday had only arrested Khitasir's march; the battle of to-day has disorganized and almost destroyed his army.

The king realises that the war cannot be continued, and the same evening his envoys present themselves before Rameses and implore his mercy. The Egyptian camp is full of joy. Since the cessation of the strife the soldiers have scattered all over the plain, spoiling the dead and collecting booty. The Egyptian does not usually decapitate his enemy; he cuts off the right hand or some limb, and carries it to the scribes, who inscribe it against his name. Pharaoh himself deigns to preside in his chariot over the registration of the hands (Fig. 108). The Khita messengers find him surrounded by the bloody trophies. He interrupts his work to receive them. If he followed his secret inclinations he would prolong the war and try to put an end to the resistance of the obstinate Khita for ever; but he is not sure that his army is still sufficiently large, after the losses it has borne, to be able to hold the field for long. The remnant of the Khita is still formidable; Kadesh is strong and will not yield

Fig. 108.—Registering the Hands cut from the Prisoners.

without a long siege. During this time Khitasir is capable of assembling a new army, Southern Syria may revolt, and a check, even if insignificant in itself, will compromise the results of the success already gained. Rameses, therefore, resigns himself to accept the enemy's overtures and to receive the letter presented by the messengers. It is from Khitasir himself and couched in the most humble terms. 'This is to satisfy the heart of Pharaoh, of the god who voluntarily diffuses his vivifying influence, of the lord, the valorous bull, who loves the truth, of the supreme king, who protects his soldiers, of the hero with the invincible sword, the bulwark of his soldiers in the day of battle, of the King of Upper and Lower Egypt, Rauserma-sotepenra, son of the Sun, Rameses Miamun. Thy servant Khitasir speaks to thee, to lay before thee that, being thyself the son of Amen, formed of his substance, as he has delivered all lands unto thee, the land of Egypt and the land of the Khita unite to lay their services at thy feet. Ra, thine august father, has given strength and victory unto thee; deign to spare us, thou whose souls are great! Thy valour has weighed heavily upon the nation of the Khita, but is it good for thee to kill thy servants? Thou art their master; will thy face be always angry towards us, wilt thou not calm thyself? Yesterday thou hast appeared and thou has killed hundreds of thousands; if thou appear to-day, no one will be left to be subject unto thee. Abandon thy designs, oh, victorious king, the genius that delights in battles. Grant to us the breath of life!' Rameses summons his council, and communicates to it the message received from the king of the Khita; his generals deliberate as a matter of form, and convinced, like himself, of the necessity of peace, they advise him to be magnanimous. 'Behold, now, this is excellent! Deign to be calmed, O sovereign, our master! If mercy be not extended to Khitasir, to whom should it be granted? He adores thee; consent then to calm thy wrath.' On the morrow the prayer was granted, and Rameses triumphantly commenced his journey back to Egypt. It was less a peace than a truce; the war soon recommenced, and continued with variable success for sixteen years longer. However, as Rameses grew older he no longer accompanied the army in person; whilst his generals fought for him, he built temples, founded new towns, and reconstructed the majority of the ancient cities. After laborious negotiations peace was at last concluded, and a day was fixed for the exchange of the silver tablets, upon which solemn treaties were usually inscribed. The ceremony took place upon the 21st Tôbi at Pa - Rameses Miamun in the Delta. Tartisabou, the messenger of the Prince of Khita, solemnly presented to Pharaoh the tablet which his master had entrusted to him, and received one bearing the hieroglyphic text of the treaty. This text recalled the past agreements between the kings of Egypt and the princes of Khita in the time of Rameses I. and Seti I. It contained a stipulation that peace should be eternal between the two peoples. 'If any enemy march against the countries that are subject to the great King of Egypt, and he send to the great Prince of Khita, saying, "Come, lead thy forces against them," the Prince of Khita will obey the words of the King of Egypt, and will destroy his enemies; but if the Prince of Khita prefer not to obey in person he will send archers and chariots from the land of Khita to the King of Egypt to destroy his enemies.' A similar clause secures the Egyptian support for the Prince of Khita in time of need. The following articles are destined to protect the commerce and industry of the allied nations, and to render the action of justice secure amongst them. Every criminal that should attempt to evade the laws by taking refuge in the neighbouring country should be given up to the officials of his people; every fugitive who was not a criminal, every subject carried away by force, every workman who should move from one territory to another to dwell there should be sent back to his people, but this expatriation should not be regarded as a crime. 'The man who is thus sent away shall not be considered guilty of a fault: his house shall not be destroyed, nor his wife, nor his children; his mother shall not be killed; he shall not be smitten in the eyes, nor in the mouth, nor in the feet; nor shall any criminal accusation be brought against him.' The articles of the treaty were loyally observed on both sides. Rameses married Khitasir's daughter, and the latter came some years later to pay a friendly visit to his son-in-law. Henceforth, 'the peoples of Egypt were of one mind with the princes of Khita, which had not been the case since the god Ra.'

Rameses lived for many years longer. He died

in the sixty-seventh year of his reign, sixty-two years after the battle of Kadesh, which he had won by his personal courage. His funeral was magnifi-

Fig. 109.—Rameses II., from a photograph of the Corpse preserved in the Boulak Museum.

cent, and his mummy reposed in the tomb which he had prepared during his lifetime in the Valley of the Kings. It could not rest long in peace. As a precaution against robbers, it was transported to the tomb of Amenophis I., where it remained for nearly two centuries with the great Pharaohs of the preceding dynasties, Amasis I., Thothmes I., his grandfather, Rameses I., his father, Seti I., and the princesses of their family. Thebes declined in power, a king of the twenty-second dynasty wished to be quit of the accumulated dead, and buried them pell-mell in a corner of the mountain, so carefully hidden that they remained there for twenty-eight centuries. Towards 1871, some fellahs in quest of antiquities discovered this group of Pharaohs, which they regularly exploited for ten years, selling a scarabæus here, a papyrus there, some pieces of stuff, some jewels, funeral statuettes, all the property of former kings. Everything that escaped pillage was in 1881 transported to the Boulak Museum, and Rameses, freed from his bandages, saw the light of day once more after an interval of more than three thousand years. Now he sleeps his last sleep in a hall in the museum under a glass case. He is no longer in our eyes as in those of our forefathers, the hero of a doubtful legend, or still less, a name detached from a form, floating in the imagination of the learned, without colour or outline. He is tall and well formed. His head is long and small, the skull bare; a few tresses of white hair still cling round the temples and the nape of the neck. The forehead is low and narrow, the eyebrow well formed, the eye small and close to the nose, the check-bone prominent, the ear round and delicately curved. In his venerable immobility he still retains an expression of pride, of sovereign majesty. His head has been measured, the capacity of his brain has been gauged, an inventory has been taken of his funeral wardrobe, and if any one wishes to see him as he appeared at the time of his death, here is his portrait (Fig. 109), taken from a photograph.

# LIFE IN ANCIENT ASSYRIA.

## CHAPTER XI.

### A ROYAL RESIDENCE: DUR-SARGINU.

Sargon wishes to found a city—Choice of a site—The gods consulted —Laying the foundation—Brickmaking—Death of Sargon—Dur-Sarginu abandoned by the kings—The outer wall—The gates: the winged bulls—Their office at the gates of the city—The streets, the houses, the population—The palace and its storehouses—The harem—The royal apartment and its decoration—The priests and their position in the State—The Tower of the Seven Planets.

In the twelfth year of his reign, upon a favourable day, Sargon, the great king, the powerful king, king of multitudes, king of Assyria, founded a city and a palace, according to the will of the gods and the desire of his heart. In the royal cities, where hitherto the king had dwelt, everything too vividly recalled the glory of the sovereigns who had preceded him. The inscriptions related in detail the history of their lives, the bas-reliefs depicted their hunting exploits and their battles. Tiglath-pileser built the centre of the palace, one of the Shamshi-Rammanu added the two wings, Assur-nasir-pal raised the many-storied tower, and Shalmaneser restored the buildings of the harem. Sargon wished for a city which should belong to him only; where the past should commence with his reign.

After meditating night and day, and carefully seeking the spot most suitable for his project, he decided upon the village of Magganoubba, at some distance to the north-east of Nineveh, situated in a large plain which extends from the banks of the Khosr to the mountains of Mousri. Every year the land produces two harvests, so that it is called the Plain of the Double Springtime. One of the streams that water it contains sulphur and has remarkable properties; for, though in other parts of the valley of the Tigris the natives and even foreigners are tormented by an eruption of large painful spots, which last for a year and then leave an indelible scar, those persons who drink of its waters either escape the disease or are rapidly cured. The site has, therefore, great natural advantages, and yet the three hundred and fifty princes who have succeedeed each other upon the Assyrian throne have lived near it for centuries without thinking of profiting by them. Sargon, better advised, determined to dwell there, and at once dispossessed all the inhabitants of the village. Some received in silver and copper the sum that they had paid for their fields, according to their title-deeds; others, who preferred land to metal, received in exchange for their patrimony a territory of the same value. It was necessary to conduct this preliminary operation with great care and justice, so that there should be no cause for justifiable complaint: if but one of the former owners of the soil had been unjustly treated, his maledictions would have brought ill luck to the new city.

The foundation of a city is a religious act, and each detail in the arrangements is marked by long and complicated rites. It does not suffice to trace out an enclosure, to plan streets, to open markets, to assemble haphazard several thousands of families: if the founder wishes that his work should last and prosper, he must draw within its walls not only a human population, but a divine one, too; he must invoke a number of gods, who will not leave the town and will undertake to protect the inhabitants. Sargon, before commencing his enterprise, devoutly consulted Hea, the king of the gods, and his sister Damkou. He went to the temple of Ishtar, queen of Nineveh, and in the sanctuary itself he implored the goddess to bless his scheme. His request found favour in her eyes. She ordered him to commence the works, and relying upon the promises of the divinity, who never deceives her votaries, he immediately assembled his labourers and collected materials of all kinds. The city, erected upon a regular plan, was to form an almost perfect square, of about seven hundred acres. The angles exactly corresponded with the four points of heaven; the sides were traced on the soil by means of a *banquette* twenty-five yards wide, built of slabs of calcareous stone hewn from the neighbouring mountains. To sanctify this structure and to avert evil influences, figurines in baked clay, representing the great gods of the country, cylinders covered with inscriptions, and amulets of various form, were placed in different parts of it, particularly in the openings reserved for the gateways. But the Assyrian architects, servile pupils of the old masters of Chaldea, never willingly use stone; as soon as the wall was a little more than three feet high they continued the work in bricks up to the top.

The bricks destined for public buildings are holy, and can be made only at certain seasons. They are prepared under the auspices of a particular god, Sivan, lord of foundations, and only during the month to which he gave his name. The king, therefore, came during the first days of Sivan (May, June), and encamped with a large suite in the plain of Magganoubba. An altar had been erected; he lit the fire, poured a libation into the consecrated brass vase, killed a bull, and with uplifted hands he prayed that Sivan and his father, Bel, the architect of the universe, would consent to direct the works (Fig. 110). The clay was then taken, freed from the stones which it contained, mixed with chopped straw and water, kneaded by the feet, moulded, and dried in the sun. The brick is nearly a square of about thirteen inches, sometimes two, sometimes four inches thick; it is stamped on one side with the name and titles of the king who manufactured it. Two months later, in Ab, the building commenced; it lasted six years, and was not finished until Sargon returned from his Armenian campaign. The king did not long enjoy the pleasure of being at home in a city which bore his name, and in which every detail reminded him of his own greatness. Soon after the inauguration of the city he was assassinated at the instigation, and perhaps by the hand, of his son, Sennacherib. Dur-Sarginu,* raised by a whim of its

Fig. 110.—The Royal Sacrifice.

founder to the dignity of a capital, is now only one of the numerous residences of the King of Assyria. It might usually be taken for a dead or, at all events, a sleeping city, with deserted streets, almost empty markets, a small and indolent population. Once or twice a year it awakens: its palaces are opened, its thoroughfares become animated, the tumult of life fills it once more. Assurbanipal, tired of the noise of Nineveh, has arrived with his harem and his whole court.

The road which leads to Dur-Sarginu crosses the Khosr when it leaves Nineveh, and follows the left bank of the river pretty closely. It is a good stone road, like all in Assyria, about twelve yards wide, bordered at regular intervals with stone posts, which

* Sarginu is the correct rendering of the name of Sargon; but, except in the name of the city, I have retained the usual form, *Sargon*.

mark the distances. It ends after many turns at the gate of Ishtar, to the south-west side of the city. The defences of Dur-Sarginu are still in the same condition as Sargon left them. The outer wall runs across the plain, strengthened every twenty-seven yards by square towers, which dominate it with their crenellated tops, and project four yards beyond the curtain. It is twenty yards high, and the roadway at the top is so

Fig. 111.—One of the Gates of Dur-Sarginu.

wide that seven chariots can gallop abreast without touching each other. This great mass of building is really only a compact block of earth. The bricks, whilst still damp, are laid upon beds without mortar or cement of any kind, so that they have welded together and formed a substance which no siege battery can possibly injure sufficiently to cause a breach and lay the city open for an assault.

There are eight gates, two upon each side. They open between two towers, which only leave space for the entrance itself. Each of them is dedicated to one

of the gods of the city and is named after it—gate of
Bel, gate of Beltis, gate of Anu, gate of Ishtar. They
are covered towards the country by a small castle,
which is defended at each angle by a low tower, twelve
yards wide (Fig. 111). Five of them are large enough
to admit animals as well as men. The peasants enter by
them every morning, pushing their cattle before them
or driving carts heavily loaded with vegetables and
fruit. They pass through the first building, cross a
large paved court, then penetrate between the two

Fig. 112.—Transport of the Bull.

towers, under an arched gateway forty-seven yards
long, broken at almost equal intervals by two trans-
verse galleries. Eleven steps placed in front of the
court prevent animals and carts from entering it.
Two gigantic bulls with human heads stand at the
entrance of the passage, the face and chest turned
towards the outside, the body placed against the inner
wall; they seem waiting for an enemy, and are accompanied by two winged genii half concealed behind them.
The arch which separates them, and which is supported
by their mitres, is decorated by a band of enamelled
bricks, upon which more genii facing each other in pairs

are holding fir cones; a many-coloured rosette is in the centre.

The transport and placement of these stone monsters proved no light task. The blocks were quarried in the mountains of Kurdistan, and were then brought down to the banks of the Zâb. Here they were roughly hewn into shape so as to lighten the weight, then

Fig. 113.—A Winged Bull.

placed upon sledges, drawn by squadrons of foreign prisoners, who afterwards with cords and levers hoisted them upon their stands, where the sculptors finished them (Fig. 112). They are now the mystic guardians of the city, which ward off not only the attacks of men, but the invasion of evil spirits and of pernicious maladies (Fig. 113). Every day the old men and idlers of the vicinity assemble at their feet. Standing, crouching, sitting upon the benches and stools they bring with them, they gossip about their affairs and regulate the destinies of the State without any fear of being disturbed. During the winter they are warm in the sunshine of the front court, and during the summer it is always cool under the arches. The judge of the district sometimes holds a sitting and gives judgment there, the merchants drive their bargains and discuss their business, whilst the politicians, always well informed, exchange the last news from abroad—that the Governor of Egypt, Psammetichus, son of Necho, has driven an Assyrian garrison out of Memphis, or that the Cimmerians have burnt Sardes and killed Gyges the Lydian.

Dur-Sarginu, through being built all at once, has none of the irregularities observed in older cities. The streets, which start from the gates, retain in every direction the width of the roads they continue. They are paved in the same way, have side-ways, or foot-paths, and are intersected at right angles. The houses which border them are usually one-storied. The door is narrow and high; it seems to be concealed in a corner of the façade. Scarcely a window breaks the unity of the wall, and the terraced roofs are surmounted by conical domes, or half-cupolas, which open inwards (Fig. 114). Strangers lodge in vast inns, situated near the ramparts. There is no outward distinction between them and the private houses. The traveller enters, and finds himself in a large rectangular court; in the centre is a well, shaded by a sycamore-tree; all round are stories of small rooms, one above the other, in which the guests spend the night, and some large ones which are used for stables for the beasts of burden and storehouses for the merchandise.

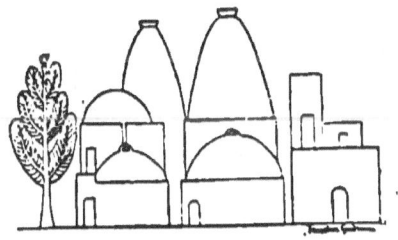

Fig. 114.—Assyrian Houses.

Towards the centre of the town the houses become richer and more beautiful, the traffic increases, luxurious chariots are seen amongst the crowd of pedestrians. The common people and the burghers are of many different types, of various origin and physiognomy. The Assyrian conquerors are great movers of men. They pride themselves upon transplanting nations like trees, and upon sending the tribes from the North to the South, from the East to the West. After each of their campaigns thousands of captives are exiled, and go to colonise some distant country, of which the native population will probably fill the vacant places in their own land on the morrow. Sargon filled his city with people gathered from the four quarters of the world, from mountains and plains, from cities and deserts; then he set over them, to keep them all in check, a handful of Assyrian soldiers, priests, and magistrates. Now, after sixty years have passed, the descendants of these forced colonists have adopted the language and customs of their conquerors. They might be taken for Assyrians from their speech and dress, but their features betray their foreign extraction; one still retains the aquiline profile of the Hebrews of Samaria, another has the fair hair and blue eyes of the Aryan Medes, a third displays the purest Armenian type, and many, who have sprung from mixed marriages, blend the characteristic features of three or four distinct races. The mixture is not so great at Nineveh, Assur, Kalakh, and the ancient cities, yet it exists there, and more than one family boasts of the purity of its Assyrian blood, who would find a barbarian prisoner amongst their ancestors if they could trace their genealogy back to its primitive source.

The royal palace is upon the north-east side of the city, half within, half without the enclosure (Fig. 115). Like the majority of important civil or religious edifices it is erected upon an esplanade of brickwork, formed of two rectangles joined like a T, a hillock

Fig. 115.—The Royal Palace of Dur-Sarginu (from Perrot and Chipiez).

built by the labour of man, which raises the foot of the walls far above the surrounding roofs. It is accessible from the city only; pedestrians reach it by a double staircase constructed in front of the platform, horsemen and carriages by a gently sloping ascent, which commences at the right flank of the building and ends on the east side of it, at the foot of high crenellated white walls. The king dwells there as in a turret, from whence he can see the whole country, and

Fig. 116.—Triumphal Gate at the Entrance to the Palace (from Place).

which he could defend long after the city had fallen into the hands of the enemy. Two principal gates correspond with the two ways of access; the one to the north-east leads directly to the royal apartments, the other is turned towards the city and overlooks the double staircase. Two high masts, surmounted by the royal standard, designate the entrance; they are visible from a great distance (Fig. 116). The door is placed between two towers, their base ornamented by winged bulls and human-headed figures. Two still larger bulls stand at the right and left of the entrance, a band of enamelled bricks defines the centre, and higher up, just below the battlements, an enamelled picture represents Sargon in all his glory. This triumphal arch is reserved for the king's use; two lower and less richly decorated side-doors admit the crowd.

The immense court into which they open is still a public place, which tradesmen, merchants of every kind, supplicants, and even mere sightseers, enter without the least difficulty. Thousands of persons are attached to the sovereign's household, and to the administration of his business: some as chamberlains, treasurers, scribes, eunuchs, military chiefs; others as soldiers, footmen, and cooks. There is a perpetual movement of detachments relieving guard, couriers starting or arriving with their dispatches, officials who are going to an audience or coming from it; files of donkeys bring provisions; morning and evening hundreds of male and female slaves descend in procession to draw from the tributaries of the Khosr the water required for such an immense number of people. The warehouses fill three sides of the court; here cellars for wine and oil, there stores of iron weapons, further on the room for copper, and one for the precious metals and jewels; the king's treasury, where he keeps the spoil of the vanquished nations, or the taxes collected from his people. The kitchens join the bakeries, the horse and camel stables communicate with the chariot house. The buildings that fill the southern corner a little beyond the stables are occupied by the servants of the palace; each family inhabits a little dark room; they are dressed and fed at the king's expense, and do all the menial work of the establishment. A small door in the southern angle of the court leads to the harem. Assyrian women of the lower classes enjoy almost unlimited independence. They go about as they like through the streets and roads, wearing a long dress of shaggy material, their feet bare, their head and face uncovered. They frequent the markets, visit their friends, attend to their business, and are quite unrestrained in their actions; they can dispose of their own property, inherit, buy and sell on their own account, bear witness in a court of justice; in short, they are the equals, or very nearly so, of their husbands. Women of higher rank possess the same rights in the eyes of the law, but practically they have very little real liberty. All the luxury and all the comfort that wealth can procure they have or they

Fig. 117.—One of the Gates of the Harem at Dur-Sarginu (from Place).

take, but they must remain at home; when they go out they are surrounded by servants, eunuchs, or pages, whose close ranks prevent them from seeing much of the outer world. The queens are completely slaves to their dignity, and remain almost invisible during their whole lives, receiving members of their family and of the household only.

When Sargon founded his city he had three legitimate wives, and to each of them he granted a distinct establishment; his harem, therefore, contained three compartments, or rather three houses. The first is isolated in the southern angle of the palace; the two others communicate with a square court, which serves as the common hall. Two benches covered with enamelled bricks run the whole length of the façade. Two gilded bronze palm-trees frame the opening; the palm, as we know, is the emblem of grace and fecundity, so that no subject could be more suitable for the decoration of a harem (Fig. 117). The internal arrangement of the three houses is precisely similar: an ante-room wider than it is long, a drawing-room, of which one half is unroofed, the other half is covered with a semi-dome, a staircase with eleven steps, and the bedroom (Fig. 118). The walls are coated with white stucco, and bordered with a black plinth; the floor is flagged or carefully bricked; here and there mats, carpets, stools, armchairs, low tables, and in the alcove a wooden bed, raised upon feet, with its mattress and coverings.

After marriage the life of the queens is passed in this prison: dress, embroidery, needlework, and housekeeping, long conversations with their slaves, the exchange of visits, and the festivals, with dancing and singing, with which they entertain each other, serve for occupation and amusement. From time to time the king passes some hours amongst them, or invites them to dine with him and amuse themselves in the hanging gardens of the palace. The wives of the princes and great nobles are occasionally admitted to pay homage to them, but very rarely, for fear they should serve as intermediaries between the recluses and the outer world. Yet a thousand intrigues are carried on beneath this apparently monotonous and simple life. The wives, who divide the affection of one man, cannot feel any friendship for each other. The least mark of interest shown by the master to either of them is a source of anxiety to the others; if the favour increase, anxiety becomes jealousy, and jealousy a mortal hatred. The neglected wives forget their former quarrels and unite against the favourite, the eunuchs take sides, and war commences—a war of artifice and treason, which ends in crime. A few drops of poison often dispose of

Fig. 118.—A Bedroom in the Harem at Dur-Sarginu.

a rival who appears to exercise too much influence over the sovereign.

The royal dwelling lies on the other side, away from the harem and the great court. It faces the south-east, towards the point where the ascent ends on the ramparts of the city. The king, without leaving his chariot or his horse, can penetrate to the very door of his private apartments. He alights in front of the monumental entrance, as usual guarded by a squadron of winged bulls in painted plaster, crosses the threshold between two lines of motionless sentinels and slaves, bowing low, their arms crossed on their breast; passes through a yard and a passage, then at last reaches the court of honour in the very centre of the palace. He occupies about twenty rather small rooms, decorated in a very simple style, where he sleeps, eats, works, receives visitors, and superintends the majority of current affairs under the protection of his eunuchs and in the company of his secretaries. The other rooms consist of state drawing-rooms, all alike, in which the crowd of courtiers and viziers wait for an audience or for the passage of the master. A shaded light falls from above, through round windows pierced in the arched roofs. Long bands of bas-reliefs in plaster, painted in bright colours, ornament the walls for about nine feet of their height. They depict scenes from the life of the founder of the city. Sargon, standing, receives one of his ministers, who offers him the necessary equipment for war or for a journey. Each object is carried by an eunuch: the cups and drinking-horns ornamented by the muzzle of a lion; the throne, mounted upon two wheels and harnessed like a chariot (Fig. 119); the armchair; the

Fig. 119.—The King's Wheeled Throne carried by two men.

P

low table, intended for meals and sacrifices; the war-chariot, a double seat, a tripod, and, closing the procession, a cup-bearer, who carries the metal bowl in which he rinses the master's cup between the bumpers. Further on, Sargon is hunting the gazelle or the lion. Elsewhere he is riding at the head of his army, across the plains of Syria or the mountains of Armenia. The artist has amused himself by reproducing the details which gives to each country its special physiognomy: a mountain is covered with pines and cypress, a district is planted with vines; the rivers appear to open, showing us the animals they contain—fish of various kinds, shells, tortoises, crabs; even the eels and frogs on their banks are represented. Formerly the sculptors covered their work with long inscriptions, which passed over the bodies of the persons represented, and disfigured them. The new school is less prodigal of writing. A few short phrases still explain the subject of the picture and the details of each scene, but long texts are relegated to the back of the plaster slabs, and are turned to the wall. The Assyrian monarchy is already old enough to have experienced the vicissitudes to which the best-constructed palaces are exposed. However solid the work may be, however powerful the dynasty may appear to be, the day will inevitably come when new cities and new royalties will displace the ancient ones. When Dur-Sarginu is abandoned, when its halls are empty and its walls crumbling, the hidden inscriptions will be found and will relate their stories to posterity, so that the glory of Sargon shall be told even in the ruins of the city that he founded.

The gods have not been forgotten; they dwell on the north-east of the platform, near the palace gardens, between the harem and the king's house. An irregular building has been reserved for them, containing the same kind of rooms that we have seen elsewhere, with white walls, black plinths, a few frescoes representing arabesques, animals, or symbolic genii. There, in an isolation almost as complete as that of the women, the priests and sacred slaves pass their time in studying the mysteries and celebrating the ritual. The King of Assyria is not the direct descendant of a god, like Pharaoh of Egypt; he is a man born of a human father, and in all the annals of his genealogy, to the remotest generations, he will find but men like himself. Nevertheless, he is the supreme head of the national religions: he sacrifices in the name of the people, presides at the solemn festivals, alone penetrates into the sanctuary, sees the gods face to face, and speaks to them. He never undertakes anything without consulting them, never enters upon a campaign without receiving some favourable oracles encouraging him to do so; he first deducts for them one tithe of the booty taken from the enemy, and he even extends to their priests the effects of the gratitude he vows to them in exchange for their protection.

However, his piety does not blind him to the point of allowing the priesthood to acquire any undue influence in the affairs of the State. Pharaoh has been seen to bow before the pontiffs of Theban Amen, and to forcibly dispute the crown with them, but no Assyrian monarch ever bent the head before the clergy of Shamash or Assur. Yet the descendants of Sargon profess a special devotion for the Queen Ishtar, the goddess of Nineveh and Arbela: Esarhaddon called her his mistress, and saw her in the battle-field charging the enemy before him. Assurbanipal invokes her, and invokes no other god in the most solemn circumstances; the veneration which he feels for her enriches her priests, but does not incline him to allow them any share in the government. Thus, whilst in Egypt the temple is built for eternity in calcareous stone, in granite, or sculptured sandstone, and the palace in light materials that do not resist the action of time, in Assyria the palace is greater than the temple in architectural grandeur and beauty of decoration. The king, his officers, wives, and treasures, occupy more than three-quarters of the platform; the priests are relegated into a corner as it were, the last thought in the plans for the royal citadel. The priests, but not the gods. Just as the crenellated terraces of the palace rise far above the pavement of the city, so the summit of their temple uplifts itself still higher above the battlements of the palace. An ancient story, well known to all the dwellers by the Euphrates, and which the Hebrews of Jerusalem have recorded in their books, relates that after the deluge, in which humanity perished, the inhabitants of the land of Shinar said unto each other: 'Come, let us make bricks, and burn them thoroughly.' And they had brick for stone, and bitumen for mortar. And they said: 'Come let us build a city and a tower, whose top may reach unto heaven;' but the gods were alarmed at their audacity and confounded their language, so that they were dispersed over the whole earth. The tower was never finished, and many people say that the great tower of Bel at Babylon is a fragment of it.

The first Chaldean architects differed from the master-masons of Egypt in not seeking the grandeur of their sanctuaries in the development of horizontal lines; they made them as high as they possibly could without risking their stability, as if they would ascend to heaven. Their *ziggorât*—so they are called—seen at a distance recall the stepped pyramids near Memphis; they are really storied towers, formed of cubed bricks laid one above the other, and joined by an ascent, which winds like a cornice from the top to the bottom of the edifice. The tower of Dur-Sarginu rises forty-five yards above the esplanade (Fig. 120). It has seven stories, consecrated to the divinities of the seven planets, each painted with the colour of its deity—the first in white, the second in black, the third in purple, the fourth in blue, the fifth in vermilion, the sixth in silver colour, the last gilded. It is massive, and contains no hall; but the upper platform supports a small cupola covered with plates of gold: two stone altars, a statue of Ishtar, a bed, and the implements for the sacrifices, form the whole furniture of this miniature chapel. This is the room of the goddess, which the priests and

Fig. 120.—The Tower of the Seven Planets at Dur-Sarginu (after Place).

the king only may enter without committing sacrilege. Her spirit is here attached to the statue like the doubles of the Egyptian idols;* from hence she watches over the people that live at her feet, foretells the calamities which threaten them, and teaches them by the voice of her prophets how to weaken, if not to avert, the

* For an explanation of the *double*, see p. 43 and following of this volume.

impending evil. Every morning the gilding of the chapel and of the upper story is illumined by the rays of the sun, and resembles a fire which all day burns between heaven and earth, and which marks the position of the city a long distance off. The weary traveller salutes it as soon as he catches sight of it, and quickens the speed of his horses in his impatience to arrive; when he resumes his journey the reflection accompanies him, and seems to brighten his way long after the tumult of the city has died away, and the palace buildings have faded into the distant horizon.

# CHAPTER XII.

### PRIVATE LIFE OF AN ASSYRIAN.

The boats on the Tigris—Dangers and annoyances of commerce—A merchant's house: the terraces, furniture, food—Protective amulets—Exorcism for the safety of the family and house—Purchase of an estate—Drawing up and signing the deed of sale—Marriage by auction—An offer of marriage—The contract and the wedding festivities—The virtues of a good wife.

THE merchant Iddina has returned from Babylon, where he had gone on business. He trades between that city and the Naïri,* and is therefore continually travelling. Every year he buys the produce of certain vineyards lying towards Amidi, and personally superintends the construction of the boats in which he carries the wine. Their form is very curious. They are round baskets made of osiers or willows, covered with skins sewn together. Some of them are very large, and can carry a weight of five thousand talents.† A layer of straw is placed at the bottom, upon which the jars of wine are carefully packed, then more straw is laid over them. The crew always includes at least two rowers and one or more asses. At the end of the journey the merchant sells the straw and wine, then dismantles the boat, which cannot be taken to Naïri by the Tigris on account of the rapidity of the current, sells the baskets for what

* The Naïri is the country in the upper basin of the Tigris between the lake of Van and the Euphrates.
† About 260,000 pounds in round numbers.

he can get, loads the asses with the skins, and returns to his home by land.

This commerce is attended by many dangers. The Tigris is in many places a capricious, violent torrent. More than one boat, drawn into an unexpected eddy, founders with all its cargo, or is thrown upon the bank and so much damaged that the owners are obliged to rebuild it. The inhabitants of the river banks are usually robbers and unreliable guides; they stop and pillage the voyagers, or force them to buy a free passage by presents. Lastly, the Assyrian governors and Babylonian officials are greedy, unscrupulous men, who must be conciliated by gifts in kind or money, and a large portion of the merchandise remains in their hands. All this diminishes the merchant's gains and increases his risk; yet the profits are so large that a great many men devote themselves to the river trade, and enrich themselves by it. Besides, the roads are no better, and if men wait until there is complete safety in this world before they attempt any commerce, they may remain at home all their lives and never be able to start. There is perfect security for travellers in Assyria itself, from Nineveh to Arbela, or from Arbela to Kalakh and El Assur. The kings insist upon the police being implacably severe, and, except in civil war, a man may travel alone without fear of robbers. But as soon as he gets beyond the centre of the empire the security diminishes, and the merchants dare only venture in caravans across the Syrian provinces or foreign lands; and even the strongest parties are not safe from a disaster. Not only the nomads and professional bandits are always roaming round them, and force them to exercise perpetual watchfulness, but the inhabitants of the villages, the small local nobility— even the kings, not content with the regular tolls, which they can legally exact on the road—have no scruples about attacking them on the way. The merchandise is divided amongst the pillagers, or goes to enrich the royal treasury; the men are massacred or sold as slaves. The merchant perpetually sways between wealth, slavery, or death.

Iddina's house stands at a short distance from the gate of Ishtar. It is larger and higher than the neighbouring houses, but there is no other external difference between them. It opens upon the street by a small arched gateway, followed by a dark, narrow passage, which passes through the thickness of the buildings and opens upon a large court, round which the rooms are arranged. A kind of verandah extends all round; posts planted in the earth support a light awning, which is fastened to the wall. The rooms are narrow, oblong; a few are arched, a few others covered with a flat ceiling supported by the trunks of palm-trees. The majority of them are storehouses for the provisions and household wealth; a small number only are inhabited. They are all surmounted by a terrace, which is reached by a steep brick staircase; from it there is a view over the surrounding houses. The Assyrian women spend a good deal of time upon the roofs. They remain there all the morning until driven away by the noonday heat, and they go back as soon as the sun declines in the horizon. There they perform all their household duties, chatting from one terrace to the other. They knead the bread, prepare the cooking, wash the linen, and hang it out to dry; or if they have slaves to relieve them from these menial labours (Fig. 121), they instal themselves upon cushions and chat or embroider in the open air. During the hottest hours of the day they descend and take refuge indoors. The coolest room in the house is often below the level of

Fig. 121.
A Slave kneading Dough.

the courtyard, and receives very little light. The floor is paved with slabs of polished plaster of Paris, which resemble a fine grey and white marble, and the walls are covered with a layer of fine plaster, soft to both eye and touch. They are watered several times a-day during the summer, and the water refreshes the air as it evaporates.

The furniture is very simple, even amongst the rich burghers. It is chiefly composed of chairs and stools of various forms, mounted some upon straight feet, others upon crossed legs. As a rule, the household sleep upon mats, but the master's and mistress's rooms contain wooden bedsteads raised upon four lion's feet, with a mattress and two coverings.* A baking oven is built in one corner of the court, skins of wine and jars full of water hang to cool from the lintels of the porch, a fireplace in the open air supports a large saucepan, in which a joint of meat is boiling. The Assyrians eat a good deal and drink still more. The poor are forced to content themselves with a little bread, a few vegetables prepared with salt and oil, and the fish which swarm in the river. The rich have as varied and abundant food as the Egyptian nobles. They repose upon beds of ivory or valuable wood as they dine, and scent themselves profusely before commencing their repast. The men and women are served separately in solemn banquets, but in every-day life they meet round the same table, or rather round the same dish.

Amulets are placed on every side, in every corner of the house; they are intended to protect the inhabitants from the evil eye and evil spirits. The Assyrians believe that the world is full of demons, eternally occupied in laying snares for men. They are rarely, if ever, seen, yet they are continually felt in the air, upon earth, at the bottom of the waters; they are as numerous as the motes of dust which dance in a sun-

* Compare, for the picture of a bed, Fig. 118, p. 208.

beam. They cannot be warded off except by incantations and talismans. The surest method of getting rid of them is to place in a very prominent position a statuette which represents them; then an incantation is recited or graven upon this portrait of themselves, which keeps them at a distance. The figures of one of the most formidable demons, the South-west Wind, which by its inflamed breath dries up the harvests and consumes men and animals with fever, are therefore hung above all the doors and upon the terraces. Iddina possesses them of every size and every material, in bronze, red jasper, yellow stone, and baked earth. The demon possesses a dog's body, standing upon eagle's legs, arms furnished with lion's claws, a scorpion's tail, two pairs of wings, and an emaciated human head with goat's horns. He is so ugly that the mere sight of his own image drives him away (Fig. 122).

Fig. 122.—The South-west Wind: a bronze statuette.

Other images of the same kind are buried beneath the stones of the threshold, so as to bar the entrance to all destructive spirits. As a rule, they bear the head of a different animal, and their form is unknown to our world. Many of them are only the national gods, who are obliged by a formula to keep guard over a private individual: Bel, wearing his tiara and horns; Nergal, with his lion's muzzle; Nebo, Merodach, and Ishtar.

We see, then, that a divine army is needed to combat the evil spirits which menace our poor humanity. 'They are the creation of hell, the great worms which heaven has let loose upon the earth, the terrible ones, whose howlings break forth in all parts of the city, who fall amongst the waters of heaven, the sons that issued from the bosom of the earth. They roll round the high beams, the large beams, like a crown. They pass from house to house, for the door cannot shut them out, no bolt can prevent them from entering; they glide like serpents beneath the door, and creep through the joints of the hinges like a puff of wind. They estrange the wife from the arms of her husband, drive the free man from the house in which he was born, and inspire the threatening voice which pursues him from behind.'* The gods charged to repulse them have each their special post, where they wait to fight them. Nergal is on the top of the wall and beneath the threshold; Hea and Merodach are in the passage, to the right and left of the gate; Naroudi is in the earth near the bed. Since all labour merits some reward, food and cups full of liquid are offered to these guardians night and morning, and they are invited to regale themselves. 'Oh, you, the sublime ones, children of Hea, eat and drink well, so that ye may keep watch that no evil can penetrate amongst us.'

Iddina, upon his return home from a long voyage, rapidly repeats a formula which should ward off from his home anything fatal he may have brought with him. 'The pestilence and fever which might carry off my people; disease, consumption, which might devastate my land, injurious to the flesh, destructive to the body; the evil incubus, the evil spirit, the evil imp, the evil man, the evil eye, the slanderous mouth, the slanderous tongue, may they be driven away from the man, the

---

\* This allusion is either to the voices sometimes heard in the night, or to effects of the voice of the magician which unceasingly pursues the man against whom an incantation has been directed.

son of his god, may they be driven from his body, from his bowels. May they never come near my body, never wound my eye, never come behind my back; may they never enter my house, never cross the beams of my roof, never descend into my dwelling. Double* of heaven, conjure them! Double of the earth, conjure them!'

As soon as Iddina has placed his asses in the stables and seen the bales of merchandise carried into the storehouses, his wife, Noubta, tells him everything that has happened during his absence—the conduct of the servants, the quantity of materials that they have woven and dyed. 'The weaver, Mousidnou, has come to borrow five-sixths of a mana of silver, which our son, Zamamanadin, has lent him, and which he will repay in a year; the interest is so calculated that it will double the capital in the time.' Iddina expresses his satisfaction with the investment his son has made. Zamamanadin is more than twenty years old; he is strong, elegant, well educated, and begins to manage the business almost as well as his father. For the last two years Iddina has confided to him the management of his fortune whilst he is absent on his journeys to Naïri, and Zamamanadin has already brought more than one delicate transaction to a successful issue. Now he is thinking of marriage, and wishes to acquire an estate in the neighbourhood of Dur-Sarginu, capable of producing an income that, joined to the share of profits allowed to him by his father, will enable him to maintain a family. He thinks that he has found a place likely to suit him, and the owner is not too exacting; it lies just beyond the Khosr, almost halfway from the village of Saïri. The land is fairly extensive; it takes thirty-five measures of wheat to sow it, they say, and it will be easy to verify the amount. It is good corn land, which has belonged to Nabouirib

* Double is here taken in the sense it has above, page 43 of this volume.

for a long time; but he is thinking of selling it because he is now too old to cultivate it himself, and all his relations are engaged in the town in more lucrative pursuits than that of a labourer. He first asked seven mana for it, but he soon lowered his price, and Zamamanadin hopes to obtain it for five. Iddina carefully notes down this information, and promises to conclude the bargain himself as soon as he has settled his own business. He was lucky enough to obtain at a reduced price, in the market of Babylon, several bales of wool dyed in Tyrian purple, which a Sidonian merchant, who was anxious to return home, desired to get rid of at any sacrifice. It is a material of incomparably fine texture and of great beauty, and if the chief of the eunuchs would but mention it to the queen they might sell it for three times its value, including the expenses of delivery at Dur-Sarginu. Half the price should be for Zamamanadin, and it would amply suffice for the purchase of the wished-for estate.

The chief of the eunuchs, prepossessed in favour of the Tyrian purple by the gift of an amulet finely engraved with Hea, the fish-god, between two worshippers, managed so well that the queen at once bought all the bales. The day after the sale Iddina went to Saïri to examine the estate for his son. The aspect is good, the land excellent. A stream crosses it and divides it into two unequal parts; the smaller could be easily converted into a vegetable garden—one or two water-swings placed upon the bank would supply the water necessary for market gardening. The matter drags a little for some days, then the sale is arranged after much bargaining and some mutual concessions; the price is five manas, and a day is fixed for sealing the contract before Judge Nabousakin. On the twenty-fifth of Tebet, in the morning, the two contracting parties meet at the gate of Ishtar, each accompanied by a scribe and some witnesses (Fig. 123). The title of scribe is not so common in Assyria as it is in

Fig. 123.—A Scribe, from the figure restored by M. Heuzey in the Exhibition of 1889.

Egypt; the officers, nobles, and officials of high rank disdain it, and leave it to the professional writers who draw up documents for the administration and contracts between private individuals. The scribes are provided with several tablets of baked clay, still soft enough to take an impression, yet hard enough for it not to be easily defaced or lost once it has been made. Each scribe takes one of them, which he lays flat in the palm of his left hand, and taking in his right hand a triangular stylus, its point cut like a bezel, commences to write. The marks obtained by gently pressing the instrument upon the clay resemble a corner,* or a metal nail. The scribe commences on the left below the upper edge of the tablet, and soon covers both sides of it with remarkable dexterity. The two scribes engaged by the contracting parties and the one belonging to the judge write the formulas at the same time, for every public deed must be drawn out at least three times. Formerly two copies only were made, and they remained in the hands of the two contracting parties; but sometimes it happened that skilful but dishonest people altered the writing to their own advantage. The Chaldeans invented an ingenious method of preventing frauds of this kind. The tablet, once sealed, they covered it with a second layer of clay, upon which they traced an exact copy of the original deed. The latter became inaccessible to the forgers, and if a dispute arose and some alteration was suspected in the visible text, the case tablet was broken before witnesses, and the deed was verified by the edition preserved inside. Now all important deeds are copied three times, two of the tablets are given to the interested parties, the third is deposited with a royal notary. The work ended, the scribes compare their writings to see that there are no omissions in either of them. Then the judge reads the deed of sale aloud:

* This is why modern scholars have called the writings the cuneiform characters.

'A field large enough to require thirty-five measures of seed corn to sow it, of wheat land, situated in the town of Saïri, bounded by the property of Irsisi, by the field of Shamasshoumouzir, by the field of Shamassalim, by the public pasture meadows; Iddina has acquired it for five manas of silver.

'The price has been definitely settled, the field has been paid for, and the buyer has entered into possession, so that the contract cannot now be cancelled.

'If, in time to come, any one wishes to contest the sale, be it Nabouirib, be it his sons, or be it his brothers, and he wishes to bring a claim against Iddina, against his sons, or against his sons' sons, to demand that the contract be cancelled, he shall pay ten manas of silver and one mana of gold to the treasury of the goddess Ishtar, who dwells in Nineveh, and moreover he shall repay to the buyer tenfold the price of the sale; he may bring the claim, but he cannot win by the action.

'Before Madie, Binshoumedir, Naboushoumidin, Mousezibil, Habasle, Belkashdour, Irsisi, Kannounai, Bahe; Nabousakin, judge.

'In the month of Tebet, the 25th, in the eponymy of Sharnouri.'*

The reading over, the contracting parties and the witnesses each signed in the usual place and way. Iddina and his witnesses placed a nail-mark upon one side of the tablet, and this mark, accompanied by the note, *Nail of Iddina, Nail of Binshoumedir*, is their signature. Nabouirib and the scribes fix their seal at the top and upon the back of the tablet, and a few words placed above or at the side, name the owner of the mark. The seals used are of hard stones of every kind, in red or green jasper, agate, cornelian, onyx, rock crystal; a few are in amber or metal. They are

* This deed is authentic, and dates from the reign of Esarhaddon (December, 673 B.C.). I have transported it, intact, to the reign of Assurbanipal, simply changing the name of the real buyer to that of Iddina; I have also transformed the Assyrian measures to modern ones that are nearly equivalent.

Q

often shaped like a cylinder, sometimes like a truncated cone, with a slightly convex base, and are engraved with figures of the gods or goddesses, sometimes alone, sometimes receiving the homage of their worshipper; the owner's name frequently accompanies the scene (Fig. 124). Each witness rolls his cylinder or stamps his seal upon the clay, and the judge, the last of all, legalises the signatures. The clay tablets are then placed in an oven and are rapidly transformed into so many solid bricks. Iddina, at once, by a new series of deeds, transfers to his son the land he has just acquired. Zamamanadin's dowry is now settled; Noubta can at once search for a daughter-in-law.

Fig. 124.—Assyrian Cylinders.

Marriage is both an act of civil law and a rite of domestic worship. It follows engagements made by two parties, consecrated by one or several formal contracts, drawn up by a scribe, and sealed by witnesses, an authentic copy of each deed being deposited with one of the notaries of the town. The lady Noubta will have no difficulty in finding a wife for Zamamanadin. A young man, rich, good-looking, and with an honourable profession, can choose almost as he likes amongst the young girls in the district; there are very few that would be withheld by their families. Noubta only hesitates between the various fashions of marrying authorised by custom, and wonders which of them will be the best for her son and for herself. Shall she buy her future daughter-in-law? It is said that formerly, in Babylon, a fair was annually held in one of the markets of the city for the sale of girls. A public crier put them up to auction, one after the other, commencing by the most beautiful, for whom all the would-be husbands disputed at a high price. The plain ones followed, but instead of selling them for money, a dowry proportioned to their ugliness was given to them. This sum was levied from the sale of the beauties. The auction ended, the couples were formally married, and the women followed their husbands to their new home.

Now customs have changed; women are no longer bought in public, but generally from relations. Nikhteqarraou, one of Noubta's neighbours, procured in this way the young Tavas-hasina as a wife for her son Zikha. Tavas-hasina was pretty, industrious, well educated, but poor; her parents were only too happy to secure her future by a matrimonial sale. In these cases the price is never high; Nikhteqarraou paid eighteen drachms of silver* for her daughter-in-law, and she is well worth it. The dyer, Nabouakhidin, who lives at the corner of the street, managed still better. He did not pay anything for Banatsaggil, the musician; he contented himself with inserting a clause in the contract by which he bound himself to pay an indemnity of six manas in silver† if he should repudiate her to marry a second wife. It is true that six manas form a large sum, but he, therefore, took precautions so that he should not pay it knowingly, for a second clause adds that should Banatsaggil ever fail in her duty she shall be put to death with the sword. Now death is not the usual punishment for an unfaithful wife; she is simply deprived of her clothes and turned into the street, where, henceforth, she lives as she may. The capital punishment is only mentioned to enable Nabouakhiden to avoid paying the six manas should he feel inclined to divorce Banatsaggil; he will have mercy upon her if she consents to forego her dowry. Noubta does not guard against misfortunes so far off; marriage by coemption appears to offer great advantages to her. A daughter by purchase does not bring with her that arrogance and those pretensions

\* About 67 francs 50 cents of silver money in weight (2*l*. 16*s*.)
† Six manas of silver about equal 1350 francs in silver weight (54*l*.)

to occupy the first place, which are so often the despair of mothers-in-law. It is to her interest to be gentle and obliging, to respect the habits of her new family; a dispute with her husband's parents might entail divorce, and send her back to poverty. In fact, she is her husband's slave, his chattel, and the law so completely regards her in that light that, if by chance, her father or any of her family wished to reclaim her, they would be punished by a fine, the penalty reserved for people convicted of unreasonably contesting the validity of a deed of sale; in the case of Tavas-hasina, the fine is fixed by the marriage contract at the sum of ten manas of silver.*

Daughters-in-law at a low price are not scarce. But Noubta determines to inquire, before choosing one of them, whether amongst her friends or her friends' friends she cannot find a girl rich enough for Zamamanadin to marry without paying for her, or even settling a dowry. And it happens that Nikhte-qarraou is on visiting terms with the wife of a merchant named Soulaï, who lives near the gate of Shamash, and who has several marriageable daughters. Bilit-sounou, the eldest, is nearly thirteen years old; she is tall, slender, with bright red lips, large eyes, thick, black eyebrows, meeting above the nose. She knows how to manage a house, can sing, play the harp, embroider without a pattern, read and write fluently; no girl of noble birth could have received a better or more complete education. The father is a good man, honest, respected throughout the whole district for his integrity; he owns a draper's shop, with a good connexion, and his mother, who still lives, possesses a great deal of land, which she will bequeath to him. Noubta obtains an introduction to the harem of Soulaï; the young girl pleases her, the marriage is arranged between the women, and ere long there is only the official request to be made for her.

* Ten manas of silver are about 2250 francs of silver money in weight (90*l*.)

Iddina powders and scents himself, puts on his best fringed robe, then goes to Soulaï's house, and, after a few compliments, explains his errand: 'Will you give your daughter Bilitsounou in marriage to my son Zamamanadin?' Soulaï consents, and without further delay the two men arrange the dowry. Both fathers are generous and rich, but they are also men of business habits. One begins by asking too much, the other replies by offering too little; it is only after some hours of bargaining that they finally agree and settle what each knew from the beginning was a reasonable dowry —a mana of silver, three servants, a trousseau, and furniture, with permission for the father to substitute articles of equal value for the cash. The marriage day is fixed for that day week, the 10th Adar. The preparations do not take long. The young girl has, during the last year, woven and embroidered all the materials required for her clothing and for the ornamentation of her room. The three slaves given to her were born in the house and know their mistress since her infancy. The bed, seats, chests, and hardware which furnish a harem are bought ready-made in the market. The chief point for the bride is the adornment of her person, so that she may find favour in the eyes of her husband when she unveils herself before him on their wedding day, and he sees her face for the first time. She bathes herself, carefully anoints her body and hair with essences, dyes the palms of her hands and her nails red with henna, powders her cheeks, and darkens her eyebrows. Her friends rally round her to assist her, to counsel her, and above all to chatter noisily from morning till night, these days of waiting being reckoned amongst the happiest of a woman's life.

On the morning of the 10th, the friends of the two families having assembled in the bride's house, the scribe who is to draw up the marriage contract appears. The two fathers and the bridegroom are in festival dress, and do the honours of the house. The astrologer has been consulted, and has declared that the day is lucky and the omens favourable. The men assemble in the reception-rooms, the women are grouped in the harem round the bride, the time has come for accomplishing the usual formalities. Iddina rises and makes his offer aloud. Soulaï accepts it, and announces the dowry he will give, amidst the approving murmurs of the assembly. Bilitsounou now enters, escorted by her friends and by the women of the two families. She is placed by the side of her bridegroom; Iddina, seizing her hand and that of Zamamanadin, lays them palm upon palm, then ties them together with a thread of wool, the emblem of the bond which henceforth links the wife to the husband; then he invokes the double of Nebo and of Merodach, as well as the double of the King Assurbanipal, and prays them to grant long years of happiness to the young couple. Only a free man has the right of conducting this symbolic ceremony, or of calling upon the gods to witness a marriage which is being celebrated in their name. As soon as he has ended his prayer, all present join their blessings to his own, carefully blending with them all the formulas considered infallible in averting the evil eye and all the malignant influences from the young couple which too profuse compliments never fail to attract towards those who receive them.

However, the scribe, who has carefully watched the scene to see that everything is done correctly, now commences to write upon a clay tablet the formal marriage contract. The terms are very simple and clear: 'Iddina has spoken to Soulaï, saying, "Give thy daughter Bilitsounou in marriage to my son Zamamanadin." Soulaï has consented, and has given his daughter Bilitsounou one mana of silver and three servants—Latoubaranou, Illasillabitiniziz, and Taslimou —as well as a set of furniture and a field of eight canes, as a dowry from Bilitsounou to Zamamanadin. He has remitted to Zamamanadin, as a guarantee of the mana of silver, which he will pay by-and-by, his servant Nanakishirat, who is worth two-thirds of a mana, and he adds nothing as security for the other third of a mana still due; when he pays the mana of silver, Nanakishirat will be restored to him.' The witnesses place a nail-mark or a seal upon the tablet. The bride's grandmother, the lady Etillitou, wishing to prove the satisfaction the marriage has given her, adds two slaves to the three which Soulaï has bestowed upon his daughter, and this gift forms the substance of a supplementary deed drawn up in the same fashion as the first. 'The lady Etillitou gives, of her own free will, to the lady Bilitsounou, the daughter of Soulaï, her eldest son—Banitloumour and Bazit, her two servants, in addition to the three servants which Soulaï, her father, has given to her. If any one should make a claim to revoke this gift, may Merodach and Zirpanitum decree his ruin; may Nebo, the scribe of Esaggil, cut short his future days.'\*

The prayer which follows the binding of the hands has invoked the blessings of heaven upon the union of the two young people; by it, and by it alone, is religion blended with marriage. As soon as the reading of the contract is over, Soulaï commands that tables should be brought in, and he invites the guests to eat and drink with him. The remainder of the day is passed in banquets and amusements—dancers, singers, players upon the harp and upon the flute, jugglers who perform feats of strength, story-tellers who relate fables or merry tales. The house, usually so closely shut, is freely opened to-day, and offers its hospitality to whoever will accept it; the whole neighbourhood comes to congratulate the parents of the bride and bridegroom, and to share in the rejoicings. Evening arrives, and now Bilitsounou must leave her father's house for ever. She weeps, clings to her mother, and delays the time of starting, as every well-bred girl should do. At last she leaves, on foot, surrounded by her companions, and

---

\* These contracts are authentic; I have only modified a few names and a few details to bring them into harmony with each other, and with the general tenor of my narrative.

advances by torchlight, to the sound of those piercing cries by which women habitually show their joy upon important occasions. A crowd assembles to see the procession pass, with its musicians and jesters, its train of slaves, furniture and chests preceding the bride. Zamamanadin waits for her in the midst of his groomsmen, and welcomes her upon the threshold of the house. The festival recommences—wine, banquet, musicians— and it continues even after the young couple have retired to the harem.

The rejoicings are prolonged for several days more; then life resumes its usual course in the two houses. Bilitsounou is soon accustomed to her new life, and Noubta congratulates herself upon her choice. The bride is a true type of the virtuous women, whom the wise of all countries delight to praise. 'The heart of her husband trusteth in her, and he shall have no lack of gain. She doeth him good and not evil all the days of her life. She seeketh wool and flax, and worketh willingly with her hands. She riseth also whilst it is yet night, and giveth meat to her household, and their task to her maidens. Her lamp goeth not out by night. She layeth her hands to the distaff, and her palms hold the spindle. She spreadeth out her hand to the poor, yea, she reacheth forth her hands to the needy. She is not afraid of the snow for her household, for all her household are clothed with scarlet. She maketh for herself cushions of tapestry, her clothing is fine linen and purple. She openeth her mouth with wisdom, and the teaching of kindness is on her tongue. She looketh well to the ways of her household, and eateth not the bread of idleness. Her children rise up and call her blessed, her husband also, and he praiseth her, saying: Many daughters have done virtuously, but thou excellest them all.'*

---

\* Prov. xxxi. Since this description represents the ideal, not of Jewish women only, but of Oriental women in general, I have allowed myself to adapt it to an Assyrian.

# CHAPTER XIII.

#### DEATH AND THE FUNERAL.

Man and his protecting deity—Prayer to the protecting deity against disease—The god Headache—The exorcist: exorcism to drive away the god Headache—Consultation in the public square—Death and burial—The destiny of the soul after death—The Chaldean tomb—Allat and Hell—The soul received amongst the gods.

A FEW weeks have passed since the marriage. Iddina insensibly falls into a languid, melancholy condition, for which there is apparently no reason. Every man at his birth is placed under the protection of a god and goddess, whose servant, and almost son, he then becomes, whom he always speaks of as his god and goddess, without any further designation. The deity watches over his *protégé* by night and by day, less to defend him against visible dangers, than to preserve him from the invisible beings which perpetually roam amongst men and assail them from all sides. If the man be pious, devout towards his god and towards the divinities of his country, if he celebrates the prescribed rites, recites the prayers, offers the sacrifices—in a word, if he be righteous—then the divine aid will never fail him; the gods will grant him numerous descendants, a happy old age, many days before the moment decreed by destiny when he must resign himself to leave the light. If, on the other hand, he be impious, violent, unfaithful, 'his god will break him like a reed,' will destroy his posterity, shorten his days, and deliver him to the demons which glide into his body and torment him with disease before he dies. Iddina asks himself what unknown crime can he have committed that his god appears to withdraw from him. He invokes the goddess Ishtar, and describes the malady which preys upon him. 'My days are passed in sighing, my night in weeping, the months are a torment unto me, my year is a perpetual cry; all my strength is chained in my body, my feet stumble and fail as though they were loaded with chains; I lie down roaring like a bull, I bleat like a sheep in my distress. . . . And no god has come to mine aid, no hand has been stretched forth to help me; no god has had pity upon me, no goddess has come near to me to help me.'

Assyria, unlike Egypt, has no sacred school of medicine where the rational diagnosis and treatment of complicated diseases is taught. It only produces sorcerers or exorcists, skilful in casting out the demons in possession, whose presence in a living body is the sole cause of disorder and death. The general appearance of the patient, the manner in which he bears the crisis, the words he utters in delirium are to these clever individuals so many signs which reveal the nature and sometimes even the name of the enemy they have to contend with. The most terrible of these evil spirits are called fever and pestilence; fortunately, Iddina's symptoms do not point to these dread visitors. He passes the greater part of each night in a profound slumber, from which he awakens at intervals, the mind disturbed, the eyes swollen, with a singing in the ears, and a noise like hammers beating in his brain. It is the god *Headache* that possesses him, and the sorcerers prepare to drive him away. The formulas used against him are very ancient: they come from Chaldea, and are preserved in some old books, written in such mysterious language and characters that only a very few learned men can understand them. The magician whom Noubta summons to her husband brings with him some of the most efficacious charms against the malady described to him. He carefully examines the patient's eyes and face, inquires about the commencement of the illness, and the various phases through which it has passed, then declares that the case is more serious than he had supposed. Iddina is the victim of witchcraft, practised by some one whom he has offended, and who is taking revenge by slowly killing him with fire. The imprecation which some magician has pronounced against him pursues him continually; it will kill him if the effects cannot be averted by a counter-spell which will induce Hea, the supreme god, and Merodach to use their great power in his service.

Medical exorcisms are religious ceremonials, which should be celebrated within the precincts of a temple. Since Iddina is already weakened by the days of suffering which he has borne, the magician consents to attend to him in his own house. He, therefore, arrives with his books, a packet of herbs, which he has carefully gathered himself, and the necessary objects for preparing a charm. He takes off his shoes, purifies himself, and, entering the sick-room, lights a fire upon the ground of herbs and aromatic plants, which burn with a clear, almost smokeless, flame. The first part of the charm, which he recites, describes the enchantment from which his patient suffers. 'The imprecation,' he says, in a firm rhythmical voice, 'the imprecation, like a demon, has fallen upon the man; the voice of the magician has fallen upon him like a scourge; the malignant voice has fallen upon him, the noxious imprecation, the sorcery, the headache. The mischievous imprecation is slaying this man like a lamb, for his protecting god is withdrawn from his body, his protecting goddess has left him, and the voice which scourges him has spread itself over him like a garment, and paralyses him.' The evil which the magician has wrought is terrible, but the gods can still repair it, and already Merodach is aroused, Merodach has looked upon the patient, Merodach has entered the house of his father, Hea, saying, 'O my father! the malignant imprecation has fallen upon the man like a demon.' Twice he speaks to him and says, 'I do not know what this man should do, or what will cure him.' Hea replies to his son, Merodach: 'My son, what is unknown to thee, and what can I tell thee that thou knowest not already? All that I know, thou knowest also; go, then, my son, Merodach, lead the man to the purifying bath, and drive away the sorcery which is over him; drive away the witchcraft, the ill that tortures his body, whether it be caused by the curse of his father, or the curse of his mother, or the curse of his eldest brother, or the pernicious curse of a stranger! Let this malediction be removed by the charm of Hea, like a clove of garlic, being peeled, or a date, being cut in pieces, or a branch covered with flowers which is torn away! The witchcraft, oh, heavenly double conjure it! oh, double of the earth, conjure it!* The gods arm themselves in favour of the patient, and Hea, the sovereign of the world, deigns to indicate the remedy. Let the invalid take successively a clove of garlic, a date, and a branch covered with flowers, and throw them into the fire piece by piece, as he recites an incantation; however strong the malediction may be, its effects will be destroyed.

However, Iddina has purified himself according to Hea's command; he has washed his feet, hands, and face, and has sprinkled his body with perfumed water. These preliminaries ended, the magician places himself in front of the brazier with the patient, peels the clove of garlic, which the god demands, and burns it, murmuring the formula, 'Even as this garlic is peeled and thrown into the fire, the flame consumes it, it will never be planted in the garden, it will never be refreshed by the water of a pool or of a trench, its roots will never penetrate the earth again, its stalk will

* Double is here used in the sense given it by the Egyptologists (see p. 43).

not grow or see the sun again, it will never serve as food for the gods or for the king; even so may Merodach, the general of the gods, drive this witchcraft far from Iddina, and loosen the power of the devouring evil, of the sin, of the fault, of the perversity, of the crime.' And Iddina repeats after him, in a faltering voice: 'The disease, which is in my body, in my flesh, in my muscles, may it be cast off like this clove of garlic, and consumed in one day by the devouring flame; may the witchcraft depart, that I may still see the light for many days to come.' The magician then cuts the date into small pieces, and whilst it burns he resumes his monotonous chant: 'Even as the date is cut up and thrown into the fire, the ardent flame consumes it, he who gathered it can never replace it upon its stalk, it will never be served at the king's table; even so may Merodach, the general of the gods, drive the witchcraft far from Iddina and break the power of the devouring evil, of the sin, of the fault, of the perversity of the crime.' And again Iddina repeats: 'The disease which is in my body, in my flesh, in my muscles, may it be cut like this date and consumed this day by the devouring flame; may the witchcraft depart, that I may still see the light for many days to come.'

The ceremony is prolonged, and the fire successively consumes the branch of flowers, a flock of wool, some goat's hair, a skein of dyed thread, and a bean. Each time the magician repeats the formula, introducing two or three words that characterise the nature of the offering: the leaves of the branch can never be reunited to the tree, nor used for the dyer's work; the wool and the hair can never return to the animals that wore them, nor be used for making cloth. Iddina keeps up to the end, in spite of his weakness; but as soon as the last words are uttered, he falls back exhausted upon his bed and nearly faints. The swoon of a patient is regarded as a good omen in these cases; it proves that the charm is working. The struggle taking place in the body between the benevolent gods and the evil spirit is always so great that few men can bear the reaction without suffering from it. The sick man becomes excited, he trembles all over, utters groans or lamentable cries, rolls upon the ground with so much force that it is difficult to restrain him; great prostration succeeds to this attack, marking the temporary victory of the sick man over his disease. The magician then recites a final incantation, in which he once more invokes Hea, Merodach, and lastly, the god of fire, who has so kindly lent his aid to the rites of the exorcism: 'O fire! powerful lord, who exaltest thyself in the land! hero, son of the abyss, who art exalted in the land! O god of fire! by thy sacred flame thou hast established the light in the house of darkness! Thou determinest the destiny of everything that has a name, thou blendest copper and tin by thine heat, thou refinest silver and gold, thou makest the wicked to tremble in the night. Grant that the limbs of this man, who has once more become the son of his god, may shine with purity, that he may be pure as the heaven, brilliant as upon the earth, that he may shine as the centre of heaven, and that the malignant tongue which had enchanted him may lose all its power over him.'

Two days pass by, yet the exorcism, although repeated night and morning, does not produce any beneficial effect, it only seems to increase the patient's weakness. Iddina does not become 'the son of his god again;' it would rather seem that his god departs from him, and delivers him to death without further resistance. An old custom still exists in Babylon of carrying the sick to the public square, and there exposing them to the gaze of the passers-by. The latter draw near, ask the symptoms, the means used to decrease the malady. If they have had, or still have, any one amongst their relations suffering from the same ailment, they describe the remedies that have cured them. This practice is also common in Assyria, like many other Chaldean usages, and Noubta at last resolves to try it. She wraps Iddina in his woollen coverings, places him upon a bed, and two slaves gently carry him to the gate of Ishtar. The judges are sitting there, all the idle men of the district are assembled in the front court, peasants and foreigners are coming in and out of the city; if there be any chance of obtaining competent advice, it must be there sooner than anywhere else.

The sight of Iddina rouses various feelings in the crowd. Several fear that the illness is infectious, and that the demon in possession may be tempted to leave the patient and throw himself upon them; others feel more curiosity than fear or sympathy; friends sorrowfully dwell upon his changed appearance, and murmur to each other sad reflections upon the instability of life. The officious crowd round the bed, question, exchange conjectures, and propose remedies to which the family listen anxiously. 'The exorcisms have failed? Which were they? Has the incantation of the seven demons been recited? Has the charm of Eridou been tried? Take the wool of a young sheep, and let a sorceress—a sorceress, not a sorcerer—bind it upon the temples of the sick man, to the right and left. The knot must be tied seven times running, seven different times; a cord must then be tied round the patient's head, another round his neck, another round each of the limbs, in order to chain his soul if it wish to escape, then the magic waters should be poured upon him.' Another declares that he has been cured by magic; an earthen figure of himself was made, then a libation of wine was poured over it, a charm was recited, and the malady disappeared. Or you can mix six different kinds of wood, pound them with a piece of serpent, add some wine and some raw meat, then form a paste of the mixture, and let the patient swallow it. This recipe is infallible; it is found in an old and highly esteemed book that King Assurbanipal has had copied for his personal use. The open air, the sun, the noise at first revived Iddina, but now they oppress him and add to his exhaustion. When he reaches home, he falls into a profound stupor, from which neither exorcisms, nor remedies, nor the despairing appeals of his wife and children can rouse him. Two more days, a slight rattle in the throat, some shivers, a few convulsive movements of the limbs show that life is not quite extinct; but on the evening of the third day, a little before sunset, he yields his last breath, and Shed, the god of death, takes possession of him for ever.

The peoples of the Tigris and Euphrates resemble the Egyptians in their noisy and disorderly expressions of grief. As soon as a man dies his relations and connexions, particularly the women, rend their garments, scratch their cheeks and chest, cover their head with dust and ashes, and utter loud howls of sorrow, which disturb the whole neighbourhood and force it to share in their mourning. But if the external marks of grief are similar, the method of treating the corpse is quite different. The Assyrians certainly believe that the life of man is prolonged beyond this world; they know that one part only of the elements which compose it dies upon this earth—the other continues to exist beyond it, if not for ever, at least for some time to come. However, they do not share the Egyptian belief that the immortality of the soul is indissolubly linked with that of the body, and that, after death, it perishes if the flesh, which it inhabited, is allowed to decay. In the Assyrian creed, the soul is certainly not indifferent to the fate of the body it has quitted; the pain it feels at death and the discomforts of its new state are increased if the corpse is burnt, mutilated, or left unburied as food for the birds of prey. Nevertheless, this sentiment is not carried so far as to lead the Assyrians to feel the same necessity for escaping corruption that induces the Egyptians to transform themselves into mummies. The corpse is not subjected to the injections, repeated baths in preserving fluids, and laborious bandaging which render it indestructible : it is perfumed, hastily dressed, and buried as soon as a change takes place in it, only a few hours after life is extinct.

Whilst the family weep and lament, some old women wash the body of Iddina, anoint it with scented oil, wrap it in a state robe, rouge the cheeks and blacken the edges of the eyelids, place a collar round the neck and rings upon the fingers, fold the arms over the breast, then lay the corpse upon the bed, with an altar at the bed-head, where the usual offerings of water, incense, and cakes are prepared. The evil spirits always hover round the dead, either to feed upon the body or to use it for their witchcraft; if they glide into a dead man at this time he may be transformed into a vampire, and return later on to suck the blood of the living. The family, therefore, by their prayers invite benevolent genii and the gods to watch over him. Two of them, although invisible, stand at the head and the foot of the bed, and stretch a hand over him to bless him (Fig. 125). These are the forms of Hea, and, like Hea, they are clothed in fish-skins. Three others take their stand in the mortuary chamber, ready to strike any one who attempts to enter it; one of them has a human head, the others have a lion's head upon a human body. Others, again, hover above the house in order to repulse the spectres who try to penetrate through the roof. So that, during the last hours which the corpse passes upon earth, it is carefully guarded by a legion of gods.

The funeral procession leaves the house early in the morning. The dead man is laid upon a bed carried by several men. It is preceded and followed by a group of hired mourners and musicians; then come the relations in their sacks of coarse dark material, very narrow and without any folds; then the friends, acquaintances, and people from the district who wish to pay the last respect to their neighbour. The cries used are the same as in Egypt, the same exclamations break the silence: 'Alas, Iddina! Alas, my lord! Alas, my father!' In the intervals the friends exchange comments upon the vanity of human things, which, under the same circumstances, always furnishes an inexhaustible subject of conversation to the survivors. 'It is the same with us all! The day of death is unknown to us all. Thus goes the world: he was alive in the evening, and in the morning he died at daybreak!' The procession slowly leaves the town, and proceeds towards one of the cemeteries where the people of Dur-Sarginu rest. No one must seek in Assyria for monumental hypogea or pyramids like those of Egypt. There are no mountains running to right and left of the stream, of stone soft enough for galleries or funeral rooms to be hewn out of them, or hard enough to prevent the chambers, once hewn, from crumbling upon themselves. Nineveh and the majority of the great cities of Assyria and Chaldea are surrounded by large, low plains, where all that is buried quickly decomposes under the influence of the heat and damp; vaults dug in the soil would be soon invaded by the water in spite of masonry, the paintings and sculptures would be spoilt by the nitre, the objects of furniture and coffins destroyed. The house of the Assyrian dead could not, therefore, be like that of the Egyptian, a *house for eternity*.

Yet he dwells there, and his soul with him. An attempt is made at the time he leaves our world to give him the food, clothes, ornaments, and utensils which he may require in the next. Well treated by his children or heirs, he protects them as well as he can, and wards off evil influences from them. When they abandon and forget him, he avenges himself by returning to torment them in their homes; he brings illness upon them, and crushes them by his curse. If through an accident he remained unburied, he would become dangerous, not only to his own family, but to the whole country. The dead, unable to procure for themselves the necessities of an honest life, are pitiless for each

Fig. 125.—Death and Hell. In the centre the dead man lies upon his funeral bed, watched by the gods; hell and its divinities are in the lower division.

other; if any one goes amongst them without a tomb, without libations or offerings, they will not receive him,. and will not give him even an alms of bread out of their scanty provisions. The spirit of the unburied corpse, having neither dwelling nor means of subsistence, wanders through the cities and the towns, and supports himself by rapine and the crimes he commits against the living. He glides into the houses during the night, reveals himself to the inhabitants under horrible disguises, and terrifies them. Always on the watch, as soon as he surprises a victim he springs upon him, 'the head against his head, the hand against his hand, the foot against his foot.' The individual thus attacked,

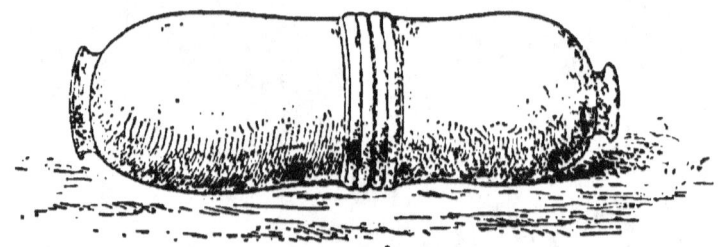

Fig. 126.—Chaldean Coffin in Baked Earth.

whether man or beast, will never escape from him, unless magic can furnish some very powerful weapons of resistance against him; the vampire figures by the side of spectres and ghouls amongst the demons, whose fury is averted by invoking the doubles of heaven and of earth.

The most ancient Chaldeans constructed their tombs in brick, like their homes and palaces. They were large vaults arched with corbels, in which one or more persons could be buried at once. They also used simple pots of baked earth, in which the corpse was placed, or two long cylindrical jars, in which it lay at full length, and which was closed with bitumen (Fig. 126). Sometimes the tombs were small round or oval buildings, raised upon a clump of bricks, and covered with a dome or a flat roof (Fig. 127). The house was not large, and occasionally the inhabitant could hardly enter it, unless he were bent almost double. In the smallest of them he had only his clothes, jewels, bronze arrows, and a vase of copper or metal. Others contained a set of furniture, less complete than those with which the Egyptians encumbered their hypogea, but sufficient for the requirements of a spirit. The body was extended, fully dressed, upon a mat impregnated with bitumen, the head leaning upon a cushion or

Fig. 127.—Round Chaldean Tomb.

against a flat brick, the hands laid upon the breast, the shroud kept in place by straps round the legs and ankles. Sometimes the dead man was laid upon the left side, the legs slightly bent, the right hand thrown over the left shoulder and plunged in a vase as though he wished to take it and raise it to his mouth. Clay jars and dishes were placed round him containing the daily food and drink, the wine which he preferred, some dates, fish, fowls, and game, even a boar's head, and, as in Egypt, offerings in stone, which replaced real offerings, and lasted longer (Fig. 128). The man carried his weapons as well as his provisions—a lance;

some javelins, his state walking-cane, the cylinder with which he sealed his deeds during his lifetime. By the side of a woman were placed ornaments and spare jewels, flowers, vials of perfume, combs, rouge-needles, and cakes of the black paste with which she darkened her eyelashes and eyebrows.

The tombs, placed one against the other, were covered with sand or ashes in the course of years; then, later on, the site was used for new tombs, so that at last, in Ourouk and many parts of Chaldea,

Fig. 128.—Interior of a Chaldean Tomb.

they have formed mounds, which increase and continue rising day by day. They are less crowded in Assyria, and less solidly built, so that they quickly disappear without leaving any trace above the ground, and whoever seeks for them must disturb a great deal of earth before he finds what remains. The monuments of the kings only are still recognised. It is said that the royal palace contains the tomb of Nimrod, the fabulous founder of the city and empire.* The

* Ctesias relates that Semiramis had buried Nimrod in the interior of the palace of Nineveh. The tradition which he quotes is certainly older than the epoch at which he wrote, and I have not felt that I ventured too much in carrying it back to the time of the Sargonides.

storied tower is built over it, and distinguishes its site from afar off. It is possible that the popular tradition is right on this point, as upon many others which it asserts, although its testimony is scarcely credited. For instance, it is known that the majority of the kings repose in the cities where they resided, under the protection of the gods of the city. The Babylonian chroniclers carefully register, behind the name of each prince, the name of the palace in which he was buried; and as to the sovereigns of Assyria, the old Ninevites still remember the *fêtes* which Sennacherib gave in their honour when he restored their tombs, which had been half destroyed during the wars and the revolutions of the preceding century.

No one now believes that the small case of baked earth in which the body reposes will be the eternal dwelling of the soul. It is supposed that far from us, some say beneath the earth, others at the oriental or southern extremities of the universe, there is a gloomy country, where all those who still exist of the past generations live together under the rule of the god Nergal and the goddess Allat. A river ends there which flows from the primitive waters of the ocean, in the midst of which our world is plunged. It is surrounded by seven walls and closed by seven doors, guarded by an inexorable porter. The shades can only enter it with an order from the goddess. They are immediately deprived of all that they brought with them, and are led naked before Allat, who judges them and assigns to them their place in her realm. Those who displease her are subjected to frightful tortures; they endure hunger and thirst, leprosy preys upon them for ever, all the diseases attack and devour them without killing them. Those who escape these agonies drag out a gloomy, joyless existence. They are hungry and thirsty, yet they have nothing but rubbish and dust to eat and drink. They are cold, and are only given one garment of feathers, the great dark wings of the birds of night, upon which they perpetually flutter to and fro, uttering plaintive cries. Once admitted to this dismal realm they never leave it, unless sent by special order from the gods above to terrify and torment the living. They have no recollection of their life upon earth. Family, friendship, gratitude for services rendered, all are for ever effaced from their memory; they only retain an immense regret that they have left the light, and a great desire to return to it. Allat could satisfy them if she liked. The threshold of her palace is built over a spring; the waters which flow from it restore life to those who bathe in or drink of them. They spring forth as soon as the stone is raised which imprisons them. But the spirits of the earth, the Anunaki, watch over them with jealous care. 'They are seven, they are seven, in the hollow of the abyss they are seven; they are neither males nor females, but are as the torrents which are poured out; they take no wife, they have no children, they know neither pity nor benevolence; they do not listen to prayer or supplication; they increase the discord in the mountains; they are the enemies of Hea, the messengers of death, and the agents of Allat.' Sometimes they scatter over the earth in the form of poisonous winds and raise a storm, sometimes they press into the battle-field and mercilessly cut down the heroes. Hea only is powerful enough to wrest a few drops of the life-giving water from them; but even then they give it reluctantly and with many protestations against the will of the supreme god.

This wild, gloomy conception of life, in common with others in a single kingdom, is still worse than the idea of prolonged existence in the tomb to which it has succeeded. In the tomb, at least, the soul was alone with the body to which it had been linked; in the house of Allat it is lost in the midst of the genii which issue from the night. It is surrounded by those formidable shapes which, scarcely defined in dreams, have already persecuted it upon the earth. None of these demons have a simple face in any way resembling humanity, but they present a mixture of man with animals, of animals together, in which the most repulsive features of each species are artistically combined. A lion's head stands upon a jackal's body, with eagle's claws and a scorpion's tail, and the creature is always roaring, howling, hissing, demanding rebellious souls to torture or destroy. The leaders of these monsters, the servants of Allat, are called pestilence, fever, the south-west wind. Allat herself is, perhaps, more hideous than the people over whom she reigns. She has a woman's body, clothed with hair and ill-proportioned, a grimacing lion's head, with the wings and claws of a bird of prey. In each hand she brandishes a large serpent, an animated javelin, which unmercifully bites and poisons the enemy. Her two children are lions' cubs, which she nurses herself. She travels through her empire, not riding upon a horse, but standing or kneeling upon it, so that she crushes it by her weight. Sometimes she goes and personally explores the river which flows from the world of the living; she then embarks with her horse upon a fairy boat, which moves without sail or oar. Its prow is terminated by a bird's beak, the poop by a bull's head (Fig. 125). Nothing can escape from her, nothing resist her; even the gods cannot enter her kingdom without dying like men and humbly owning themselves to be her slaves.

At last, however, a time came when the human conscience revolted against this savage dogma, which condemned all mankind to perpetual misery in utter darkness. What! kings who were good and kind to their people, heroes who destroyed monsters, soldiers who unhesitatingly sacrificed their lives on the field of battle, are to perish in the same obscurity as tyrants, slaves, and cowards? Their power, their courage, their virtues could only shorten their sojourn in our world of light, and precipitate them to the bottom of hell before their time! It was then believed that the gods, separating them from the crowd, welcomed them into a fertile island lightened by the sun, and separated from our world by the unfordable river which leads to hell. There grows the tree and flows the river of life; some privileged men occasionally enter it before death and return with their youthful health and strength restored to them. At first this happy land was placed in the marches of the Euphrates, towards the mouth of the river; later on, when the country was better known, beyond the sea. Then, as the discoveries of the merchants or the wars of the conquerors enlarged the limits of the horizon in which the first Chaldeans had confined themselves, the mysterious island receded further and further towards the west, then towards the north, and finally almost disappeared in the far distance. At last the gods of heaven became hospitable, and received heroic souls into their own kingdom upon the summit of the *Mountain of the World.*

This mountain occupies the southern region of the universe; one side of the starry firmament leans upon its summit; the sun escapes from its eastern flanks every morning to return to it on the west. When a hero dies his spirit rises from the earth like a cloud of dust driven before the wind; as soon as it reaches the region of clouds the gods hasten to meet it, and greet it like one of themselves. 'Come,' they say, 'wash thine hands, purify thine hands; the gods, thine elders, will wash their hands and purify their hands with thee,' to take their share in the banquet of immortality. And now, 'eat pure food from pure dishes, drink pure water from pure cups, prepare to enjoy the peace of the righteous.' Hea himself, the sovereign of the gods, deigns to assign a place for his guest in the sacred domains, and transfers him to it with his own hands; he gives him honey and fat, and pours the water of life into his mouth; with it he regains the power of speech of which death had deprived him. Yet, as he reposes upon a luxurious bed, he can look down upon the earth and all its miseries. At first the privilege of the heroes, this future existence has now become the general inheritance. Henceforth a man has only to live well upon earth—and by living well I mean to be devout towards the gods, regular in the celebration of their festivals, offering to them many prayers and gifts—and he will receive a welcome on the other side of the tomb. Merodach and his wife, Zirpanitum, will 'make him live again;' he will go, come, speak, eat, drink as he likes, enjoy the sun and the light. The kingdom of Allat now contains only the past generations, those who have lived and died in the earliest ages of the world. They are still there in the shadow, standing round the thrones upon which the ancient kings are seated round Ner, Etana, and all the old prediluvian heroes. The men of the present day are more fortunate. The years which they pass amongst us are no longer darkened like those of their ancestors by the ever-present image of eternal night. Piety will render them worthy of heaven, repentance will blot out their sins, and the gods will receive them into their own dwellings.

The tomb of Iddina is provided with food and furniture. This is more from respect for the ancient rites, than from any belief in the ideas which they formerly expressed. No doubt many of the people, and even many of the higher classes, still imagine that the soul dwells near the corpse and regales itself upon the food lavished upon the dead. But Iddina's relations do not share the popular creed. They know that the soul of their beloved one has flown to heaven during the funeral. They feel sure that the benevolent gods have protected its flight and preserved it from the malignant demons. When they shall also leave this earth they hope to meet it upon the summit of the *Mountain of the World*, amongst the 'silver clouds.'

# CHAPTER XIV.

## THE ROYAL CHASE.

Assurbanipal: his taste for pleasures and the chase—The state of affairs in Elam: the nephews of King Teumman take refuge in Assyria—The start for the lion hunt: the gazelles, stags, the wild asses—Crossing the river—The camp, the royal tent—The auroch and the auroch hunt—The sacrifice upon the return from the chase—The lion of Assyria and lion-hunting in the marshes—Hunting the captive lion in the royal parks—An embassy from Teumman.

ASSURBANIPAL was young when he ascended the throne. He was not yet thirty years old when Esarhaddon, his father, chose him from amongst his sons, and proclaimed him as his successor at Nineveh in the presence of the nobles and of the army: the following year he became king. He is tall, vigorous, and well made; his face is wide, the eyes are boldly opened, the nose straight, the mouth hard and proud, the hair long and wavy. His predecessors were passionately fond of war and of conquest; they lived, and sometimes, like Esarhaddon, they died in camp. Assurbanipal does not care to put himself into harness. He usually leaves to his generals the management of all military operations, and as they have been trained in a good school, the affairs of the country do not suffer. It is not that he is incapable of commanding and fighting like any one else, if necessary, but he is naturally indolent, voluptuous, devout, fond of luxury and the arts, still a bold rider and mighty hunter before the gods.

He has come to Dur-Sarginu for some weeks, hoping to escape the annoyances of politics, but in vain; at Dur-Sarginu, as at Nineveh, his position as king weighs heavily upon him. The messengers that arrive morning and evening from all parts of his empire always disturb his rest and spoil his pleasures by their news. Babylon is moving secretly; the Urartu are stirring and threatening the northern frontier; Egypt is always intriguing and privately stirring up the small princes of Judea, of Moab, and the Philistines; the Cimmerians, vanquished by Ardys, son of Gyges, and by his Lydians, appear likely to invade Cilicia; the Medes have killed one of their chieftains who was devoted to Assyria, and have replaced him by one of his cousins, whose hostility is manifest; Elam is arming openly, and the king is only waiting for a pretext to enter upon a campaign. Teumman is a 'devil incarnate,' whose cruelty and pride are unlimited. He had scarcely ascended the throne when he wished to seize and murder the children of his brothers Urtaki and Ummanaldash, who had reigned before him. Warned by some faithful friends, they fled with their servants, and large bands of the Elamites accompanied them to Assyria. Assurbanipal welcomed them kindly, partly through natural generosity, but greatly through interest. These young men with barbarous names and uncouth speech— Ummanigas, Ummanappa, Tammaritu, Kudourru, Paru —are the legitimate heirs to the Susian throne; they still have numerous partisans in the country who would certainly revolt if they were supported, and who, in case of war, would probably cause a diversion, which would be greatly in favour of the Assyrian army. In the meantime Assurbanipal receives them with the greatest hospitality, and treats them like princes of his own family rather than like strangers. He assigns to each of them houses, a suite, a sufficient income, and almost royal state; he frequently invites them to his table, and to-morrow he will take them to hunt lions beyond the Zâb, in the direction of the Median mountains.

The lion is not found now in the vicinity of great

cities, where they formerly abounded. They must be pursued far into the country; and the hunting expeditions planned against them resemble an excursion into an enemy's territory rather than a hunting party. The king takes one part of his guard and starts at sunrise. Dur-Sarginu is surrounded by villas and gardens, watered by canals supplied by the Khosr. The procession, crowded between the walls which border the road, becomes elongated and seems interminable; however, the houses soon become more scattered, the clumps of trees lighter, cultivation ceases, meadows commence, and the small army of sportsmen can easily deploy, as though in battle order.

From thence to the banks of the Zâb the ride is charming, the grass is abundant, and the sun warms the fields, whilst it does not yet scorch them. The undulating plain extends to the horizon, verdant and perfumed. The flowers are so thick in places, and so close to each other, that they might be taken for a coloured carpet spread over the ground; the dogs as they run amongst them become striped with yellow, pink, and blue. Every moment a frightened hare or a covey of partridges rises almost under the horses' feet. The herds of gazelles and wild goats which graze in the distance become anxious; they raise their heads, scent the wind, look on every side for one moment, then with a sudden movement scamper away and are lost in the horizon. These animals run so fast and so long that the swiftest hounds can rarely overtake them. However, a few greyhounds are slipped against them, and accidentally start a band of wild asses (Fig. 129). The wild ass is a very pretty animal, with grey, shining hair, and such rapid paces that it easily outstrips the horses. It utters a cry, gives a kick, and gallops out of range, then stops to see who comes; as soon as the enemy approaches, it starts again, then stops, restarts, and continues the same manœuvres without any fatigue as long as it is followed. Twenty horsemen start in pursuit, less in the hope of catching them than to breathe their horses and enjoy the pleasure of galloping across the fields. In returning they have the

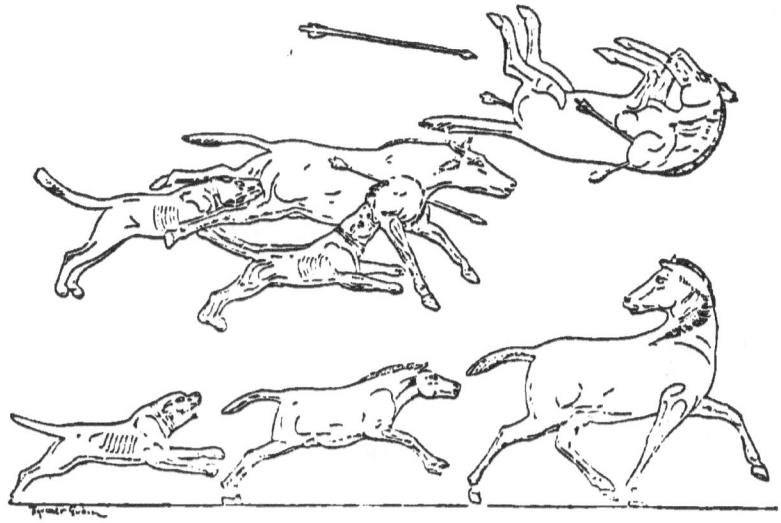

Fig. 129.—Hunting the Wild Ass.

good luck to surprise a family of deer that were quietly feeding in a small hollow; an old stag, pierced by two arrows, bravely turns upon the dogs, and his resistance gives the young fawns time to escape.

Fig. 130.—Assurbanipal and his Suite.

Assurbanipal never deigns to pause for such small game. He slowly drives across the plain, upright, impassive in his state chariot (Fig. 130). A large sunshade embroidered with red and blue shelters him from the sun. The coachman, who sits to the right, regulates the horses' steps so as to avoid jolting as much as possible; two eunuchs, clinging to the side of the chariot with one hand, wave their large flyflaps with the other. The chariots belonging to the Susian princes follow next, then those of the viziers, then a body of lancers on horseback; pedestrians, the trains of dogs, the men in attendance, the mules laden with provisions or necessaries for the sport, close the line. The party halt for one hour in the middle of the day, and rest in an improvised camp in the evening near a torrent still swollen by the melting snows.

Fig. 131.—The King crosses the Stream in a Boat, the Horses swim behind.

On the morrow, towards sunset, it reaches the Zâb almost unexpectedly, so completely is the river concealed by its deep banks, in the midst of this level plain where nothing betrays its presence.

Messengers had been dispatched in advance, so that everything was prepared for the crossing. Assurbanipal and the Susian princes embark upon two boats. The riders crowd pell-mell into fishing barques. The horses swim over, held by the grooms or fastened to the boats (Fig. 131). The foot soldiers always carry a large empty skin. They inflate it (Fig. 132), tie up the opening, and throw themselves into the water with it. Half carried, half swimming, they soon cross a river without laying aside their weapons (Fig. 133). In about half an hour the river is crossed. The camp is fixed a little further away, upon a dry, sandy spot, with sentinels and advanced posts as in time of war. The majority of the troops hastily pitch tents or sleep in the open air as well as they can. A little dry wood, brought from Dur-Sarginu, some dried grass hastily collected in the vicinity, and in a few moments a fire is kindled. The saucepan soon boils under the watchful eye of a comrade, or of one of the women who accompany the soldiers, and all the men who are not on duty eat and drink at their ease, seated in groups of three or four. Each nobleman has his own tent pitched near to the royal pavilion. The latter is a kind of temporary palace of rather complicated construction. Ten posts are placed in the ground in two parallel lines, united at

Fig. 132.—Foot Soldiers blowing out their Swimming Skins.

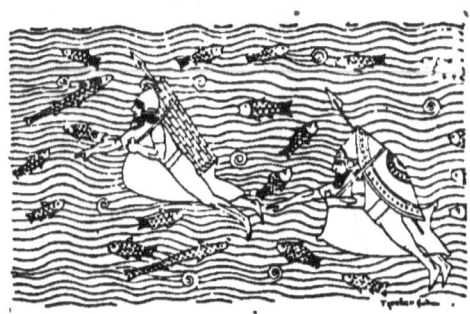

Fig. 133.—Crossing the River upon the Swollen Skins.

the top by cross-beams, and secured upon the outside by cords pegged to the ground, then over this framework pieces of coarse linen or bands of felt are stretched, closing the sides (Fig. 134). The space inside is a kind of flattened ellipsis. The central part, where the fire burns, remains unroofed, so that the smoke may escape easily. The two hemi-cycles at the end are covered with half-domes of linen or felt of unequal height, each supported by a branched post. The door is placed at one end, beneath the smallest of the cupolas. The furniture is the same as in an ordinary house—a folding table with gazelles' feet, stools, an armchair, a complete bed. The vessels for eating and drinking are suspended to the branches of the post. Outside, an altar is erected to the gods, by the side of a stable in which the horses find provender and shelter against the night chills (Fig. 135). A herd of cattle, sheep, and goats, penned behind the stable, provide fresh milk and meat for the royal table night and morning. Assurbanipal is willing to risk his life, but he will not dispense with the comforts to which he has been accustomed from infancy.

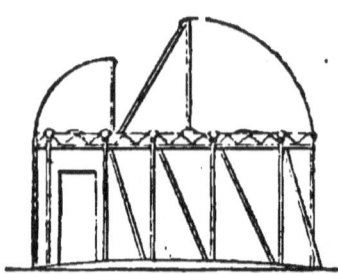

Fig. 134.—The Royal Tent.

Fig. 135.—The Royal Stable.

The huntsmen have not yet found any traces of lions, but they declare that at a little distance to the north-east they have seen some wild oxen. The auroch has become very rare during the last half-century. The kings of Assyria have so furiously hunted it that they have almost exterminated the species; the specimens seen from time to time in the plain, either alone or in herds, descend by chance from the mountains of Media or Armenia. Assurbanipal receives the huntsmen's report with great pleasure, augmented by the fact that he has never had an opportunity of rivalling the prowess of his ancestors against the auroch: he takes counsel with some of the old officials, who had hunted with his grandfather, Sennacherib, in their youth, and arranges the details of his expedition for the morrow with as much zest as though he were planning a battle. The pleasure is greater, because the auroch can only be taken by a particular stratagem. He is not dreamy and gentle like the domestic ox; but he is extremely large and strong, one of the fleetest and most cunning animals in creation, quite as suspicious at the approach of strangers as dangerous in attack. The hunters, therefore, divide into two bands. The first cautiously makes its way to the back of the troop and scatters as a semi-circle behind it; then, suddenly rushing forward with loud cries, it drives the animals towards the spot where the king is posted. Assurbanipal has left his state chariot in the camp—it is too heavy and crowded with servants. He goes alone with his coachman in a war chariot, low and light, provided with a lance, bow, and quiver; a horseman, armed with various weapons, leads a horse behind him by a rein. In fact, the chariot is not suitable for use at all times. It sticks fast in marshy soil, breaks against the stones, upsets over rough, uneven ground, or at least jolts so much that the soldier, shaken in his balance, cannot use his weapons; the horse is, therefore, serviceable as a supplement to the chariot. The oxen, disconcerted by the enemy's cries and by the sudden apparition, hesitate for a moment before moving. Then an enormous beast, of formidable appearance, lowers its head, bellowing with rage, and rushes upon the nearest horseman so quickly that he has not time to avoid it; the enormous creature raises beast and man with one blow from his horns, and throws them into the air as easily as if they were a bundle of hay, then crossing the line of the galloping horsemen, he flies towards the mountains, no one daring to follow his retreat. The remainder of the troop scamper off in a different direction, where the plain seems empty, and find themselves in the midst of the hunters. In less time than

Fig. 136.—The King kills the Auroch with his poignard.

we can speak, three of the bulls are rolling on the ground, pierced with several arrows; the four others, but slightly wounded, turn short round and gallop towards the river. Assurbanipal follows the largest of them, which, he is almost sure, is wounded in the shoulder; then gradually he overtakes it, skilfully drives his chariot beside it without checking speed, and, laying aside his bow, grasps one of the poignards he wears in his belt. With one hand he seizes one of the animal's horns, with the other he plunges his weapon into his neck; the short, wide blade divides the spine, between the neck and shoulder, the bull falls like a stone (Fig. 136). A flight of arrows arrests the fugitives before they can reach the water; the whole herd is killed, except the old bull that escaped at first.

The return to the camp is a triumphal march. As soon as the sentinels signal the arrival of the party, soldiers, slaves, women, all who are not bound by etiquette or military duty, hurry to meet it and form two lines, watching the procession. The sight of the seven bulls, each carried by five or six men, almost causes them to forget the respect due to royalty. They exclaim upon the size of the animals, the strength of their horns, the savage aspect given by their manes; they praise their master's skill, and loudly thank the

Fig. 137.—The King giving thanks to the goddess Ishtar for his sport.

gods who have favoured him with such rare and terrible game. Assurbanipal has left his chariot in front of his tent, and now prepares to return thanks for his success to the lord Assur and the lady Ishtar of Arbela (Fig. 137). Two priests with their harps are waiting to commence the hymn of praise. The bearers place the aurochs on the ground and arrange them side by side in a single line. The king, accompanied by his fly-flap and sunshade-bearers, stands on the right, the bow in his left hand. He takes the cup full of sacramental wine, which the vizier presents to him, touches it with his lips, then partly empties it over the victims whilst the musicians play. The same evening an eunuch will start for

Nineveh to have the new exploit graven upon stone. The picture will display the departure, the chase, the death, the solemn entry, and an inscription placed above the last scene will tell posterity the name of the victor: 'I, Assurbanipal, king of multitudes, king of Assyria, whose power is secured by Assur and Beltis, I have killed seven aurochs; I have strung the mighty bow of Ishtar, queen of battles, against them, I have made an offering over them and poured out wine upon them.'* The flesh and the fat are not very good, particularly when the animal is old, but the head and skin are carefully removed and prepared, then deposited in the royal treasury. The ancient kings of Assyria highly prized trophies of this kind. Tiglath-Pileser I. boasted nearly six hundred years ago of having brought a large number back from Syria, with elephants' tusks and a Nile crocodile, which Pharaoh had given him. 'I even took some young aurochs,' he added, 'and made herds of them.' This was a preserve which he wished to secure for future occasions, for he certainly never intended to break these gigantic brutes in for harness, nor to reduce them to the condition of domestic cattle. No doubt later on other sovereigns endeavoured, if not to tame them, at least to keep them in parks; but none of their attempts appear to have been successful, and we do not find in any of the annals of Assyria that herds of aurochs were maintained, either born in captivity or simply preserved long in the royal parks. Already their name for many contemporaries is a word that has lost its exact meaning. They no longer know whether it designates a real animal or one of those fantastic monsters that peopled the world in the earliest days of the creation. The commemorative bas-reliefs sculptured upon the walls of the palaces will soon be

* As yet no auroch hunts have been found upon Assurbanipal's monuments; all the preceding details are taken from the pictures of Sennacharib. The text of the inscription is taken from the bas-reliefs, which represent the king hunting the lion; I have replaced the lion by the auroch.

the only mementoes of their real form.* Two days passed in a vain search for lions; on the third, when the king was thinking that he had better move the camp, a fellah, still trembling with his fright, came in and warned him that the same morning two lions had robbed him of a sheep in the outskirts of the village he inhabited. The lion of Assyria and Chaldea is smaller and less fierce than the lion of Africa. It is easily tamed when young, and as it grows older retains its affection for the master who feeds it and treats it well. The kings always keep one in the palace for their own amusement, but we do not find it trained to follow them into battle and fight against their enemies, like the lions of the Pharaohs of Egypt so often do.† In a wild state it inhabits the marshes on the borders of the river or canals. By day it crouches in the thickets, and leaves them only at the last extremity; at night it goes in search of food, trying to surprise a gazelle or a wild ass. When game is scarce it prowls around human habitations; a sheep, an ox, a horse, a dog, anything will do for it, but it rarely attacks a man. The lion is hunted with large dogs, supported by well-mounted riders; but the dogs and horses must be trained first, or the sight and smell of the animal scares them away. The dogs used for this purpose are large mastiffs, with rough tangled coats, black upon the body, reddish upon the head and limbs; the tail is curved, the lip pendant, the jaws wide (Fig. 138); it is said that when they have fastened on their prey they will let themselves be torn in pieces, but they will not let go their hold.

Assurbanipal, delighted with this unexpected good luck, at once orders the marshes, in which the maraud-

* The name *rimou*, Hebr. *rem*, has, in fact, been misunderstood in the few pages in the Bible in which it is mentioned; before the cuneiform texts were deciphered it was usually translated *licorne*, *unicorn*.

† See p. 174, the account of the tame lion belonging to Rameses II, and its share in the battle of Kadesh.

ing lions have taken refuge with their prey, to be surrounded, then pauses a moment to examine them before he enters. A spongy soil, rather below the level of the plain; at first a few pools of stagnant water scattered here and there, then some clumps of reeds and water-plants, and a real forest of giant rushes twelve or fifteen feet high. One or two paths beaten by the fishermen, who venture into these dangerous places, wind through the thicket; a river passes through it and separates into ten branches, of which several appear to be navigable and flow into the Zâb at a little distance away. Assurbanipal places a boat full of soldiers across the widest of the streams. Their duty is to cut off the lion's retreat if it tries to escape and swim across to the marshes and the plain beyond. He places the lines of beaters, then mounts a horse, the quiver at his back, the bow in his hand, and commands the dogs, hitherto held in leash by a keeper, to be loosed. The brave animals at once rush into the thicket, closely followed by the king and the grooms, who carry his weapons and lead his second horse.

Fig. 138.—The Dog used for hunting the Lions.

A loud baying sounds above all the voices, then the

angry roar of a wild beast, harsh and short. As he approaches one end of a large clearing, the king perceives two lions at the other extremity, both slowly retreating, followed at a respectful distance by half-a-dozen dogs. An arrow shot at a gallop strikes the lioness between the ribs (Fig. 139); as she turns to spring, a

Fig. 139.—The King shoots an Arrow at the Lion whilst in full gallop.

second pierces her shoulder, and a third enters the spine above the loins. She falls, then rising upon her fore paws, and painfully dragging her paralysed hind quarters, she waits for the attack, her neck firm, her head threatening (Fig. 140). A lance-thrust in the jaw kills her as she moves. At first her companion seemed inclined to defend her, but his courage failed at the sight of this sudden execution, and four arrows striking him at the same time completely disconcerted him (Fig. 141). He bounds into the thicket and disappears, the dogs following. Assurbanipal rushes after them, but the soil soon gives way under the weight, his horse sinks up to the pasterns in the mud, and can scarcely free himself. The king hastily dis-

Fig. 140.—Death of the Lioness.

mounts, gives the reins to a groom, and tries to follow on foot to the river's bank.

The baying of the hounds, so loud but one moment ago, is now lost in the cover, and he has nothing to guide him. At every step he slips upon a leaf, stumbles against a root, or entangles his feet in the young shoots and fallen branches. The rushes surround him so that he cannot see anything; perhaps the lion is there, almost touching him, without his knowledge. And, in fact, a sudden opening in the green mass which imprisons him suddenly shows him the beast, standing on the bank but twenty steps away, strongly defined against the reflecting bottom of the river, absorbed in the contemplation of the boat which bars his passage. He is evidently questioning in his lion's brain which is his wisest course: to give battle upon the water and force a crossing, or to turn back into the thickets of the marsh. The arrival of the king decides the question, and leaves him but the choice of two enemies. His rage at being tracked so closely revives his spirits. His tail lashes his sides, he wrinkles his face, shakes his mane, and with unsheathed claws and open mouth rises upon his hind legs to end the battle at one blow. Assurbanipal, who was waiting for this moment,

Fig. 141.—The Wounded Lion.

Fig. 142.—The King kills the Lion with his Lance.

at once seizes his ear with the right hand, and plunges a lance into his breast (Fig. 142). The weapon, driven home, pierces the body through, touches the heart, and comes out behind the shoulder. He proves to be a savage old lion, of extraordinary size, about six feet long from the tip of the nose to the root of the tail, and it would be hard work to drag him through the marshes. Fortunately the boat is there; the lion is carried to it, and suspended to the poop by the paws tied together, the head and tail falling over the water. Then the king embarks and gives the order to row back to the Zâb, so as to return to the camp. The

Fig. 143.—The Lion attacks the Royal Boat.

channel, wide enough in some places to form pools, is very narrow in others. In leaving one of the narrow points a loud roar startles them all, and a large wounded lion springs from the reeds, clears the six feet which separate him from the boat at one bound, and clings with his claws to the edge of the vessel (Fig. 143). But the king has already greeted him with an arrow full in the chest; the crew have set upon him with spears, he is killed immediately, then hauled up, and hung on the other side of the poop as a pendant to the first lion. The three bodies are carried back to the camp (Fig. 144), then presented to Ishtar with the same ceremonies that had celebrated the triumph over the wild bulls, and the sculptors were ordered to represent the hand-to-hand struggle of the sovereign and his savage foe. 'I, Assurbanipal, king of peoples, king of Assyria, alone on foot, in my majesty, I seized a lion of the desert by the ear; and by the mercy of Assur and Ishtar, queen of battles, I pierced its loins with my lance, with mine own hands.' But the chase is not always so successful, and often in these later years the king has left Nineveh with much pomp, only to return with empty hands after a fortnight or three weeks of useless riding to and fro, without seeing anything but gazelles and wild goats. The times are past when the old Tiglath-Pileser could boast of having killed one hundred and twenty adult lions, sometimes following them on foot, sometimes on horseback, or even in his chariot. Now, probably, the whole of Mesopotamia does not contain so many, and every expedient is tried to procure them. They are sometimes imported from those fortunate countries which possess more than their princes care to have—from Chaldea, Arabia, Elam, and even from Africa. The purveyors have invented various methods of taking them alive. Here is one of the most simple: A large, deep pit is dug, and edged with a low wall of dry stones, as though it were an ordinary fold; then a strong post is placed in the centre, its top showing a little above the wall, and a living lamb is fastened to it. The lion, attracted by the plaintive bleatings of

Fig. 144.—The Lion taken back to the Camp.

the poor little creature, looks at the wall, easily jumps it, and lands at the bottom of the hole. The hunters, who are concealed near, run up, and allow it to exhaust itself in useless efforts to escape, then to get hungry, and finally after some time they lower with cords an open cage, in which they have placed a piece of roast meat. As soon as the lion has gone in to feed, they close it, and haul their prisoner to the surface, still furious and stupefied by its misfortune.

The lions, forwarded to Assyria by the nearest route, are sometimes kept in large walled parks, in which they enjoy relative liberty, herds of goats being provided for their food. From time to time the king comes to enjoy the amusement of the chase. Often, also, the cage is placed in the centre of a plain, surrounded by an unbroken line of soldiers; it is still a park, but temporary, and the wall is of men, not of brick or stones. The square formed, the keeper raises the trapdoor, and takes refuge in an open railed safety-box built for him on the roof of the cage (Fig. 145). The animal rushes out, stretches itself, looks round, then sees the enemy and comprehends the situation.

Fig. 145.—The Lion Leaving its Cage.

This imitation hunt is copied from the real expeditions, the same weapons are used, the same methods of attack by arrows, spears, on foot, on horseback, or in chariots, but the lion has not the right to escape. Whenever it tries to break the line the soldiers repulse it, and force it to return and encounter the attacks of the sovereign. The fate of the auroch awaits the lion, and the time draws near when the sculptures will be the only testimony to the careless bravery with which the Assyrian kings pursued it, even in its lair. It is doubtless written in the book of destiny that Assurbanipal will not complete the campaign so brilliantly commenced. Whilst he dedicated his lions to Ishtar, a special dispatch from his grand vizier, who remained at Dur-Sarginu during the expedition, to transact the royal business, begged him to return immediately. An ambassador from Elam had just appeared on the frontier coming from Teumman. He requested an audience, and whilst the demand was made in the most correct terms, it contained no allusion to the object of the visit. But no one doubted that he had received orders to demand the extradition of the princes, and the people that accompany him made no secret of the fact. 'Teumman knows,' they say, 'the friendship which Assurbanipal has conceived for the nephews of Urtaki, and would be sorry to disturb it. He does not wish that they should be entirely restored to him, the bodies may be kept; he only wishes for the heads, and will hold Assyria free to do as she likes with the rest.' To refuse the audience meant an immediate declaration of war, and the grand vizier dare not assume so much responsibility. Assurbanipal is less annoyed than might be supposed at the message which recalls him. The success of his expedition has excited him, and the war with Elam does not alarm him any more than the war with the lion. He returns to the city with the same order and with the same pomp as he left it. The Susian princes, who know that their destiny is in the balance, anxiously watch his face, and joyfully notice that it does not betray any mental preoccupation. The soldiers, who see in war a new opportunity of pillage and the rapid acquirement of wealth, openly rejoice at the thought of a campaign, of which the end is not even doubtful, and the good people of Dur-Sarginu, who cheered the king when he started, greet his return yet more warmly as they see the aurochs and lions carried home.

# CHAPTER XV.

### THE ROYAL AUDIENCE: PREPARING FOR WAR.

The Assyrian court; its luxury, and in what respects it differs from Egyptian luxury—The king's costume—The embroidery: through it the forms of Assyrian art are diffused over the world—The jewels—The king's ministers and their functions: the *Tartan* and the *Limmou*—The embassy from Elam: the various races from Elam—Declaration of war—The Assyrian army: its method of making war—The dangers of a coalition, and the means used to prevent it—The dispatches forwarded to the governors and military commanders.

THE day fixed for the audience has arrived. Assurbanipal wished that the Elamite ambassadors should receive every mark of consideration, and the whole court is assembled to do them honour. The Assyrian royalty is perhaps the most luxurious of our century. Its victories and conquests, uninterrupted for one hundred years, have enriched it with the spoil of twenty peoples. Sargon has taken what remained to the Hittites; Sennacherib overcame Chaldea, and the treasures of Babylon were transferred to his coffers; Esarhaddon and Assurbanipal himself have pillaged Egypt and her great cities, Sais, Memphis, and Thebes of the hundred gates. The foreign gods, Khaldia the Armenian, Melkarth of Tyre, Chemosh of Moab, Ptah, Amen, and their troops of divine animals have been humiliated before Assur, and the sacred vases from their temples are piled high in the chambers of the Ninevite palaces. Commerce has followed in the direction opened by the armies. Now foreign merchants flock into Nineveh, bringing with them the most valuable productions from all countries—gold and perfume from Southern Arabia, ivory from Africa and the Chaldean Sea, Egyptian linen and glass-work, carved enamels, goldsmith's work, tin, silver, Phœnician purple; cedar wood from Lebanon, unassailable by worms; furs and iron from Asia Minor and Armenia. The least of the nobles who lives near the king unites, in his palace and upon his person, the natural productions and manufactures of the whole world.

The same wealth formerly existed on the banks of the Nile; but Egypt was more refined, and never displayed her opulence with so much ostentation. Pharaoh and his nobles loved, and still love, elegance and perfection rather than rich ornaments and furniture. They wear little, and their garments are of simple white linen, but the quality is so light and fine that the form and colour of the body are visible through it, and contact with it is a caress to the limbs. On the contrary, the Assyrians seek for heavy, stiff materials, shaggy and loaded with fringes, overweighted with many-coloured designs and embroideries. Their garments envelop them completely from neck to ankle, but they drape badly, and encircle the bust and hips almost without folds. Even the women seem to prefer a style of dress which enlarges them and conceals their natural shape as much as possible; the wadded cases in which they imprison themselves give them a stiff, awkward appearance, which contrasts most unfavourably with the supple grace and easy movements of the Egyptians.

Assurbanipal has carefully powdered himself. His hair and beard, perfumed, combed, divided in rows of curls, one above the other, fall over his shoulders and chest. He wears for the occasion one of his most resplendent state costumes. A high mitre, shaped like a truncated cone, exactly follows the outlines of his forehead and temples; it is of white wool, striped with blue. A wide band, ornamented with rosettes in golden thread, holds it in place upon the forehead; the two ends are tied behind and fall upon the neck. The short-sleeved dress is of very deep blue, embroidered with rosettes in red cotton; it is fastened round the waist by a wide sash carefully arranged in three folds, edged at the ends by a fringe of which each thread is

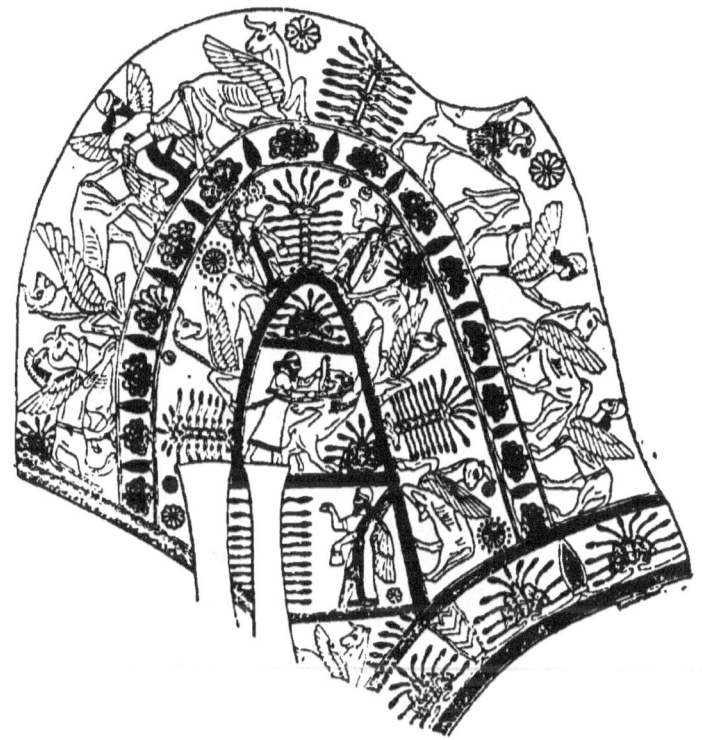

Fig. 146.—Fragment of an Assyrian Embroidery, from a bas-relief reproduced by Layard.

decorated by four rows of glass beads. A vest is passed over the robe, covering the shoulders and descending halfway down the back. The material of which it is made is almost hidden by heavy embroidery. Borders of flowers and palm-leaves surround religious scenes, in which the king adores the sacred tree, or struggles with a lion or with two winged sphinxes, or presents a bow and arrow to various divinities (Fig. 146). The

T

design is most carefully and boldly drawn, and if a little overloaded, as a whole the details are so varied and beautiful that they fairly astonish those who are not aware of the manual skill of Assyrian women. They execute, or rather paint, with their needles these fragile pictures. Their reputation has extended to foreign lands, and not only nations civilised for many years, like Syria and Egypt, but even the half-savage peoples of Greece or distant Etruria greatly appreciate their work.

The embroidered stuffs from Nineveh and Babylon are in fact one of the wares which the Phœnicians export with the greatest profit, and which render Assyria and Chaldea celebrated in lands where the fame of their arms has never penetrated. The images of gods and animals, natural or fantastic, represented upon them have been copied by the artisans of these different countries in their own materials, upon their jewels, their vessels in stone or metal. As they are ignorant of the signification of these figures, they separate them or group them arbitrarily, without any thought except to compose some harmonious decorations. They have even blended types borrowed from other nations, particularly from the Egyptians, and this mixture of contradictory elements excites the amusement or wrath of learned Assyrians, when one of these grotesque works accidentally falls into their hands. It is even said that some of these barbarians have imagined that they recognised portraits of their gods and heroes in the figures of the Ninevite gods or kings. Thus, the Hellenes took possession of the superb group which represented the giant Gistubar strangling a lion with one arm and carrying it away with him. They believed it to represent Hercules, the son of Zeus, who formerly killed a gigantic lion in this way; thus the portrait of the old Chaldean hero has become that of their national god. This is really one of the most curious and unexpected effects of commerce

## THE ROYAL AUDIENCE: PREPARING FOR WAR. 275

between the various nations; the material form has become detached from the idea which inspired it, and has gone to the other end of the world to clothe a different idea, and give it the body it lacked.

The jewels match the costume. The Assyrians have retained the use of ear-rings for men, which the Egyptians have rejected for some centuries. Those worn by the king to-day are very simple and of an ancient form, resembling those worn in the time of Sargon. They consist of a simple ring of gold, decorated with three balls upon the sides and ornamented by a pendant shaped like a spindle and adorned with a few balls. The bracelets are of a more elaborate design. Two are usually worn upon each arm. The first, placed very high towards the shoulder, is a golden reed rolled upon itself; two lions' heads stop the ends of the spiral. The bracelet for the wrist is a golden circle, closed by a rosette with ten petals. The effect of these jewels is rather heavy; it produces the feeling that the owner is conscious of his wealth, and has told the artist to use a great deal of the gold. But the work, examined closely, shows immense skill; the lions' heads are expressive, the petals of the rosette are arranged with exquisite taste. The way in which the various motives are disposed is most ingenious. No doubt the Assyrian goldsmiths would succeed as well as the Egyptian if they were not obliged to work for clients who value jewellery for its massive appearance and its weight.

The necklet is not so important in the Assyrian costume as it is in the Egyptian; it consists of a gold ring, to which the divine emblems are attached—the lunar crescent of Sin; the four-rayed disk of

Fig. 147.—The King's Necklet.

Shamash, the sun; the triple-pointed thunder of Adar (Fig. 147). It forms an amulet rather than an ornament, and the necessity for respecting the immovable types of the symbols has preserved its ancient form almost unaltered; just as we see it upon the sculptures worn by the old kings, so it is round Assurbanipal's neck to-day. The beauty of the sword a little compensates for the simplicity of the necklet. It is worn almost horizontally, nearly at elbow height, so that the

Fig. 148.—An Assyrian Sword.

Fig. 149.—The King in his State Costume.

left hand usually rests upon the pommel when it is inactive. The rather short hilt is of turned ivory; four lions' heads in gold are attached to it near the junction with the blade (Fig. 148). The sheath is of wood, overlaid with gold; it is decorated towards the point with two golden lions, standing upon their hind legs, apparently playing with each other. The profusion of gold produces a better effect than might be supposed. The pale yellow of the metal softens the otherwise rather crude tones of the vermilion, blue, and white materials. The king, thus apparelled (Fig. 149), really looks what he wishes to be considered—the image of the gods upon earth. Foreigners, and even his subjects themselves, when they are first admitted to his presence upon state occasions, secretly think that they see in him the likeness of Assur, and should the god deign to come amongst us and reveal himself in a living form, he would surely resemble the king.

After dressing in his private apartments, Assurbanipal crosses the courtyard shaded by a parasol, which a servant holds over him; then he seats himself at the end of the audience hall upon a large carved armchair between two eunuchs, who fan him unceasingly (Fig. 150). His ministers and attendants stand on either side of the throne with the princes of his family. The highest in rank amongst them, the first in the empire after the king, is the Tartan, who has the supreme command of the troops. The duties which he fulfils have always been considered very important in

Fig. 150.—The King upon his Throne.

a military monarchy like Assyria; but they have become so heavy through the conquests of the last few years that Assurbanipal has been obliged to divide them. He has instituted a second Tartan, who exercises the same power as the first, but over one half of the empire only. Whilst this one, the Tartan of the left, holds authority over Commagene and the north-western provinces, the ancient Tartan on the right dwells near the sovereign, and commands in the provinces of the south and east. He is assisted by four viziers of less position—the mayor of the palace, who regulates the royal household; the chief of the eunuchs, who rules over the women; the Toukoulou, who is at the head of the priesthood; lastly, the regent, who manages the financial department and the civil administration. From all time the Assyrians have had the habit of designating each year that passes by the name of an eminent personage, who is supposed to have directed its events, and whom they call *limmou*. For instance, they say that a certain town has been destroyed, or certain people conquered, Shamsi-ilou, Adar-malik, or Atar-ilou being *limmou*. The reigning sovereign is always *limmou* during the year which follows his accession to the throne; after him, the great officers of the crown receive the same title in the order of precedence which their position gives them— first the Tartan, then the mayor of the palace, then the chief of the eunuchs, and so on, until the list of officials being ended, the hierarchy brings back the king's name for the second time, then those of his ministers.

The crowd of courtiers and officers of less rank arrange themselves in lines by the walls of the hall. Their costume is very similar to that of the king. They wear the same close-fitting fringed robe, the same short sword, the same bracelets and golden earrings: the head-dress is different. The lesser nobles are bareheaded, the others wear a fillet passed round the forehead and tied at the back; the fillet worn by the viziers is wider than the others, and is ornamented with golden rosettes. They have all a proud, haughty expression, strongly marked features, and energetic carriage. They are usually of middle height, but thick-set and robust. Their arms are bare, and the development of the muscles denotes extraordinary strength; whilst the outline of the body, so far as it can be defined through the thick robes, confirms the promise of great vigour given by the arms. They are a race of soldiers built for conflict, prepared and trained by the fatigues and perils of the chase for the fatigues and perils of war. Seeing them, it is easy to understand how, in spite of their small numbers and the limited extent of their territory, they have succeeded in subduing all the peoples of Asia, and in defeating the armies of Pharaoh.

The Elamite embassy is headed by two noblemen of high rank in the court of Susa, Umbadara and Nebodamiq. The customs and civilisation of the Susians in many ways resemble those of Assyria and Chaldea, but with something less polished, more savage about them. The costumes worn by the two ambassadors are similar to those of Assurbanipal's courtiers. They wear the long robe of brilliant colours, bordered with fringe; the sword and bracelets. Umbadara has only a fillet round his head; Nebodamiq wears a round cap, fastened upon the temples by a ribbon (Fig. 151). The men who form the suite are of varied physiognomy and costume. Some of them are dressed like their leaders, but more simply. They closely resemble the Assyrian type—strong curved nose, large eyes, long face, middle height. Others have woolly hair, flat nose, projecting mouth, thick upturned lips, short crisp beard; they would be taken for negroes but for their white skins. They are natives of the provinces near the sea. Lastly, some are tall, slender, with straight nose, blue eyes, and a few of them with fair hair. They belong to the independent tribes that inhabit the mountains situated beyond Susiana, and they are connected with those Persians and Medes that call themselves Aryans. These brave soldiers have endeavoured latterly to unite

Fig. 151.—An Elamite Nobleman.

their scattered clans in a single nation, obeying one king. Their success might prove a serious danger for Assyria, for they are bold, enterprising, and, above all, numerous. If any one can induce them to forget their mutual feuds, can group them round one leader, and discipline them, nothing can long resist him. Other nations may be superior in tactics, weapons, and confidence in themselves; he will crush them beneath the masses of his soldiers.

Luxury is not as visible amongst this varied group as in the court of the Assyrian monarch. The colours are equally brilliant, but the embroideries are less beautiful, the gilding and jewels less rich; not that the Elamites are less fond of gold, but they possess less of it. Their appreciation of their relative poverty both humiliates and irritates them. The race hatred which they feel for the Assyrians adds to their natural insolence, and the looks which they have encountered since they crossed the frontier encourage them to believe that the powerful Ninevites are secretly afraid of them. They almost hope their mission will fail; a war would give them the treasures displayed with so much ostentation, as though in defiance of their mission.

Umbadara and Nebodamiq, introduced by an eunuch, advance slowly, the eyes lowered, the hands crossed on the chest, between the double lines of courtiers. When they reach the throne they prostrate themselves, kiss the ground before the king's feet, then, upon a sign, rise and stand motionless before the sovereign. Usually the envoys of foreign princes remain kneeling during an audience. Assurbanipal, who wishes to spare the pride of the Susians, exempts them from this part of the ceremonial, and allows them to speak to him almost face to face. No one appears before a sovereign with empty hands, and even under these circumstances Teumman has not broken this rule of international courtesy. Umbadara and Nebodamiq, after the first salutations have been exchanged, offer the presents they have been entrusted with — gold and silver vases, precious stones, and valuable stuffs. They then open the subject of their message, and communicate their master's proposals to Assurbanipal. Peace exists between Assyria and Elam; should they not endeavour to maintain it by every possible means? Teumman wishes to do everything in his power to please his brother Assurbanipal. Yet the latter has received and treated with great distinction certain Elamite subjects, the sons of former kings, who, after conspiring against their legitimate sovereign, have fled to escape the just punishment which awaited them. If Assurbanipal consents to drive them away, or to deliver them to the ambassadors, he will have no ally more faithful than the King of Elam; if not, it is war.

The conclusion of the speech was foreseen. Assurbanipal's reply was equally certain: he was resolved not to betray the princes, who had relied upon his generosity. He and his counsellors have not decided without some hesitation. Elam is a military power of the first rank, stronger than Armenia, Chaldea, or Egypt, and its kings have always successfully resisted the most furious attacks. The Assyrians assert, in their official chronicles, that Sargon defeated Ummanigash, who reigned over Susiana during his life, and that he imposed a tribute upon him; but the annals of Elam and Chaldea relate another version of the story. In reality Sargon was defeated, and Assyria was invaded and devastated with impunity. Sennacherib boasted of having defeated the forces of Minanou near Khaluli. Minanou on his side declares that he almost entirely annihilated the Assyrian army in the same battle; and if we look at the matter without prejudice, we cannot help thinking that he was right. Sennacherib, after this so-called triumph, was obliged to return home, and took no further steps against Elam for some years. The effects of this victory curiously resemble those of a defeat.

War against Elam is therefore a dangerous thing; the Assyrians have quite as much to lose by it as to gain. Still, they have decided in favour of war. Assurbanipal declares that he cannot possibly accept the proposals of Teumman; he knows the courage of his soldiers, the skill of his generals, and with the aid of Assur and Ishtar—of Ishtar particularly, the queen of battles—he hopes to win. Umbadara and Nebodamiq, who have dared to bring him the challenge from the enemy, shall not return to Susiana; they shall remain at Nineveh, prisoners with their suite, until the gods have decided between their king and the King of Assyria. At a word from the Tartan they are seized before they can attempt any resistance and taken away; only the secretary and two or three of his servants are liberated and sent back to the frontier. They are to inform Teumman of the result of the embassy, and to give him a letter, in which Assurbanipal advises him to give up his evil projects, under penalty of incurring the anger of the gods.

The war once decided on and declared, Assurbanipal hastens to take the measures necessary to commence it with vigour. The Tartan of the right, Belnahid, commences giving his orders as soon as the audience is over, and before nightfall couriers have already started in every direction with secret letters for the governors of the provinces and the allied sovereigns. All the administrative machinery is arranged in view of war, for war has for many centuries been the normal condition in Assyria. The troops are therefore ready to march at the first signal, and to move from one end of the empire to the other. They are almost entirely recruited in Assyria itself, and in the districts of Mesopotamia which have always belonged to the sovereigns of Nineveh. A few detachments of little importance accompany the governors of the provinces to their residence; they form the nucleus of an army, and their fidelity can be absolutely relied upon.

Around them, in case of need, the governors can assemble the troops raised among their native subjects and those brought by the vassal princes. The majority of the army is concentrated round the royal residences at Nineveh, Kalakh, or in the always threatened provinces which border Elam and Chaldea. The organization is so perfect that the regiments can be mobilised in a few days, and sent wherever the king has declared the war. They strengthen the regiments which garrison the frontier, and usually form with them a sufficiently numerous army to equal, if not to surpass, in numbers the forces which the enemy can bring against them.

The divisions scattered in the other provinces remain almost inactive during this time. Since their departure usually gives the signal for a general insurrection in the country which they occupy, they are only called out in the last extremity, when it is a question of repairing a defeat or of filling the vacancies caused in the ranks by a murderous campaign. Thus each war unduly prolonged, or costing a large number of men, threatens to entail the dissolution of the empire. The Assyrian, knowing this, is therefore merciless to the cities he takes and the peoples he conquers. Not content with pillaging houses and ruining the fields, he massacres whole families, and no torture appears too cruel to punish those who have resisted him. He impales some, flays others alive, puts out the eyes or cuts off the lips of his prisoners—without counting the children and young girls whom he carries into slavery. His rule, established by force, is only preserved by force. The day which sees it weakened upon one point, will also see the hatred now silently repressed break out with new force; the countries outwardly most resigned to slavery will not hesitate to rebel, if a chance of regaining their liberty should occur. The couriers who carry tidings of the war against Elam to the governors, at the same time deliver orders to watch over their provinces with the greatest vigilance, so as to guard against any hostile movement, and to crush the slightest insubordination without mercy. Assyria has really but one army to place in the field, and cannot therefore contend with more than one enemy at a time; if forced to divide her forces and to fight both against a foreign enemy and against her rebellious subjects, she would be too weak numerically to struggle for many years in succession, and would at last succumb.

The fear of an alliance between the natives dwelling at a distance, with the object of a simultaneous attack from Assyria, although formerly chimerical, is now but too well justified. When Pharaoh invaded Syria at the head of his bowmen and chariots, if the Ethiopians should rise against their viceroy at the same time, it was only an unfortunate coincidence, nothing more. The people who then inhabited the basin of the Orontes had so little direct communication with those who dwelt upon the banks of the Upper Nile, that the idea never occurred to them of endeavouring to combine together against their common enemy. Revolts, which then failed miserably, would have destroyed the Egyptian power if any joint effort had been made, forcing Pharaoh to defend his northern and southern frontiers at the same time; as it was, Pharaoh had time to move his troops from place to place, and to crush one by one those adversaries who would have overwhelmed him had they supported each other. The same thing happened to the ancient Assyrian conquerors, Tiglath-Pileser, Assur-nasir-pal, Shalmaneser II. Elam, Urartu, Chaldea, the kings of Damascus and the Hittites were attacked separately, and never thought of forming a coalition. Each nation in its own land valiantly defended itself as long as possible, but even neighbouring tribes did not think of allying themselves together — the Susians with the Babylonians, the Hittites with the Phœnicians and the kings of Damascus, the latter with the Hebrews, the Hebrews with Egypt. All these nations, invincible if they had combined, were conquered because they remained isolated.

However, during the last century communications have become so rapid and easy between the different countries that the kings and cities now menaced by Assyria have agreed to unite in their resistance to her. When Sennacherib assailed Judea, king Hezekiah of Jerusalem entered into an alliance with Merodach-Baladan: the diversion made by the Chaldeans saved the Jews for some years. This lesson has not been lost. Since then all the nations have tried to join together against Assyria, whose policy has been to prevent the formation of a league at any price. There is a perpetual coming and going of secret messengers, conclusion of tacit alliances, conventions of mutual assistance between the most varied countries and princes. Gyges of Lydia makes a treaty with Psammetichus of Egypt, and promises to help him. Psammetichus in his turn forms an alliance with the small sovereigns of Southern Syria; the latter are always in correspondence with Chaldea, and Chaldea always inclines to side with Elam against Assyria. The union of so many nations would be irresistible if they could only be induced to act together, but as yet no one has succeeded in doing so. The distances between the allies are so great, some are impatient, others so slow and undecided, and it is said the watchfulness of the Assyrians is so active, that the best-planned schemes end in a check. Elam strikes a blow before Babylon is ready; Egypt will not take the field if she can help it; Judea, Moab, Ammon, the Philistines, Nabatei, and Arabs wait until Pharaoh's bowmen have entered Syria before they march. But the Assyrians advance at full speed, crush Elam or Chaldea, kill some hundreds of Arabs, sack a few Syrian cities. Pharaoh, always prudent, retires to Africa. The danger is averted, but it exists; the coalition will soon be re-formed. When it can arrange its movements so that all its forces can take the field at the same time, the Assyrians will require great luck and marvellous energy to escape ruin.

Couriers hurry in every direction. The instructions they carry to the governors are couched in firm direct terms, without any flowery language and without any repetitions. Here, for instance, is the message sent by the king to Belibni, who commands a detachment in the land of the Pukudu,\* towards the mouth of the Euphrates:—'A letter from the king to Belibni: may the greeting I send thee bring happiness to thee! With regard to thy rule over the people of Pukudu on the banks of the Kharrou, to whomever the house of his lord is dear, let him henceforth tell his lord all that he has seen and heard. And now do not fail to let me know everything that thou mayest hear with regard to them.'† Change the proper names and you will have, if not the form, at all events the substance of all the dispatches sent by the king to his generals on the evening of the audience and on the following days. They were to redouble their vigilance, not to allow any movement amongst the people under them to pass unnoticed, to transmit to the palace as quickly as possible the least item of information which they could collect. Their work is less brilliant than that of their comrades, who form part of the chief army; but it is scarcely less important. If each of them preserves peace in his province, if he prevents any insurrection or represses it before it has time to strengthen and extend, Teumman, thrown upon his own resources, will not be able to stand before Assurbanipal, and Assyria will conquer Elam once more.

\* The Pukudu were an Aramean tribe, which inhabited the marshes at the mouth of the Tigris and Euphrates, near a canal or river derived from the Tigris, and named the Kharrou.

† This dispatch is genuine, but it relates to one of Assurbanipal's wars against Chaldea and Elam, some years later than the one I have chosen for my subject here.

# CHAPTER XVI.

### ASSURBANIPAL'S LIBRARY.

The old Chaldean literature—Assurbanipal orders the principal works to be copied for his library—The royal annals: account of the death of Gyges the Lydian—Money in Lydia—The goddess Ishtar The *Descent of Ishtar into Hades*—The poem of the creation—The poem of Gistubar—Gistubar struggling against the monsters—His dream—He captures Eabani—His struggle against Ishtar—Death of Eabani—Cure of Gistubar.

ALTHOUGH sanguine as to his ultimate success, Assurbanipal cannot help feeling anxious as he thinks of the chances of the war, and this anxiety prevents him from sleeping. He calls one of the eunuchs on guard at his chamber door, and sends him to find the librarian of the palace: he wishes to have the tablets that chronicle the chief events of his reign brought to him, so that he may re-read the accounts of his former victories, and so revive his confidence.

The Assyrians can write with a cut reed upon prepared skins, wooden tablets, and even upon the papyri brought from Egypt by the caravans. They then use a cursive character derived from the Phœnician alphabet. The scribes use this writing for registering the booty taken during a war, the tributes, taxes, and the business of current administrations, which do not require the minutes to be preserved for a long time. When the subject of the work is history, literature, judicial acts, or official documents that must be deposited in the archives, they resort to the old Chaldean characters and clay tablets.* This system has some inconveniences, and

* See in Chapter XII. the detailed description of these tablets.

a great many advantages. The books of baked earth are inconvenient to hold, heavy to handle, the characters are not clearly defined against the yellow colour of the clay; but, on the other hand, a work cut upon brick and incorporated with it, incurs less danger than a work written in ink upon rolls of papyrus. Fire cannot hurt it, water cannot injure it for a long time, and if it is broken the pieces are still good; provided they are not reduced to powder, they can generally be readjusted and the text deciphered, with the exception of a few letters or some words of a phrase. The inscriptions found in the foundations of the most ancient temples, several of which are twenty or thirty centuries old, are, as a rule, clear and legible, as though they had just left the hands of the scribe who traced them and the potter who baked them. The hymns, magic incantations, lists of kings, annals, hymns composed almost at the commencement of history, thousands of years before the Assyrian empire, although exposed to the accidents of twenty conquests, to the destroying fury of man and the assaults of time, have yet resisted them all, and have come down to us intact; this would certainly not have been the case had their authors confided them to the papyrus, like the Egyptian scribes. The chief danger they encounter is to remain forgotten in the corner of a room, or buried beneath the ruins of an edifice; then they sleep, so to speak, for many years, or even centuries, until the day when a chance excavation, or the intelligent search of a learned man, discovers them and restores them to the light.

Assurbanipal is fond of old books, particularly of the old sacred works. He collects the scattered specimens from the chief cities of his empire, and even employs scribes in Chaldea, Ourouk, Barsippa, and Babylon to copy for him the tablets deposited in the temples. His principal library is at Nineveh, in the palace which he built for himself upon the banks of the Tigris, and which he has just finished decorating. It contains more than thirty thousand tablets, methodically classified and arranged in several rooms, with detailed catalogues for convenient reference. Many of the works are continued from tablet to tablet and form a series, each bearing the first words of the text as its title. The account of the creation, which begins with the phrase: *Formerly, that which is above was not yet called the heaven,* was entitled: *Formerly, that which is above, No.* 1; *Formerly, that which is above, No.* 2; and so on to the end. Assurbanipal is not less proud of his love of letters than of his political activity, and he is anxious that posterity should know how much he has done for literature. His name is inscribed upon every work in his library, ancient and modern. 'The palace of Assurbanipal, king of legions, king of multitudes, king of Assyria, to whom the god Nebo and the goddess Tasmetu have granted attentive ears and open eyes to discover the writings of the scribes of my kingdom, whom the kings, my predecessors, have employed. In my respect for Nebo, the god of intelligence, I have collected these tablets; I have had them copied, I have marked them with my name, and I have deposited them in my palace.'

The library at Dur-Sarginu, although not so rich as the one in Nineveh, is still fairly well supplied. The scribe, Naboushoumidin, who has charge of it, soon takes the tablets containing the annals from their places and gives them to the eunuch. But what Assurbanipal wishes read to him in detail is less the history of his wars than the text of the oracles by which the gods have encouraged him to undertake them, and the enumeration of the miracles which they have worked for him. The exact recollection of what has been done for him in the past will disperse his fears, and give him faith in the aid they will bestow upon him in the future. 'Take the tablet,' he said to the reader, 'containing the account of Gyges, the

Lydian, and repeat it to me.' The adventure of Gyges is celebrated throughout Assyria. The scribe then reads it aloud. 'Gyges, the king of Lydia, a country beyond the seas, a distant land, of which the kings, my fathers, had never even heard the name, Assur, my divine generator, revealed my name to him in a dream, saying: "Assurbanipal, the king of Assyria; place thyself at his feet, and thou shalt conquer thine enemies in his name." The same day that he dreamed this dream, Gyges sent horsemen to salute me, and related to me the dream which he had had, by the mouth of his messengers. When the latter reached the frontiers of my empire and encountered the people of my empire, they said to him, "Who, then, art thou, stranger, whose land has never yet been visited by one of our couriers?" They sent him to Nineveh, the seat of my royalty, and brought him before me. The languages of the east and of the west, which Assur had given into my hand, none of those who spoke them could understand his language, and none of those who surrounded me had ever heard speech like unto it. In the space of my empire I at last found one who understood it, and he told me the dream. The same day that he placed himself at my feet, mine, the king, Assurbanipal, he defeated the Cimmerians, who oppressed the people of his land, who had not feared the kings, my fathers, and had not placed themselves at my feet. By the grace of Assur and Ishtar, the gods my masters, they took amidst the chiefs of the Cimmerians, whom he had defeated, two chiefs whom he chained heavily with manacles of iron and chains of iron, and he sent them to me with a rich present. Nevertheless, the horsemen that he at first sent regularly to pay homage unto me, he soon ceased to send them. He would not obey the commands of Assur, my divine generator, but foolishly trusted in his own strength, and in the wishes of his heart; he sent his troops to the assistance of Psammetichus, king of Egypt, who had contemptuously thrown off my yoke. I heard this, and prayed to Assur and Ishtar: "May his body be thrown down before his enemies, and may his bones be dispersed." The Cimmerians, whom he had crushed in my name, reappeared and subjugated his whole land, and his son succeeded him upon the throne. The punishment which the gods, who are my strength, had drawn upon his father, at my request, he told me by his messengers, and he placed himself at my feet, saying: "Thou art a king acknowledged by the gods. Thou cursedst my father, and misfortune fell upon him. Send me thy blessing, for I am thy servant, who fears thee, and will wear thy yoke."'

In one moment this glorious episode of his history repasses before the eyes of the king; he once more sees the arrival of the foreign ambassadors, their curious costumes, their embarrassment and that of the court, the time when he invoked the anger of the gods against Gyges, and the moment when the messengers of Ardys* informed him that the gods had granted his prayer. From that time Lydia has always been faithful to him; every year Lydian horsemen cross Asia to lay their master's tribute before him. It is not large, but that is willingly excused, when the length of the journey is considered; it consists of horses, stuffs, and above all, gold, which their country produces in great quantities. They have invented a very ingenious way of using it in the markets. In the royal workshops it is made into small globular blocks of a certain weight, which are marked with a stamp, with the image of a horse's head, a flower, or a fox in full gallop. The mark and the size of the blocks show their value at once, and the usual weighing is, therefore, dispensed with. This greatly facilitates all commercial transactions.† It is said that the use of this money is spreading; some day it may even reach Assyria itself.

* Ardys was the son of Gyges, and his successor upon the throne of Lydia.
† See upon this subject, p. 21.

Assurbanipal causes the account of his wars in Egypt to be read to him, then his campaigns against Baal of Tyre and the Phœnicians, and in all of them he recognises the effects of the protection which Assur and Ishtar extend over him. Ishtar, whom the Canaanites and Phœnicians revere under the name of Astoreth and Astarte, has not always been, in Assyria, the all-powerful divinity that she is now. The most ancient kings never recognised in her anything beyond ' the mistress of battles and of war, the sovereign lady, who embellished the faces of the soldiers '—a race of conquerors was certain to worship a goddess of war. They had raised two sanctuaries to her, which soon became celebrated, the one in Nineveh, the other in the small town of Arbela, beyond the Zâb, almost upon the eastern frontier of their land. They piously invoked her, but always placed her in the background, far behind Assur, Sin, and the other gods. Esarhaddon brought her out of the shade, where she had been thrown, and made her his patron. Each time he started for a new expedition he consulted her, and she answered through her priestesses; the events never falsified her predictions. The love which Assurbanipal feels for her is, therefore, a really paternal inheritance, like the throne itself. It is towards her that he instinctively turns when he has any reason for joy or sadness: he thanks her for his successes, confides his anxieties to her, and loves nothing better than listening to the books which speak of her and of her mysterious adventures. He interrupts the eunuch in the midst of his reading, between the account of a raid upon Armenia and that of an excursion against the peoples of the Taurus, and commands him to go and ask Naboushoumidin for the *Descent of Ishtar into Hades.*

This is one of the most touching episodes in the life of the goddess. Her husband, Tammuz, had been killed, and, god though he was, had been obliged to join the other dead beneath the earth, in the gloomy kingdom of Allat. There was but one way of restoring him to the light; he must bathe in and drink of the waters of that wonderful spring, which restores those who drink it.* Ishtar resolved to go and fetch some of it; but no one can enter Hades before he is dead, and Ishtar is not more exempt from the fatal law than other beings. 'To the land from whence no traveller returns, to the regions of darkness, Ishtar, the daughter of Sin, has directed her spirit; yes, the daughter of Sin herself has directed her spirit to the house of darkness, the seat of the god Irkalla, to the house which those who enter can never leave, by the road over which no one travels a second time, to the house of which the inhabitants never again see the light, the place where there is no bread, but only dust; no food, but mud; no one can see the light there, all live in darkness, and like the birds, are clad in a raiment of feathers; upon the gate and the lock on all sides the dust lies thick.' Ishtar reached the ramparts of Hades; she knocked, and addressed the doorkeeper in an imperious tone: 'Guardian of the waters of life, open thy doors; open thy doors, that I may go in! If thou do not open thy gate and let me in, I will sound the knocker, I will break the lock, I will strike the threshold and break through the portal. I will raise the dead to devour the living, the dead shall be more numerous than the living.' The doorkeeper opened his mouth, he spoke, he said to the lady Ishtar: 'Stay, O lady! do not break down the door, but allow me to go and announce your name to Ninkigal,† the queen of Hades!' The guardian descended and announced Ishtar's visit to Ninkigal: 'O goddess! thy sister Ishtar has come in search of the living water; she has shaken the strong bolts, she threatens to break down the doors.' When Allat heard this, she opened her

* See upon this wonderful spring, p. 248.
† The goddess of the dead is called Allat or Ninkigal indifferently during the narrative.

mouth and spoke: 'Thus, like grass under the scythe, Ishtar has descended into Hades, like a reed, which bends down and withers; she has asked for the waters of life. Well, what does her wish matter to me? What can her anger do to me? She says: "With this water I would revive my husband, and he would satisfy me, like food, and quench my thirst like a beverage, which revives the faint!" If I must weep, it would not be for her, but for the heroes who have been forced to leave their wives; I would weep for the brides that thou, O guardian, hast torn from the bosom of their husbands; I would weep for the little children whom thou hast taken before their day had dawned. Go then, O guardian, and open the gates for her, but unrobe her according to the old laws.' Mortals come naked into the world, and naked must they go out of it, but the piety of their relations or friends provides them with ornaments and clothes, which they hope to take with them. The law of Hades does not allow them to retain anything, and the demons take all their possessions away before presenting them to the queen.

The guardian went and opened the door: 'Enter, O lady, and since the city of Coutha rejoices because of thee, so may the infernal palace rejoice because of thee.' He let her pass through the first gate, shut it upon her, and took off the crown she wore upon her head. 'Why then, O guardian, hast thou removed the crown from my head?' 'Enter, O lady; I obey the commands of Allat.' And at each gate he took off some of her jewellery, her ear-rings, her jewelled necklet, the veil which covered her bosom, her enamelled waist-belt, her bracelet, and her ankle-rings; at the seventh gate he took off her last garment. Therefore, when Ishtar descended into Hades, Allat saw her and treated her with contempt. Ishtar lost all patience and reproached the queen bitterly. Allat, to punish her, called Namtar, the demon of pestilence, her messenger of death, and gave the rebel into his hands: 'Go, Namtar, take Ishtar and lead her from my presence. Sixty times strike her with disease, pour disease of the eyes into her eyes, disease of the loins into her loins, disease of the heart into her heart, disease of the head into her head; upon her and upon each of her limbs pour disease.' Now whilst she suffered the pangs of Hades, all nature was mourning for her loss—animals, men, the gods themselves, all were perishing, and the world would have been depopulated had not means been found of rescuing her from the tomb which she had entered.

Hea, the supreme god, the king of the universe, who alone can violate the laws which he has imposed upon creation, determined to recall her and to grant the boon, for which she had descended into the realms of Allat—the water of life, that would restore Tammuz to life. Hea, in the wisdom of his heart, made a man, he created Assousounamir the eunuch: 'Go then, Assousounamir, turn thy face towards the gates of Hades, let the seven gates be opened before thee, that Allat may see thee and rejoice in thy presence. When her heart is at peace and her anger appeased, adjure her by the great gods, then turn thy head and go to the retreat of the stormy winds, command the house of the stormy winds, where the pure fountain is imprisoned, and let Ishtar drink of its waters.' Allat dare not disobey the commands of the master of the gods; she called Namtar and told him to prepare everything, so that life might be restored to the goddess. The spring is hidden far down beneath the threshold of the palace; the stone must be broken before the water will appear, and even then it will not produce its full effect unless the *Anunaki*, the seven mysterious spirits who preside over the preservation of the earth, are present. 'Namtar went and struck the solidly constructed palace, he broke the threshold, invoked the spirits of the earth, and seated them upon a golden throne, then poured the water over Ishtar and led her towards the daylight.' He restored her garments and ornaments as she passed from door to door; when she had returned to the entrance he informed her that henceforth the life of her husband was in her own hands. 'If Allat has not yet given thee the life thou hast so dearly bought, come back to her and claim Tammuz, the husband of thy youth. Pour the water of life over him, anoint him with precious scents, and clothe him in a purple robe.' Nature revived with Tammuz: Ishtar had conquered death.

The form of this work is modern, but the original conception and the development are very ancient: the descent of Ishtar into Hades was already sung by the earliest masters of Chaldea, with several other works that we still read with admiration. The poets and priests knew how to compose grand religious poems with a skill and wealth of imagination that scribes of later generations have never equalled. It is natural that this should be so. In their days the earth was still newly created, and they felt the gods were nearer to them than we can do. When they described the first days of the world, they and their audience had no difficulty in imagining the events of the beginning of the centuries; they knew them through the direct revelation of the gods who had shared in the work. In the time when the heavens above were not, and the earth was not named, the primordial water-deep engendered them, and Moummou Tiamat, the Ocean Chaos, was mother of them all. The waters formed but one mass, the fields of corn were sterile, and the pastures were not yet grown. In these days the gods had not yet appeared, they had no names, and their destiny was not yet fixed.' All things issued from the water, the earth, the heaven, and mankind.

The old inspired singer then narrates the successive generations of the gods, and the struggles by which they triumphed over Tiamat. Merduk, or Merodach, of Babylon, the sun-sovereign, was their champion. 'Go,' they said to him, 'and cut short the days of

Tiamat, and throw her blood to the winds. He had the bow prepared so as to make a weapon, he brandished the club and fastened it to his side, he seized the boomerang and held it in his right hand. When he had suspended the bow and quiver upon his shoulder he launched a flash of lightning before him, and instantly an impetuous speed filled all his limbs. He who fears no rival entered the chariot of fate, and stood firmly there; his hand fastened the four pairs of reins to the edge of the chariot.' Thus armed he threw himself upon Tiamat and attacked her. 'He brandished the club and crushed her; he broke her chest, tore out her heart, bound her and cut short her days, then threw down the corpse and stood over it. When Tiamat, who marched before them, was defeated, he dispersed her soldiers, scattered their battalions; and the gods, her allies, who marched beside her, trembled, they were afraid, they turned round and fled to save their lives, so they pressed against each other in their hurried flight; but he followed them and broke their weapons.'

The longest of these old poems relates the great deeds of Gistubar. He was born in Ourouk of Chaldea, the son of a king; he would have been himself a king had not his father been dethroned by the Elamites when he was yet an infant in the cradle. Brought up in exile, he devoted himself to the royal amusement of hunting. The earth was not at that time peopled as it now is, and wild beasts waged cruel war against men: not only lions, tigers, and aurochs, which kings delight in killing now, but monsters with forms half-human joined to those of the most formidable animals. Human-headed bulls, which are now only seen in stone at the palace gates, then existed in flesh and blood, continually seen in the country. Scorpion men, satyrs, griffons, inhabited the desert and the mountain, ready to descend upon any one who crossed the boundaries. Gistubar had already destroyed a great number of them, when the gods, seeing the end of the predestined days of exile drawing near, sent him a dream. Then he revealed his dream, and said to his mother: 'I have dreamed a dream in my sleep; for it seemed unto me that the stars of heaven fell from heaven, and they fell upon my back, descending from heaven upon me. And see, as I looked suddenly I paused, and I saw a being raise his face before me, a creature with a terrible face, and claws like unto the claws of a lion.' It then seemed to him that he fought against the monster and destroyed it: then he awoke.

Dreams do not come by chance; they are the messengers of the gods, by which they announce the future to those who can understand them, but Gistubar could not find any one to interpret his dream. At last some one told him of a monstrous genie, Eabani, whose wisdom was unequalled, but who dwelt alone in the mountain. He had the bust and face of a man, the legs and tail of a bull, and horns upon his head. 'He feeds with the gazelles during the night, he remains hidden during the day with the animals of the fields, and his heart rejoices over the reptiles that are in the water.' Gistubar sent his chief huntsman, Zaïdou, to take him, but Zaïdou was frightened at the sight of the monster, and returned without daring to approach him. Then the hero resorted to craft: he chose two beautiful women, Hakirtou and Oupasamrou, who enticed Eabani out of the cavern where he had concealed himself. He approached Hakirtou and listened to her song, then he became attentive to it, and at last turned towards her and seated himself at her feet. 'Hakirtou bent her face towards him, she spoke, and he listened to her words. She then said to him: "Eabani the illustrious, who resemblest the gods, why dost thou dwell amongst the animals of the desert? I wish thee to follow me to the centre of Ourouk, to the temple of Elli-Tardousi, the dwelling of Anu and Ishtar, the house of Gistubar, the strong giant, who stands like a bull before the chieftains." She spoke, and before her words all the wisdom of his heart melted and disappeared.' He followed her to Ourouk, explained that the dream foretold the hero's victory over his enemies, then married one of the women who had induced him to leave his solitude. Thus Gistubar won the affection of his servant Eabani, whom he always loved.

Gistubar then took the field, and the Elamite first experienced the strength of his arms. Houmbaba, who had dethroned his father at Ourouk, 'he killed him; took his weapons and spoiled him, then put on the insignia of royalty, he cut off his head, and put on the diadem and the crown; yes, Gistubar ornamented himself with the crown and put on the diadem. Ishtar, the goddess of Ourouk, raised her eyes and looked upon him, then seeing him so handsome and so strong, she decided that she would marry him. 'Listen to me, Gistubar, and be my husband; I will be a vine unto thee and thou shall be the trellis to which I am bound, thou shalt be my husband and I will be thy wife. I will give thee a chariot of crystal and of gold, the pole is of gold and the ornaments are of glass, and thou canst yoke thine horses to it every day. Enter our house under the shadow of the cedar-trees, and when thou art there the Euphrates will kiss thy feet. Kings will bow down to thee, nobles and princes will bring offerings unto thee, the tribute of the mountain and of the plain. In thy parks thy sheep shall bear thee twins, in thy stables thy mule shall come to demand its burden; thine horses shall always gallop with thy chariot, and thy bull shall have no rival in bearing the yoke.' Gistubar heard her, but repulsed her with a mixture of contempt and fear, asking her what she has done with the mortal husbands that she has married during her long life as a goddess. Tammuz, whom she mourned so deeply; Alala, the eagle, whose wings she clipped; the powerful lion, whose claws and teeth she extracted by sevens; the untamed horse who carried her in battle; and Taboulou, the shepherd; and the gardener

Isoullanou; all died before their time. 'And I, I will not ascend to thee to fall again, for thou lovest me but to treat me as thou hast treated them.'

Ishtar thus rejected, hurried to throw herself at the feet of her father Anu, the sovereign of the Gods, and implored his vengeance against the hero who has insulted her. 'My father, create a divine bull and launch it against Gistubar.' Anu granted the prayer of the goddess and created the bull, but Gistubar entrusted the faithful Eabani with the task of fighting against the adversary. 'He also assembled three hundred heroes, so that they could replace Eabani if he were killed, and he made two ranks for the battle and one rank to fight against the divine bull. Then the creature lowered its horns against this third row, but Eabani conquered it. Eabani pierced the body of the bull, he seized it by the top of the head, and plunged his poignard into the nape of its neck. Eabani opened his mouth, he spoke, he said to the hero Gistubar, "Friend, we have succeeded and we have destroyed the enemy; but, friend, let us reflect upon the consequences, and fear the power of Ishtar. Divide the limbs of the bull." And Ishtar ascended the wall of Ourouk, she tore her garments and uttered a curse. "I curse Gistubar, who has insulted me and killed the divine bull!" But Eabani heard the words of Ishtar, and he cut off the limbs of the divine bull and threw them down before her. "Here is the reply to thy curse; I accept it, and as I received it from thee, I turn it against thee." Ishtar assembled her servants and lamented with them over the limbs of the bull.' Gistubar consecrated the horns and the skin to the Sun-god.

Still the hatred of Ishtar pursued him, and despairing of finding an enemy capable of vanquishing him in a fair contest, she called disease to her assistance, and disease overcame the hero. Leprosy covered his body, and the fear of death, that last enemy of man, drew near to him. Once more the gods interfered to save him; they revealed to him in a dream that he could be cured by the intercession of Khasisadra, and even become immortal. Khasisadra, the son of Oubaratoutou, was the last of the ten kings who ruled in Chaldea immediately after the Creation. When the gods destroyed mankind to punish them for their sins, he only escaped in his ark, and he repeopled the world with his descendants. Then by the command of destiny he was carried away whilst still living, and was transported to the mysterious gardens where the blessed dead reside, beyond the mouth of the Euphrates.\* Gistubar started in search of him, but his usual good luck failed him; he lost his way, and the faithful Eabani perished in the claws of a more terrible monster than any he had yet seen. The soul of Eabani joined the souls in the kingdom of Allat, but Hea, the creator, took pity upon him and commanded his son Merodach to deliver him. He rose from earth like a cloud of dust, and ascended to heaven. The gods welcomed him and feasted him. Now lying upon a sumptuous couch, he drinks pure water, and from above he watches the spectacle of human actions. 'He who falls in battle, I see him as thou seest me. His mourning father and mother support his head, his wife laments over his body. His friends stand in the plain, and he sees them as I see thee, and his orphan children cry aloud for bread, but others eat the food that was ready in his tents.'

Gistubar recommenced his journey. Henceforth he travelled alone; yet after many wanderings he reached the mountains of Mas, where the sun rises every morning and sets every evening under the guardianship of scorpion men. The latter referred him to the pilot Ourbel, who told him to construct a boat, and then took him after six weeks' delay to the dwelling of Khasisadra. There he was forced to stop, for no living mortal can cross the stream which surrounds the garden. But Khasisadra, touched by his misery,

\* See p. 250 respecting the Chaldean paradise.

related the story of the Deluge to him,* and pointed out a certain cure for his illness; saying, that not only should he not die, but at the end of his trials the gods would receive him and would confer immortality upon him. The poem ends with this consoling promise, and, in fact, Gistubar is now a god. Poetry, sculpture, and the plastic arts have immortalised his life and his adventures. He is the giant whom we have seen by the side of the winged bulls at the door of the palaces strangling a lion in his arms (Fig. 152).† The cylinders which the Assyrians wear hanging round their necks, and which they use for seals,‡ often bear as the subject of their decoration some incident of his life—his struggles against the bull and the lion, his meeting with the scorpion men, his voyage upon the Euphrates with Ourbel, his quarrel with Ishtar. If the poem which rendered his name popular should perish in the lapse of time, these numerous images and pictures would still enable inquirers to partly rewrite it.

Fig. 152.—Gistubar strangling a Lion in his Arms.

* The episode of the Deluge is fully given in M. Maspero's *Histoire Ancienne*.
† See above, chapter xi., the figure of Gistubar by the side of the winged bull.
‡ See p. 226 and Fig. 124, several of these cylinders.

# CHAPTER XVII.

### THE SCIENCE OF PRESAGES.

Chaldean astrology—Influence of the stars over the human destiny—An exact observation of the stars enables astrologers to foretell future events—The message of the stars upon the war with Elam—The books of omens and the tables of Sargon the ancient—Assurbanipal invokes Ishtar of Arbela, and the goddess answers him—The *Seers* and the interpretation of dreams—Apparition of Ishtar to one of her Seers—The gods of Elam prophesy like the gods of Assyria.

THE same anxiety which prevents Assurbanipal from sleeping impels him to question the stars and the oracles, to wrest from them the secrets of the future. The Chaldeans have known from all ages how to read human destinies in the book of heaven. The stars, far distant as they are from our earth, are not indifferent to anything that happens upon it. They are animated beings, endowed with good or bad qualities, their rays travel through space, and from a distance they influence all that they touch. These influences modify each other, combine or nullify their mutual power, according to the intensity with which they are manifested, the position the stars occupy in heaven with regard to each other, the hour of the night and the month in the year in which they rise or set behind the horizon. Each portion of time, each division of space, each category of beings, and in each category each individual animal, vegetable, or mineral is placed under their rule, and submits to their inevitable tyranny. The child is born their slave, and remains their slave until his last day; the star which prevailed at the time of his birth becomes his star and rules his destiny.

But not only individuals, peoples and kingdoms are also subject to particular stars, or to stars which govern the existence of their kings. They increase or decrease according to the perpetual impulsion given from on high; the history of their disasters and prosperity in the past is registered on the face of heaven, and that of their future disasters or prosperity is equally clearly written for those who can read the record. Astrologers have been working at this science for many centuries, and their observations, accumulated from age to age, now enable us to know the special character and virtue of each of those luminous points that brighten our nights; to calculate without many chances of error the numerous aspects they bear in relation to each other; to decide which amongst them exercise the most authority over human affairs, at what moment this authority is the strongest, and when it becomes weaker or disappears altogether. The signs which are visible in heaven, in addition to the regular phenomena, also play their part in this divination by the movements of the celestial bodies. The sun and moon do not wrap themselves in bloody vapours or hide their faces behind the clouds without some reason for doing so. When they eclipse themselves or suddenly appear inflamed with unendurable brilliancy, when fires burn on the horizon and, upon certain nights, the stars seem to detach themselves from the heavens and to fall upon the earth, these prodigies are warnings which the gods send to nations and to kings before great crises. Happy is the man whose eyes are clear-sighted to perceive them, whose intelligence is quick enough to understand them, who has the prudence and presence of mind to regulate his conduct by their predictions!

Every night from the top of the many-storied towers the astronomers are now observing the heavens, seeking to discover the signs which will reveal the issue of the coming struggle between Assyria and Elam; but it would almost seem that the heavens intended to conceal the secret. From all sides the same reports reach the king; so far, the state of the atmosphere will not allow any accurate observations to be made. Ishtar-nadinshoum, the chief astronomer of Arbela, writes: 'Peace and happiness to the king, my master; long may he prosper. On the 29th I observed the node of the moon, but clouds obscured the field of observation, and we were unable to see the moon.' Nabouâ of El Assur, and Naboushoumidin of Nineveh, express themselves in almost the same words. The latter, summing up the dispatches of his fellow-workers to present their reports to the king, is even forced to own that upon 'the 27th the moon disappeared, on the 29th it was invisible; upon the 28th, 29th, and 30th the node of the darkening of the sun was continually watched, but the eclipse did not take place.' The obstinacy with which the heavens refuse to speak disconcerts many of the people, and the most doleful rumours commence to circulate amongst the populace. A great many persons take a kind of bitter pleasure in collecting and spreading the most alarming predictions. They repeat an observation of the astronomer Nabomousessi, that 'when a cloud conceals the heart of the constellation of the Great Lion, the heart of the country is sad, and the king's star is darkened.' Now, last night a cloud passed before the Great Lion and partly concealed it; the stars, therefore, condemn the land to sadness, and what cause for depression can there be if the war with Elam is to end well? Others relate that the night before last the moon was half hidden by clouds as she rose, so that only the lower half of the disk was visible. Every one knows that the phenomenon signifies an invasion of the Assyrian territory by the enemy, and great mourning for a prince. Several confirm the predictions of the moon and the lion by that of Venus. Yesterday, the 5th of January, Venus rose just as the sun set, and this announces both a good harvest and the presence of an enemy's troops in the country; the first prophecy is welcome, but to what enemies can the star allude except the Elamites?

Thus sadly whisper those people who are anxious about the war, or whose interests are jeopardised by it; others are less gloomy, and have procured favourable omens for themselves, which they quote in opposition to the gloomy predictions of the former. Now, three times running, since the commencement of the month, Sin, the god of the moon, has disappeared early in the morning before sunrise, and now three times at sunset he has been wrapped in clouds and has refused to give light to the earth. This is a rare but very important sign; before it the usual omens lose all their signification. It means the end of Teumman's reign and the ruin of his empire. This is the explanation given by the royal astronomers of Nineveh and Dur-Sarginu, and Assurbanipal himself accepts it freely. Indeed, their predictions flatter the national pride too much for them not to be promptly received by the people in preference to those of the other astrologers. A rumour spreads through the land that Sin has declared in favour of Assyria, and henceforth all the reports sent to the king of the heavenly movements unite in promising a complete victory. The 11th of Tammuz, a greenish light; the land of Elam will be ravaged. On the 14th, towards evening, the moon and the sun were both visible, and, so to speak, balanced each other at the two extremities of the horizon; this is a proof that the gods intend bestowing additional prosperity upon Assyria. On the 16th, Jupiter was brilliant in the middle of the night; this indicates a battle in which many enemies will perish, and their bodies will remain unburied. Thus each day and each night brings its new omen, which confirms those previously recorded and increases their force.

The profound knowledge which every one in

Assyria, even the common people, possesses on these subjects astonishes foreigners, and leads them to think that there are almost as many astrologers or sorcerers as there are inhabitants upon the banks of the Euphrates. Yet it does not require much learning to enable one to understand the language of the stars, for there are a number of books which teach the people how to translate it without any difficulty. Assurbanipal's library contains at least forty of them, and these are only the principal works, the classics of this kind of study. There are many more, which have not the same authority, but which are not less attentively read and commented upon by the people. Some treat of eclipses of the moon, and the events which they announce, according to the month and day upon which they take place. Others study the movements of each planet and the influences which it exerts over the earth, either alone or where two or three appear together in the sky. Or it may be a catalogue of the prognostics to be derived from thunder. If it thunders on the 27th of Tammuz, the harvest will be good and the yield magnificent; if it thunders six days later, on the 2nd of Ab, there will be inundations or rain, the king will die, and his country will be divided; if it thunders on the 3rd, an epidemic will cause ravages in all parts, and if it is the 4th an earthquake will threaten the cities. A very useful calendar for a nation of soldiers indicates the favourable or unfavourable character of each month for military operations. For instance, Tammuz is a propitious month for commencing a campaign or fortifying a city, but it is fatal to any one giving battle in the open field or assaulting a city. Iyyar has inverse properties; it is lucky for battles or sieges, but no one should commence a war or construct a fortress during that month.

These are black books in common use, which the first comer will be able to understand after a little while. Others exact long years of careful study; they are accessible to learned men only. They cannot be used with any profit unless one watches the stars, and learns to follow their courses. The initiation is slow and painful, but those who attain it become in some degree the heralds of the gods upon earth. Destiny speaks to men through them, and each night reveals some portion of the future. Sometimes this is a dangerous honour. The kings will not undertake anything without first consulting the initiates, and they trust to them to point out the most favourable time for the execution of the royal projects. One moment's lassitude whilst they are taking their observations, one inaccurate figure in their calculations, one error in reading the stars or in interpreting the signs, may ruin the sovereign who relies upon them. Some of the kings have declared war and have been defeated or killed, but if their astrologers had been more attentive or more skilful they would have stayed quietly at home. The stars disapproved of the enterprise and predicted the fatal end, but the astrologer misunderstood their language and thought he read encouragement where he should have seen threats; the ignorance or folly of the servant led to the ruin of the master.

In Egypt the majority of the books relating to science are sacred works composed and revealed by the gods themselves.* The Assyrians do not attribute such a lofty origin to the works which teach them the courses and explain the influences of the stars: they believe them to have been written by learned men, who lived at different epochs, and who acquired their knowledge from direct observation of the heavens. Their most ancient astronomers, through contemplating the army of stars every night, thought they recognised that each of their evolutions and each of their groups corresponded with certain unvarying phenomena and events upon the earth. For instance, if Jupiter rises,

* See above, chap. vii., the divine origin of the books upon medicine used in Egypt.

shining with a brilliancy that equals the daylight, and its disk, owing to the arrangement of the gloomy bands which cross it, resembles a double-edged sword, wealth and abundance reign in the whole country, discords are soothed, and justice prevails over iniquity. The first man who observed this coincidence was struck by it and made a note of it; those who followed proved that his observation was correct, and ended by deducing a general law of the facts accumulated upon this point during many years. The brilliancy and the particular aspect of Jupiter which they described was henceforth 'a favourable augury which promised happiness to landowners and to all the land that depended upon them. During the time that it lasts, no foreigner will rule in Chaldea, but tyranny is divided against itself, justice reigns, a strong sovereign will govern. The landowners and the king are firmly established in their rights, and obedience and tranquillity reign in the land.'

The number of these observations multiplied so quickly that it became necessary to class them methodically so as to avoid losing oneself amongst them. Tablets were soon arranged, which registered by the side of the indications giving the state of the sky on certain nights, at certain hours, the record of the events that followed at the same time, or soon afterwards, in Chaldea, Assyria, and foreign lands. For instance, the astrologers are convinced that if the moon has the same appearance upon the 1st and the 28th of the month, it is a bad omen for Syria, whilst if it is visible upon the 20th, it predicts happiness for Chaldea and misfortune for Assyria. 'If it nears the same aspect on the 1st and the 27th, Elam should tremble; but if the sun, when it sets, should appear double its normal size, with three sheaves of bluish rays, the king is lost.' All these observations were collected gradually, the uncertain ones were verified, the false ones eliminated, and from what remained a code was drawn up of the signs which predict and regulate human destinies. The old Sargon of Argané, who reigned more than twenty centuries ago,* methodically arranged all the information acquired up to his reign in a great work, which Assurbanipal has caused to be copied for his library, and which fills no less than seventy clay tablets. The book was retouched under his son, Naramsin, then rearranged from time to time, so that the progress of the science has been always recorded up to date. Now it is the great classic work upon the subject; its authority is unquestioned, and reference to it closes all controversies. Whenever one of the royal astronomers is asked to explain an ordinary phenomenon or a celestial prodigy, his first care is to refer to the tablet of Sargon; if it is found there ninety-nine times out of a hundred, he contents himself with copying the passage which relates to the question put to him, adds his name, and forwards the quotation, often without daring to add a single word to it. The treasures of patience, courage, and ingenuity displayed by the old masters in the collecting of the materials for this great work, and in establishing a solid foundation for their theories, may fairly astonish us. Learned men of the present day acquire their knowledge far more easily. They only require well-trained eyes to discover in the sky the same combinations of stars that Sargon has described, and a good memory, so that they can immediately apply to their observations the passage in which the prognostics suitable to the occasion are enumerated at great length.

The month of Tammuz is entirely passed in material and mystical preparation for the conflict; a great many men have been convoked, a great many gods consulted. The army would be ready to start, but its departure is deferred, for the month of Ab, which has now commenced, is most unfavourable to the movements of the troops. The campaign will not

* The reader must not forget that the events related in this narrative took place about 650 B.C.

commence before the following month of Elul, which the calendars indicate as one of the most propitious for the opening of military operations. Besides Ab is consecrated to the great annual festivals celebrated in honour of Ishtar in the sanctuary of Arbela. Assurbanipal attends them in state with all his court. Every day he personally offers the sacrifice to the goddess; every night from the summit of the seven-storied tower his astronomers search the depths of the heavens, and read there new signs of victory. The first tidings received from Elam confirm their predictions. Teumman has suddenly fallen ill; his eyes are darkened, his lips blue, his heart has been seized by violent spasms. This is a final warning sent to him by Assur and Ishtar before striking the death-blow, and every one in Assyria takes it in this way, but Teumman paid no attention to the illness. As soon as he recovered he joined the army. It is well known, through the secret friends that his exiled nephews have retained in his court, that he uttered blasphemous words against Ishtar when he heard that his ambassadors had been arrested, and that he is quite resolved not to draw back until he has completely vanquished Assyria. 'This unfortunate king,' he said, 'whom Ishtar has rendered mad, I will not let him go until I have gone up against her and have measured my strength against her.' Every one knows Assurbanipal's love for his goddess; Teumman's insolence horrified him. The dispatch which informed him of the sacrilegious speech of his enemy, and which at the same time announced the entrance of the Elamite vanguard upon Assyrian territory, reached him in the evening long after sunset. He could not wait until the morrow to go and implore the pardon of his patroness for the insult she had suffered through her affection for him. He hurried to the temple in the middle of the night, penetrated to the sanctuary, and went straight to the prophetic statue. A single lamp burnt before it, and the uncertain light vaguely defined its motionless form, and left the remainder of the chamber in deep obscurity. The king fell weeping before the goddess and raised his hands: 'O lady of Arbela! I am Assurbanipal, the creature of the two hands, the creature of Assur, thy father, and you have created me that I may revive the sanctuaries of Assyria, and complete in their perfection the great cities in the land of Akkad. I have, therefore, come here to thy dwelling-place to visit thee and to adore thy divinity, when this Teumman, the king of Elam, who does not worship the gods, has risen against me, to fight against me. Thou art the lady of ladies, the queen of battles, the mistress of wars, the sovereign of the gods, who, in the presence of Assur, hast always spoken in my favour, to turn the hearts of Assur and of Merodach, thy companion, towards me. Now, Teumman, the king of Elam, has sinned grievously against Assur, the king of the gods, thy father, and against Merodach, thy brother and thy companion, and even against me, Assurbanipal, who have always endeavoured to rejoice the heart of Assur and of Merodach; he has assembled his soldiers, he has started his army, and is now ready for war, he has demanded his weapons that he may march against Assyria. Thou, who art the archeress of the gods, throwing thy weight into the midst of battle, do thou cast him down, and pass over him, like the whirlwind of a noxious storm.' As in Egypt,* the divine statues in Assyria are animated by the spirit of the being they represent; they hear, speak, and move. Ishtar was touched by the prayer offered by her favourite and by his sobs: 'Fear nothing,' she said to him, filling his heart with joy. 'Since thou hast come before me, since thine eyes are full of tears, I will pour my grace out upon thee.' The voice was then hushed, the silence which it had broken seemed more solemn than before, and the king finding himself alone

* See pages 52 and 62 of this volume upon the prophetic statues of Egypt.

under the doubtful light of the lamp, suddenly experienced the fear produced by the presence of the divinity; in the midst of his joy a shiver passed over him, and his blood curdled round his heart. Now that night, at the time that Assurbanipal was lamenting before the goddess, one of the seers of the temple had a dream. The sky is an open book which all may read; the privilege of consulting it is not reserved for a few men only—it is the right of all. But the gods have a thousand means of revealing the future to the men whom they favour with their love or their hatred, and dreams form the one most often used. The dreams which usually cross the sleep of men resemble a nation of aërean figures sufficiently fluid to assume at their pleasure every variety of form, and to change them as rapidly as they put them on; they move, act, and speak, and their least movement, their least action, their lightest word, are secretly connected with the events that are preparing in the life of a man or of a nation. Sometimes these messages from above are conceived in a direct language, and do not require an interpreter; future events are presented to our eyes without a veil. But usually they are expressed by symbols or allegories, and then a man versed in the art of interpreting them is required to unravel the eccentric or broken thread of their predictions.

Like the astrologers, these divines have their official manuals; the doctrine contained in them is also the result of observations collected by their predecessors in the course of ages. One of them, now in the library of Assurbanipal, teaches us what we must expect of fate if we dream of monstrous animals that unite the body of a bear, a dog, or a lion, to the paws of some other animal, dead fish, or a fish with birds. These are all fatal omens, and the dreamer should recite a prayer to the Sun as soon as he awakes, for the orb of day can weaken or even dissipate entirely the malignant influence. However spontaneous dreams may be, and however independent they appear to be of all human will, it is certain that they can be invoked by repeating certain prayers and submitting to certain rules. There are amulets which procure, for those who wear them, truthful dreams and the power of recollecting them after awakening. In solemn circumstances, the dreamer should prepare some days in advance by abstinence, fasting, and prayer, and should retire to an isolated room or into a temple to pass the night. Then, before sleeping, he mentally formulates the question to which he desires an answer, and if sleep does not come naturally, he produces it by narcotic beverages, mixed according to secret prescriptions of the divines. It then becomes a religious rite, that of the incubation, in which every moment is defined by severe rules, according to whether the gods in general are addressed, one god in particular, or merely the souls of the dead. The replies obtained would be absolutely reliable if the interpreters did not frequently mistake the value of the details which always accompany the principal episodes. From these mistakes arise many disillusions, of which the faithful complain bitterly, and which make them wrongly accuse the malignity of the gods. But the gods never refuse to send sincere dreams, when they are faithfully asked, according to the prescribed forms. Is it their fault if the senses of men are so dense that they cannot read their signification?

Most of the temples have their male and female seers, who are regularly attached to them, and whose duty consists in receiving the will of the god, either by direct revelation during the vigil, or indirectly through the medium of dreams. At Babylon a woman dwells on the summit of the many-storied tower, and waits each night for the visit of the god. In the temples of Ishtar, in that of Arbela, as in that of Nineveh, men sleep in the temple of the goddess. She manifested herself to one of them on the same night that the king prayed to her so urgently, and he related his vision in these words: 'Ishtar, who inhabits Arbela, came in before me. On her right and on her left side two quivers were hanging; she held a bow in one hand, and in the other a heavy sword. She advanced towards thee, and spoke to thee like a mother. Ishtar, the first amongst the gods, said to thee in a tone of command, "Thou hast asked for victory; where thou art, I will be also." Thou sayest unto her, "Can I go with thee where thou goest, O sovereign of sovereigns?" She then answered, "Stay thou in the place consecrated to Nebo; eat thy food, drink wine, let thy musicians play before thee and glorify thy name. For I will go down to the battle, I will accomplish my work, and thy face shall not pale, thy feet shall not stumble, thy beauty shall not fail in the midst of the battle." She hides thee in her bosom like a good mother, and wraps thee round on every side. A flame will issue from her for the destruction of thine enemies, for she has turned her face against Teumman, the king of Elam, who is odious in her eyes.'

If the oracle of the stars had allowed any doubts to remain, that which Ishtar has deigned to grant, through her seer, would remove them all. The blasphemies of Teumman have enraged the goddess; the war against Elam is henceforth her own war, and she will lead it herself. Assurbanipal need not even join the army. Ishtar commands him to remain in his palace and enjoy a peaceful life, whilst she will take his place at the head of his troops and will lead them to victory. The words of the seer are promulgated through the cities, and fill Assyria with enthusiasm. The soldiers are equally delighted with the account of the vision. They are particularly affected by the predictions. A bad omen disconcerts them, enervates their courage, and delivers them over to their enemies conquered in advance. Battalions, that would never hesitate to allow themselves to be killed to the last man in ordinary times, have frequently given way at the first onset when the predictions have been unfavourable. Their heart failed them at the idea that the powers above were not on their side, and the assurance that they risked their life for a cause already lost paralysed their arms. But if the stars are propitious, and the seers promise them support from the gods, they can be relied upon to make any effort required of them. Success springs from their faith in the oracles, and the army is already more than half victorious that knows that its gods are fighting for it.

And whilst the divinities of Assyria are thus arming for the conflict, those of Elam are displaying equal activity in their preparations. Interest would force them to do so, even if national pride were not also an incentive. The day upon which the Ninevite generals defeat their own generals will not only establish the supremacy of Nineveh and Assurbanipal over Teumman and Susiana, but that of Bel, Assur, and Ishtar over Susinag, who inhabits the depths of the mysterious woods, and who is present everywhere, though invisible to men, over Shoumoudou, over Lagamar, over Partikira, over Ammankaisbar, over Oudouran, over Sapak, and over all the divinities that the ancient kings have adored. Formerly they led their worshippers to the conquest of Chaldea, and placed a dynasty of Elamites upon the throne of Babylon; since then they have suffered some checks, and have lost the territory that they had won, but up to the present they have always defended the independence of Elam and preserved the booty which she had taken from the foreigners. The statue of the goddess Nanai, which they erected at Ourouk, is still in the great temple of Susa, where the king, Koudournankhoundi, placed it, more than sixteen centuries ago, upon his return home from his campaigns. There are a few undecided and timid men, even in the king's court, who fear the war, and counsel him against it. One of the sons of

Teumman perpetually reminds his father of the great power of Assyria, and repeats to him as often as he dare, 'Do not hope for victory.' The generals and courtiers, as a rule, do not share his fears, and the gods do all in their power to excite the courage of their defenders. Their astronomers reply to the combinations of stars so favourable to Assyria, by other combinations which foretell the coming triumph of Elam. Their seers oppose their own visions to those of the seers of Ishtar, whom they accuse of falsehood, and the contemptuous words which Teumman repeats respecting the goddess of Arbela are inspired by his confidence in the prophecies of his own priests. Their oracles predict the immediate fall of Assyria, the pillage of Nineveh, the captivity and death of Assurbanipal.

The same rivalry occurs whenever war breaks out between the two nations; the battle of men is complicated by a battle of the gods. The gods dwell in the camp, invisible; they descend into the thickest of the fight, they protect the chiefs with their own persons, and strike the enemy's generals when they can. Victors, they take the foreign gods as their prisoners and exact tribute from them; vanquished, in their turn, they bow to the law of the strongest. Their statues, treasures, and servants are taken from them, their temples are destroyed, their sacred woods cut down; they suffer slavery, perhaps death, like the people that adored them.

# CHAPTER XVIII.

### THE WAR.

Rapid march of the Assyrian army—Its arrival at Duril separates Elam from Chaldea—Teumman concentrates his army in front of Susa—Organization of the Assyrian army—The infantry—The war chariots—The cavalry—The Elamite army: its position at Tulliz—Battle of Tulliz—Death of Teumman—Registering the spoil—Surrender of Susa—Proclamation of Ummanigas as king of Susa, and of Tammaritu as king of Hidalu.

THE month of Ab is very fatal to armed expeditions, but the following month, Elul, is equally propitious, and as soon as it opens, the army commences its march. Elam is covered, upon the side nearest to Nineveh, by high, woody, almost impracticable mountains, inhabited by the half-barbarous tribes of the Kashshi. They could not be crossed without great sacrifices, and the Assyrians might leave half their army there before reaching the seat of war. They therefore usually attack Susiana by the south-western frontier, towards the spot where the waters of the Ouknou and the Ulai join those of the Tigris and the Euphrates. Even then the route is full of difficulties for the assailants. It is marshy, unhealthy, intersected with ponds, rivers, and canals, which interfere with the operations; but at all events the invaders are in the very heart of the country as soon as the watery barrier is crossed. The army rapidly marches by the side of the Tigris, and ten days after starting has already reached the city of Duril. During the last century the great wars between Assyria and Elam have been waged at frequent intervals, and Duril has acquired an importance that no one could have foreseen. Here Sargon fought his first battle against Umbanigash, a hotly disputed field, in which each party claimed the victory. He fortified it, and established a garrison and a governor, to whom Sennacherib and Assurbanipal confided the administration of a large territory. It is now the centre of an important road, which commands the lower course of the Tigris, and can interrupt, if it does not entirely cut off, the communications between Susa and Babylon.

The rapidity with which all the preliminaries of the action have been carried out disconcerts Teumman, and ruins all his plans. He had counted upon a long delay, which would have given him time to negotiate with the Aramean tribes or the small Chaldean kingdoms, and to excite them against Assyria. His manœuvres have succeeded upon one point, for the people of Gambul have openly declared in his favour; but the sudden apparition of the Assyrian vanguard cuts short his intrigues, and represses any symptoms of rebellion that might have appeared. The army is not commanded by the king in person. Assurbanipal has carefully obeyed the orders of Ishtar. He remains in his palace at Arbela, and forgets his anxiety in the midst of festivals and banquets. The Tartan of the right, Belnahid,[*] leads the campaign under the inspiration of the goddess, and, by his side, the Elamite princes command a large number of refugees. As they pass through the country, they proclaim that they do not come as enemies to place the land under a foreign rule, but as allies, who wish to reinstate the legitimate heirs upon the throne; and this declaration brings thousands of partisans to their assistance. Teumman, abandoned by the allies whom he thought

[*] The texts do not give us the name of the personage who led the campaign against Elam. As Belnahid was in high office at this epoch, I have placed him in command, to avoid the frequent repetition of the title of Tartan.

he had secured at the first sign of the arrival of the Assyrians, cannot rely upon the fidelity even of his own subjects. At the least failure, the revolution will break out, and he will be lost. Since he has but one battle to fight, he wishes to engage in it under the most favourable circumstances. He recalls the troops that he had scattered along the frontier, join to them the new contingents, and thus forms a large army, which he concentrates in the village of Tulliz, before Susa. The position is admirably chosen; it entirely masks the approaches to the capital, and commands the city itself, where the partisans of the old kings are beginning to stir. It also covers the roads which lead to Madaktu, in the upper part of the country. If successful, Teumman will regain all that he has been forced to abandon at a single blow; defeated, he can still take refuge in the mountains and there prolong his resistance.

The Assyrian army is the best-organized war machine that the world has yet seen. The Egyptians themselves, at the time of their greatest power under Thothmes III. and Rameses II., never disposed of troops so well drilled and, above all, so well equipped.* The art of the blacksmith and of the armourer has made so much progress since that date, that their best troops would have little chance of success if they were opposed to Assyrian soldiers. It is the superiority of weapons, not any superiority in courage and discipline, that has secured to the Ninevite kings since Sargon the priority over the Pharaohs of the Delta of Thebes and Meroë. Whilst the Egyptians, as a rule, still fight without any protection except the shield, the Assyrians are, so to speak, clothed in iron from head to foot. Their heavy infantry is composed of spearmen and archers, wearing a conical cap ornamented with two side pieces which protect the ears, a leather shirt covered with overlapping metal scales which

* Upon the equipment of the Egyptian soldiers see p. 81.

protect the chest and the upper part of the arms, cotton drawers falling to the shins, close-fitting breeches, and boots laced in front. The spearmen carry spears six feet long, with an iron or bronze head, a short sword passed through their belt, and an immense metal shield, sometimes round and convex, sometimes rounded at the top and square at the bottom. The archers have no shields; they replace the spear by a bow and quiver, which hang over their back. Their light infantry also includes some spearmen, but they wear a helmet with a curved crest, and are provided with a small round wicker-work shield. The archers have no breastplate, and are associated either with slingers or with soldiers armed with clubs and double-edged axes.

The spearmen and archers of the line are usually of Assyrian origin, or levied in the territories that have been subject to Assyria for a long time; the other troops are often recruited amongst tributary nations, and they wear their national costumes. They are arranged in companies, and manœuvre with a regularity which foreigners themselves admire. As early as the reigns of Sargon and Sennacherib, one of the most celebrated Hebrew prophets, that Isaiah who advised King Hezekiah in his war against Assyria, was astonished at their good discipline. 'None shall be weary or stumble amongst them; none shall slumber nor sleep; neither shall the girdle of their loins be loosed, nor the latchet of their shoes be broken.' They march with extraordinary rapidity, leaving no stragglers or lame men behind them as they go, and their generals are not afraid to impose fatigues upon them to which the soldiers of other lands would quickly succumb. They either ford the rivers or swim across them upon inflated skins. In wooded countries, each company sends forward a certain number of pioneers, who fell the trees and clear a path.

The cavalry are divided into two corps, the chariot

soldiers and the regular cavalry. The Assyrian war-chariot is much heavier and more massive than the Egyptian.* The wheels are high and thick, they have eight spokes. The body, which rests upon the axle, is square in front; the panels are full, sometimes covered with metal plates, or more often painted or decorated with incrustations. The pole is long, thick, curved at the end, with an ornament in wood or chased metal—a flower, rosette, lion's head, or horse's head. Each chariot is drawn by two horses, sometimes a third horse is fastened to their flank, but it does not usually draw, it is intended to replace one of its companions in case of an accident or a wound. The horses are harnessed rather lightly, and sometimes wear a kind of armour in thick cloth, which covers their back, chest, neck, and the top of the head; the pieces are fastened together by tags. Each chariot contains three men—a coachman who drives, standing to the left, a warrior with a bow or spear, and a groom, who protects his two comrades, but particularly the warrior, with a round shield. Sometimes there is a second groom. Their equipment is similar to that of the infantry, the cuirass of metal scales, the helmet, the bow, and the lance. This small troop has sometimes a standard, round which it rallies during the battle. A staff of medium height is placed in front of the chariot between the soldier and the coachman; at the top is a reversed crescent or a disk supported by two bulls' heads; it is decorated by two bulls, and by a standing figure of Assur shooting an arrow (Fig. 153).

Like the Egyptian chariots, the Assyrians always charge in a regular line, and there are few troops in the world that can resist their first shock. When a battalion of the enemy sees them coming, rapid and light, their darts pointed, their bows strung, they usually disband immediately after the first volley of arrows, and run away. The line is then broken, and

* See for the Egyptian chariot, p. 82.

the chariots disperse over the plain, crushing the fugitives beneath their wheels, and trampling them under their horses' feet. Each chariot forms a movable fort, with a sufficient garrison not only for fighting within the walls, but for making a sortie if necessary. The warrior gets down, kills a wounded man, cuts off a head; or, placing himself in front of his horses, well covered by his grooms, he takes leisurely aim at some leader of the enemy, hits him, then remounts and continues his course.

Formerly the chariots were very numerous in the Assyrian armies. They are less used at the present day, but tradition gives them the post of honour, and the king or the chief general always reserves for himself the privilege of leading them into the fight. It is the distinguished branch of the service, the one in which the princes and great nobles prefer to serve, and its weight often decides the fate of the battle.

Fig. 153.—An Assyrian Standard.

Yet now the cavalry commences to rival it, if not in numbers, at least in importance. It has not been long in use, and the old Assyrian kings, like the Pharaohs of the great epoch, were unacquainted with its capacity. Tiglath-Pileser I., Assur-nasir-pal, and Shalmaneser III.

had a few cavalry, but they used them more as messengers than as combatants. Sargon and Sennacherib were really the first to handle them in great masses, and to entrust them with an important part in their strategy. The horse was at first ridden barebacked; now it is covered with one cloth, or with a complete caparison similar to that of the chariot horses. All the cavalry wear helmets and cuirasses like the infantry of the line, but they have no shields; they replace the floating petticoat by cotton drawers. One half of them

Fig. 154.—Assyrian Cavalry charging: the Servant leads the Archer's Horse.

carries the sword and lance, the other half is armed with a bow and sword. The lance is eight or nine feet long, the bow is shorter than the bow used by the infantry, and the arrows are scarcely three feet long. Formerly each mounted archer was accompanied by a servant, mounted like himself, who led his horse during the battle so as to leave both his hands free (Fig. 154). The art of riding has made so much progress during the last few years that the servant has become useless, and has disappeared from the armies. Now lancers and bowmen are all trained to guide their steed by the pressure of the knees, and they may be seen galloping with flying reins, shooting their arrows as they go, or else, halting suddenly, they quietly discharge the arrow, then turn and gallop off again.

It is said that in the last war between the Cimmerians and the Lydians troops of cavalry charged each other at full gallop, then mingled and fought hand to hand, like regiments of infantry, until the flight of the weakest or the least brave. The Assyrian cavalry have not yet had the opportunity of trying this manœuvre, for the nations with whom it usually fights have only chariots to bring against it. It charges the infantry, is invaluable in the fight and the pursuit, and reconnoitres on the march of an army. It is then sent some distance in front of the mass of the troops, to search the woods, discover ambushes, examine the posi-

Fig. 155.—Assyrian Cavalry fighting in a Mountainous Country.

tion of the enemy, and point out the practicable roads and the fords in the rivers. Sennacherib, who often made war in mountainous and woody countries, in the Taurus and Armenia, on the borders of Media and Elam, owed part of his success to the judicious use which he made of his lancers and mounted archers. Their unexpected movements, the rapidity and length of their rides, dismayed the barbarians, who saw them appear at several points at the same time, as though sprung out of the ground, when they thought them still a long way off (Fig. 155). Dangerous passes were crossed, villages pillaged, crops burnt or trampled by the horses almost before the presence of the enemy was suspected, and when help came they were already far from all pursuit. If a certain number of miners and engineers trained in the construction and handling of machinery be added to the cavalry, we have a complete enumeration of the elements of an Assyrian army. The proportion of the different services is always about the same. There is, on an average, one hundred foot soldiers to every ten cavalry and every single chariot; the infantry is really queen of the Assyrian battles.

The Elamite army is organized in the same fashion as its rival, or nearly so. It has also chariots, cavalry,

Fig. 156.—Elamite War-chariot.

and infantry, but the cavalry are neither as numerous nor as well drilled as the Assyrian troops, and the chariots contain fewer men. Many of them have no body, but consist of a simple platform, upon which the soldiers sit or stand; they look more like luggage-carts than war-chariots (Fig. 156). One part of the infantry, recruited from the plains, is equipped like the Assyrian archers and spearmen (Fig. 157). The remainder is less well armed. They have no cuirass, but a simple tunic with a short skirt, and in the hair a ribbon with the two ends falling over the neck. In spite of this material inferiority, courage, vigour, skill, and tenacity render the Elamites formidable enemies. They are seldom routed, and, when defeated, the victory has always exhausted the victor so much that he has been unable to profit by his advantage, and has retired from the battle-field in almost the same condition as the vanquished.

The Tartan, who has proved their military qualities, minutely examines their position before the battle. Their line of defence is skilfully chosen. It extends from the shores of the Ouknou to those of the canal which passes before the citadel of Susa and serves as a moat against an enemy coming from Assyria. In the centre the village of Tulliz forms a solid background to the masses of infantry, whilst behind, a large wood of palm-trees is ready to receive

Fig. 157.—Elamite Archers.

Fig. 158.—The City of Susa.

the fugitives in case of defeat and to hinder the pursuit. A long line of crenellated walls, bristling with towers, is clearly defined on the horizon above the tops of the trees; these are the ramparts of Susa (Fig. 158). The city, built upon an artificial mound, like all the cities of Assyria and Chaldea, dominates the plain, and is visible at a great distance. To the south and east, immense gardens, watered by canals carefully kept in repair, make a border of foliage. Thick gloomy woods extend towards the north. The profane are forbidden to enter them, for the gods of Elam dwell there, in the mysterious chapels to which only the priests and kings have access. From time to time their images are carried to the town to receive some act of solemn public worship, then return to their retreats, amidst the devotion of the whole nation. No one amongst the people knows what passes behind the curtains of the first trees, what bloody ritual or what voluptuous mysteries are celebrated there. After each successful war a part of the spoil is carried there which never reappears; statues of the enemy's gods, precious vases, blocks of gold or silver, furniture, and stuffs. More than one object has been deposited there for twenty centuries, the spoil from Ourouk, Sippar, Babylon, and the more ancient Chaldean cities being stored pell-mell with the trophies more recently taken from the Assyrians. The mausoleums of the old kings are built in the same neighbourhood; some of them are still in a good state of preservation, others already damaged by the action of time. No history could be more tragic than theirs, for treason and murder have made and unmade kings in Elam with, perhaps, more rapidity than anywhere else, and there are few of the sovereigns united in this corner of earth who do not sleep in a bloody tomb. If we only take recent years, Susa has changed her master seven times in half a century, and three out of these seven sovereigns have been assassinated.

Teumman is surrounded by traitors, and he knows it. Simburus, one of his most powerful vassals, has already abandoned him, and has joined the Assyrian camp with his men; Umbakidinni, chief of one of the tribes of the mountain, has surprised Istarnandi, the viceroy of Hidalu, upon the upper course of the Ulai; has cut off his head and has carried it to the Tartan in token of submission. However, the Susians will not allow themselves to be affected by these successive

Fig. 159.—The remnant of the Elamite Army thrown into the River.

defections, and they receive the Assyrians' charge with their usual resolution. The battle commences by the exchange of volleys of arrows; then the war-chariots rush against each other, and meet several times without any result. One last charge, led by the exiled princes, at last breaks down the resistance of the Elamites; the uninjured Susian chariots disperse over the plain, the cavalry follows them in their retreat, and the infantry, influenced by their example, quickly disbands. One part of the soldiers hides in the wood, the other, driven back into the canal, tries to discover a ford, or to cross it by swimming to gain shelter under the ramparts of Susa. (Fig. 159). The whole plain is strewn with broken chariots, quivers, bows, lances, the corpses of men and horses. Here a group of archers still tries to resist the cavalry who harass it; further on, a wounded chief, ready to fall from his horse, raises his hand to sue for mercy from an archer who is aiming at him. A foot soldier strikes down a kneeling Susian with his club; others cut of the head of the enemy they have killed, and carry it away as a trophy. All the wounded who can still stand upright are hurrying away as fast as they can; those who are no longer able to walk, try to find a bush or a ditch in which they can hide until nightfall; it is their sole chance of life, and heaven knows it is a very slight one! Every head cut off brings praise and part of the spoil to the soldier who brings it in; the victors, therefore, carefully search the field of battle, examining the long grass and the ridges of land, as though seeking ordinary game. The birds of prey have already assembled over the field, ready to commence their odious meal. The canal is full of mutilated bodies and of drifting chariots; the Assyrian archers, standing upon the bank, shoot at the men still struggling in the water, and very few of the fugitives succeed in reaching the other side. The prophets and seers of Nineveh were right in predicting a victory. Ishtar has kept her promise, and Elam is at the feet of Assyria. Teumman, seeing the battle lost, escapes through the wood with two of his sons and his most faithful generals. He sends one of them, Ituni, to the Assyrian general to demand an honourable capitulation—not that he thinks that he will obtain it, but he hopes to stop the pursuit and gain a little time. Ituni did not even obtain a hearing, and in his rage broke his bow with his sword at the moment that the soldier who had taken him raised the sword to behead him. A few minutes later one of Teumman's cousins, named Urtaku, was pierced by an arrow and fell; as he rose an Assyrian rushed upon him, raising his club. Urtaku did not lose courage in this supreme moment. 'Come,' he said, 'cut off my head and carry it to the feet of your master: may it prove a good omen.' Then he bent his head for the fatal blow. However, Teumman's chariot had broken against a tree; his horses were too sorely wounded to carry him, or had already escaped; his faithful friends had been killed one after the other: alone, with one of his sons, he was slowly retiring on foot. From time to time he turned to shoot an arrow, and his proud carriage and sure aim discouraged the enemy; perhaps he might have escaped and found shelter if his nephew, Tammaritu, had not perceived him, and at once pursued him with some Susian exiles and Ninevite spearmen. An arrow hit him in the right leg and he fell upon one knee. Seeing that he was lost, he wished that at least he should not die unavenged. He pointed Tammaritu out to his son, and in a despairing voice cried, 'Shoot!' (Fig. 160). The shot failed, a flight of arrows disabled the two men; Tammaritu

Fig. 160.—Death of Teumman.

himself cut off his uncle's head and joyfully carried it away.

When he returned to the camp the battle was entirely ended. A few detachments still hurried over the plain, collecting the Assyrian dead and wounded, picking up the weapons, and methodically spoiling the bodies of the enemy; the remainder of the army had already returned to its former position. The camp was full of soldiers staunching their wounds or those of their comrades, cleaning or straightening their weapons, congratulating themselves upon having escaped death this once more, or lamenting the fall of a friend. Those prisoners whom it was deemed advisable to keep were already standing on one side, guarded by sentinels. The execution of the others was continued without a

Fig. 161.—Reception and Registration of the Heads.

pause; they were made to kneel in long rows, their backs to the executioner, their heads bowed so that a single blow of the club broke their skulls. The scribes standing in their large tents registered the heads cut off; every soldier brought some, threw them upon the common heap, then dictated his name, mentioned his company, and retired cheered by the hope of a recompense suited to the number of his victims (Fig. 161). The kings of Assyria delight in these hideous trophies. When they accompany the army they preside over the reception of the heads and distribute the prizes allotted to the soldiers; when absent, if the heads cannot all be sent to them, they insist upon seeing those of the principal chiefs. Teumman's head, presented to Bel-nahid, was by his orders carried all round the camp in one of the chariots taken during the battle (Fig. 162), then embalmed and sent to the palace of Arbela by an express courier; as to the corpse, it was left in the wood, and in a few days the birds or the beasts of prey will have devoured it.

If Susa opens her gates to-morrow and accepts the new sovereign offered by Assyria, Ummanigas, the son of Urtaki, the battle of Tulliz will suffice to end the war. If, on the other hand, she acknowledges one of Teumman's sons as her master, the struggle will recommence, and the gods themselves scarcely know when and how it will end. Elam has almost unlimited re-

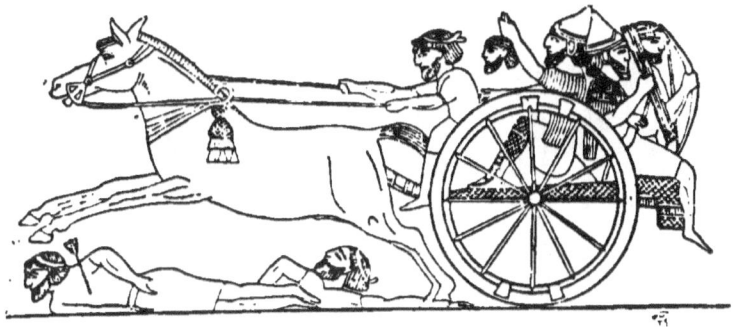

Fig. 162.—Teumman's Head carried through the Assyrian Camp.

sources in men and in captains. As soon as one army is destroyed, others can be formed equally numerous and equally determined to fight. One king is killed, another rises in his place and returns to the charge, without allowing the fate of his predecessors or his own danger to influence him in any way. Yet this once the partisans of peace carry the day in Susa, and the friends of the exiled princes decide the population to proclaim Ummanigas. Early the following morning the Assyrian guards see a long procession issue from the gates of Susa and slowly proceed towards Tulliz; it is a deputation of the army, the nobles, and the people, coming to ask for their sovereign from the victor. Several members of the royal family are at its head, in festival robes, without their weapons. The archers come next with their bows, the quiver on one shoulder, the poignard in the belt; then follows an empty chariot led by a groom on horseback, the chariot for the new king. The priests and singers of the gods march behind, beating the time with their feet, and filling the air with the sound of harps and flutes. A choir of children follows them, singing a hymn under the direction of the sacred eunuchs (Fig. 163).

The plain has been nearly cleared since the evening, and the traces of the battle have almost disappeared; but the canal is still full of corpses, chariots, broken

Fig. 163.—The Elamite Musicians marching to meet the Assyrians.

weapons, and rubbish. The painful spectacle contrasts strangely with the festival dresses and songs of the procession advancing upon its banks. Belnahid receives the chiefs of the deputation in the front of his army, and listens to their request from his chariot. He summons Ummanigas and Tammaritu to come before him, and makes them swear by their gods and by the gods of Nineveh to be always faithful allies of Assyria, never to conspire with the sovereigns of Babylon or with the princes of the Aramean tribes, and to avoid any action which could injure the interests or glory of Assurbanipal. The oath taken, he descends from his chariot, and taking them by the hand proclaims Ummanigas king of Susa and Madaktu, and Tammaritu king of

Hidalu, then he presents them to their new subjects. The princes and warriors fall down before them and salute them, whilst the musicians play and sing louder than before (Fig. 164). Elam, that on the previous evening had been content with one king, now possesses two, and ere long jealousy and ambition will cause them to turn against each other. Assurbanipal and his minister expect this: internal dissensions and the weakness of her neighbours assure the security of Assyria. Whilst the two kings and their escort solemnly enter Susa amidst the shouts of the crowd, a long line of prisoners leaves the camp and commences

Fig. 164.—The Assyrian General presents Ummanigas to the Elamites.

its sorrowful journey towards the north. Several are almost certainly doomed to torture and death; these are the generals, governors of the city, and the nobles who have most distinguished themselves by their courage, who are being led in chains before the king, and whom he rarely spares or forgives. A larger number have been allotted to the soldiers or to the public treasury. Amongst them are a few men, but the majority are women and children, who will be sold as slaves, or serve in the house of the master to whom the fortune of war has delivered them. The majority are reserved for a milder fate, and are less prisoners than enforced colonists. Assurbanipal wishes to repopulate two or three Syrian cities that he has lately sacked, and he has charged his generals to take him a few thousand Elamites. They travel in bands, under the superintendence of a soldier, the men carrying a small bag of provisions, which is no inconvenience to them, the women carrying their children in their arms

Fig. 165.—Prisoners going to Assyria.

or upon their shoulders (Fig. 165). Herds of cattle, goats, and sheep accompany them. The luggage and the sick follow in chariots drawn by mules or oxen. Many die on the road of fatigue and misery, obliged as they are to sleep in the open air upon the bare ground. Those who reach the end of the journey receive a house, cornfields, gardens, and vines; their first sorrow calmed, they are perhaps richer and happier than in their own country.

# CHAPTER XIX.

### THE FLEET AND THE SIEGE OF A CITY.

The land of Gambul and the Arameans of the Euphrates—The marshes—Bit-Iakin and the emigration of its population in the time of Sennacherib—The fleet of Sennacherib and the two elements of which it is composed: the Phœnician galleys—Embarkment, crossing the sea—The war in the marshes—The city of Sapibel—The blockade—Sapping the walls—The war machines: the ram and the rolling towers—Capture and destruction of the city.

THE campaign is ended in Elam, but it continues in the land of Gambul, where the King Dunanu and Prince Nabuzulli still resist the Assyrian armies. Gambul is one of the numerous small Aramean States which have established themselves at the mouths of the Tigris and Euphrates, half in the marshes, half upon dry land. That portion of the population that lives upon dry ground is almost identical with the Chaldeans in language and customs. They worship the same gods, obey the same laws, wear the same costume, and follow the same industries; yet the national character is affected by the vicinity of Elam, and is rougher and more warlike. On the other hand the inhabitants of the marshes are barbarians that live on the produce of fishing and hunting. Like the Delta of the Nile, that of the Tigris and Euphrates is an immense plain, always being increased at the expense of the sea by alluvial deposits. Where the soil is sufficiently raised above the usual level of the floods, cultivation has conquered, and wrests from it two good harvests every year. The cities, placed upon artificial mounds, are surrounded by evergreen gardens; date-trees and acacias grow along

z

the canals; wheat-fields extend in all directions, intersected by damp meadows, where innumerable herds of cattle graze peacefully. Where the soil is below the level of the river, the aspect is perhaps more desolate than that of the marshes of the Nile. Foul, stagnant water, half covering a thick black mud, sandy islands in seas of mud, here and there woody hillocks or plateaus of pure healthy ground, and over all a spontaneous growth of aquatic plants—water-lilies, reeds, horsetails, gigantic rushes—so thick and so strong that a man can scarcely force his way between their stems. Sparse squares of small, badly grown wheat in the glades, these are the fields. A collection of huts upon some of the highest points, these are the villages. It does not take long nor cost much to build them. Bunches of reeds are tied together, then bent and placed against each other so as to form arches; mats hung over this rudimentary framework, then covered with mud, form the walls. The inhabitants go from village to village upon flat-bottomed boats, which they manage with poles. They have hidden dens, where, in case of war, they and their families can take refuge, abandoning their homes to the mercy of the invader. To reach them it becomes necessary to enter one of the narrow canals, bordered with thickets, each perhaps containing an ambush; to cross the moving bogs, where horses and pedestrians risk being engulfed, and to brave the poisonous fevers which rise from the stagnant waters—and all this trouble is merely to carry off a few thin cattle, or take one or two dozen prisoners. What an end for the veterans who have safely encountered the dangers of twenty battles fought in the mountains of Armenia or Commagenia, in the plains of Chaldea or Elam, upon the banks of the Nile or the shores of the Mediterranean, to at last be drowned in the liquid mud of a marsh, or to fall ignominiously between two bunches of reeds under the blows of a semi-savage!

Bit-Iakin was formerly the most important of these

small states. From there came Merodach Baladan to conquer Babylon and resist three great kings of Assyria; there he returned in his old age like a boar at bay, who, after a long chase, returns to his lair to face the hunters. Continually pursued by Sennacherib, despairing of a successful resistance, he preferred expatriation to submission: he assembled his faithful servants, carried his gods with him, crossed the sea where the Euphrates flows into it, and established himself at Nagidu, upon the coast of Elam. With any other king than Sennacherib he would have been safe. In fact, the Assyrian kings feared the sea for many years, and would not willingly venture upon it; moreover, they had not been acquainted with it very long, except by hearsay, through the descriptions which the Chaldeans or the peoples of Syria gave of it. When their victories led them to the shores of the Mediterranean, they admired its beauty and enjoyed the pleasure of sailing upon it, but prudently abstained from venturing too far from the land. Sennacherib then conceived the bold project, unheard-of before, of embarking his army upon a fleet and going in search of the exiles of Bit-Iakin at Nagidu. The execution of this plan offered difficulties which would have discouraged a prince of less adventurous spirit. The only ships at his disposal in those districts belonged to Chaldean states of but doubtful fidelity, and it would not be prudent to entrust the fate of a king of Nineveh and his troops to their care. Their vessels also were arks of ancient form, heavy, round, bad seaboats, very similar to those built in ancient times under Sargon the elder and his son Naramsin. Now Sennacherib, during his wars in Judea, had seen the sailors of Sidon, and the progress which the Sidonians had made in the art of ship-building, besides the skill with which they handled their *sea-horses*.* He had not much difficulty in finding amongst his prisoners a sufficiently large

* The Phœnicians called their vessels by this name.

number of Phœnicians to construct a fleet. He established two ship-building yards, one at Til-Barsip upon the Euphrates, where they used the woods from Amanus and Lebanon, and the other upon the Tigris, at Nineveh itself, for the woods from Kurdistan.

The ships built in them were of different forms. At Til-Barsip, where the Phœnician element predominated, the style was Phœnician; at Nineveh it was Chaldean, modified by the Phœnician. The type selected was the most perfect known at that date, the galley, a vessel with a double row of oars one above

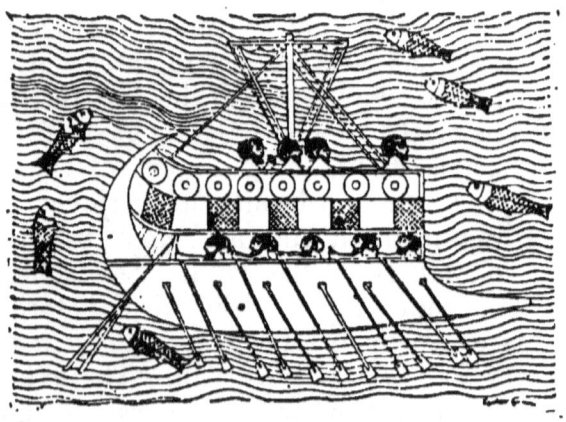

Fig. 166.—A Phœnician Galley.

the other (Fig. 166). The hull was long, low in the water, with a round keel. The poop, raised very high, was curved back upon itself like the ancient Egyptian galleys.* The front, upright and flat, was armed with a sharp spur, strongly fitted to the keel, which served to pierce the enemy's ships. The two lines of rowers were placed horizontally one above the other. The first rested their oars upon the gunnels, the others passed theirs through portholes opened in the side of the vessel. A bridge supported by vertical posts passed from one

* For the description and figure of the Egyptian galleys, see p. 166.

end to the other, forming an upper deck reserved for the soldiers and the remainder of the crew; round shields suspended upon light woodwork formed a kind of bulwark the full length of the ship. The mast, upright in the centre of the bridge, was embedded in the keel; it was held in place by two stays, which started from the top and were fastened to the front and back. The square sail was supported by a yard which could be raised or lowered at will. The ships of the other type had no spur, but had very high curves both in front and behind, and the prow was ornamented with a horse's head, which justified the name of the sea-horse. They had no masts, but were decked. They were propelled by a double row of oars one above the other. These were old vessels transformed into galleys.

The two divisions of the fleet were then ordered to meet at Bab-Salimeti, upon the Euphrates, at a little distance from the sea. The squadron of Til-Barsip at once descended the river, which is always navigable, and the voyage was accomplished without any difficulty.* The Ninevite squadron left the Tigris at Opis, to avoid the camps of the Aramean allies of Elam, always more or less hostile even when nominally at peace with Assyria. It then entered the grand canal of Arakhtu, which unites the Tigris to the Euphrates and crosses Babylon. The canal had been neglected for some time, and though it sufficed for irrigation and the passage of small boats, the mud was very deep in some places, and vegetation was so thick that it formed a serious obstacle to the passage of large vessels. However, all these difficulties were overcome, and the journey from Babylon to Bab-Salimeti was only a question of days. On its way each division had embarked the troops it was to carry, men and horses,

* I remember that Alexander, the same year that he died, caused a Phœnician fleet to be built at Thapsus, which descended the Euphrates to its mouth.

chariots, provisions, the siege machines necessary for a campaign which might last for some time. Sennacherib joined the fleet with his guard, and encamped upon the banks of the river. This was an imprudence which he would never have committed had he known more about the sea. The tides, although unknown to the Mediterranean, are very strong in the Gulf of Chaldea, and are felt some distance up the country. Their effects are particularly dangerous during the equinoctial periods, when the tides are very high. The waves then ascend and meet the current of the river; the shock of the two strong waters contending as they meet shakes the banks, carries them away, breaks down the dykes erected for the defence of the country, and inundates all the surrounding districts. This annual event occurred during the voyage of the Assyrians, much to their terror and loss. Their tents were flooded and overthrown by the waves, the king and his guard were forced to take hasty refuge upon the ships, and to remain there for five days, 'like prisoners in a large cage.'

Sennacherib then perceived, though rather late, that he had omitted to celebrate the propitiatory rites, without which it is not prudent to approach the Ocean, and he attributed his misfortune to the displeasure of the gods. As soon as the waters had retired he descended to the spot where the river loses itself in the sea, and standing upon the prow of the admiral's galley, he offered a sacrifice to the supreme god, Hea. The traditions of the Chaldeans relate that when the Babylonians still lived in a state of barbarism, like the beasts of the fields, Hea issued from the waves, in the form of a fish's head and a man's body, or some say, of a man wearing a fish's skin, and he then civilised them (Fig. 167). He taught them to build houses and temples, showed them how to cultivate the land and reap the produce; imposed laws upon them, and revealed to them the principles of science, of the arts, and of writing. Other Gods, resembling him, afterwards rose from the waves to complete his work; it is said that, even now, the sea still conceals them, but occasionally at long intervals they manifest themselves, but no one living can boast of having seen them. Sennacherib, therefore, sacrificed to the god of the Ocean, poured out a libation from a golden cup, in the sight of all the army, then threw the cup into the sea, with a golden model of the ship and the figure of a fish, also of gold. The gods soothed, the vessels unfurled their sails amidst cries of joy. The crews were composed of Tyrians and Sidonians, but also of Greeks from Cyprus, who rivalled the Phœnicians in skill and daring: they soon became accustomed to the tides, and conducted the fleet to Nagidu. The shore is dangerous, and the inhabitants were armed and waiting for them on the beach. Yet Sennacherib disembarked, took the place, and carried the fugitives back with him. No Assyrian monarch had ever attempted such an enterprise before him, and not one of his successors ever tried to rival it. Many of them have won greater victories and more of them than he did upon dry land; but he is the only sovereign who ever triumphed over the sea.

Fig. 167.—Hea, the Fish-god.

The conquest of Gambul does not require either a fleet or foreign sailors, merely a large number of the flat-bottomed boats used by the natives in crossing the marshes. A large detachment of archers and spearmen, supported by a few chosen cavalry, was thrown into the land, they captured some boats, constructed others, and borrowed some from neighbouring tribes, that dared not refuse to lend them, and then the man-hunt commenced. Whilst one portion of the troops embarked and went up the canals, the others scattered

Fig. 168.—An encounter between the Assyrians and the inhabitants of the Marshes.

fan-wise through the reeds, and slowly drove all their enemies before them. The unfortunate inhabitants of Gambul tried to defend themselves behind the widest barriers of water, and sometimes their pools became the theatre of real naval battles, which they usually lost (Fig. 168). Their boats, loaded with women and old men, were almost unmanageable, and fell an easy prey to the invader. As the Assyrians conquered the land, whole populations left their villages and took refuge in their thickest bushes, where they hoped to defy pursuit (Fig. 169). It was in vain: the cavalry followed them, famine drove them out; the resistance lasted for some time longer, but it ended in the usual way, by the death of the bravest and the captivity of the others.

Here, as elsewhere, the Assyrians proceed with methodical cruelty. The chiefs are reserved for tor-

Fig. 169.—A family of the Chaldeans taking shelter in the Reeds.

ture at the pleasure of the king. Some of the warriors taken in arms are executed on the spot, with blows from clubs; some of them are reserved for incorporation with the army. Sennacherib brought thirty thousand recruits of this kind back from his expedition to Nagidu, and they fought as bravely for him in Armenia and Cilicia as they had done against him in Chaldea. Women, children, and artisans are led into slavery, and are sent to colonise some other country, far from their native land. Seeing the minute care with which these arrangements are carried out, one wonders how it is that a country is not utterly ruined after an Assyrian army has fallen upon it. Sometimes the whole population is taken at a single blow. The towns remain empty and the land uncultivated for several years. Gradually, however, a few fugitives who have escaped the catastrophe issue from their hiding-places, or leave the neighbouring cities where they have found shelter. Their first care is to rebuild their fallen walls and their houses; they sow their fields, timidly at first, then with more courage as their numbers increase. A few years of quiet and relative peace, in which they try to avoid recalling themselves to the memory of the Assyrians, easily restore their prosperity; the families multiply with great rapidity, and new generations arise as turbulent as their forefathers. If we reckon the men whom the people of Bit-Iakin and Gambul have lost in battle, those who have been massacred or carried into captivity, all who during the last century have died in exile of hunger and misery, it would seem that the country must have been a desert for many years, yet whenever a war breaks out Assyria finds it ready—the people may be conquered and weakened, but they cannot be exterminated.

Whilst part of the Assyrian army searches the marshes, the bulk of the troops is fighting against the regular forces of Gambul. Dunanu does not venture into the open country; he waits to be attacked behind the walls of Sapibel, his capital. These are the usual tactics not of the Aramæans of the Tigris only, but also of all the small princes that enter into conflict with Assyria. They have rarely sufficient troops at their disposal to risk a battle, or if their numbers are great they are too well aware of the inexperience of their generals and soldiers to hazard life and liberty upon the chance of a single blow. They prefer a guerilla warfare, in which their knowledge of the country gives them a great advantage; they dispute every mountain pass, every river ford, and, if fortune be against them, they have still the resource of defending themselves in their strong cities. They hope to exhaust the patience of their assailants by a long resistance; and it has sometimes happened that a king of Assyria, after having besieged and taken two or three cities, has renounced the pursuit of the enterprise and has retired, taking his booty and his prisoners with him. Sometimes a revolution breaks out, or some barbarous tribe invades a province at the opposite extremity of his empire. Reasons differ, but the result is the same: the Assyrians beat a retreat, and the prince whom they are besieging is freed from them for the time. This method, almost infallible hitherto when blockade and famine were the only means of reducing a fortified city, is not quite so certain now that machines have been invented which can force a breach in the most solid walls.

Sapibel is built in a good position. It has always been difficult to take, but its strength is doubled since Esarhaddon, having taken it from the Prince Belikisha, repaired the walls, so that it should be one of Assyria's bulwarks against Elam. A deep canal, always full of water, serves as a moat to the north and west, marshes protect it towards the south, but the front opens upon a plain, and is not defended by any natural advantage. The engineers entrusted with its fortifications have therefore arranged their plans so as to rectify this deficiency. A single wall, bristling with towers made of unbaked bricks, runs the whole length of the river and marsh; a double wall faces the plain. The two parts are of unequal height; the external wall is only twelve yards high when the battlements commence, the second one is sixteen yards high, and the towers are placed about every four yards along its curtain. The whole building resembles the fortifications of Dur-Sarginu, except in the dimensions and form of gates. The latter in Sapibel have not the castle projecting from the wall in front of them; they open upon the plain, one at each end, and are directly exposed to blows from the outside. But the inner wall has only one gate, placed in the centre. Each of the three gates is flanked by two strong towers built very near each other.

As soon as the frontier scouts signal the approach of the Assyrians, Dunanu makes all his arrangements in view of a long siege. He forces the inhabitants of the country districts to take refuge with him, with their corn, cattle, and provisions of wine and oil; he then carries off the still unripe fruits and crops, so that nothing should be left for the enemy. The men receive weapons and reinforce the regular garrison; the women prepare the bread and food. The engineers heighten the towers by erecting a rough wall of large osier rounds upon a light framework hanging over the battlements (Fig. 170). The soldiers themselves take every precaution to guard the part of the ramparts confided to them, and to multiply their means of resistance. At intervals all round the walls they place heaps of stones and shingle for the use of the slingers, and of large stones to be thrown down upon the enemy if they attack the foot of the rampart. Dunanu, his brother Samgunu, and his ally Palia, the grandson of Merodach Baladan, preside over the final preparations, and encourage the men by their words. 'No doubt the enemy is powerful, but Sapibel is strong, and has already repulsed more than one attack; she will repulse this one too, if her defenders show their usual courage. The gods, who have assisted them until now, will not desert them in this new peril.'

The Assyrian vanguard advances to the foot of the

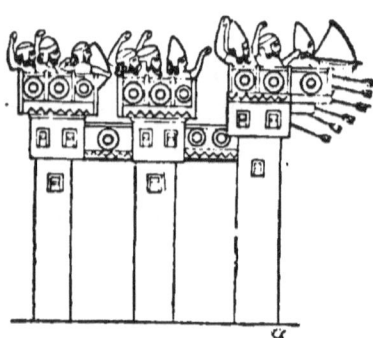

Fig. 170.—The Towers with their extra Defences.

walls, then, finding them well armed, it retires after shooting a few arrows. The captain of one of the gates, seeing them beat a retreat, imprudently pursues them. His troop is repulsed, and re-enters the town in confusion, leaving some ten men on the ground; the captain himself is severely wounded, and falls with ten others into the hands of the enemy. In these cases the Assyrians never show quarter. The prisoners were taken in front of the gates from which they had started full of life one hour earlier; there, under the eyes of their fellow-citizens who arm the ramparts, they are impaled; the posts with their living burdens are placed in a line, near enough for their friends to watch their agony, yet too far off for an arrow to reach the sufferers and end their tortures (Fig. 171). This terrible punishment is frequently inflicted by the Assyrians during a war. It is prompted in some degree by natural cruelty, but also by calculation. It is a slow, painful death, for the victims often linger two or three days in great agony; and since new prisoners are daily added to their numbers, if the siege is long the posts at last stand like a forest between the two armies. This lamentable spectacle often weakens the courage of the besieged, and leads to treason in the garrison; but it produces no effect upon the defenders of Sapibel. The Assyrians, after examining the city on various sides, have realised that it will not yield without a regular siege, so they have decided to commence operations.

Fig. 171.—Prisoners impaled by the Assyrians.

Their first precaution is to erect upon the plain, just beyond range of the ramparts, an immense entrenched camp, in which their whole army can dwell

350  THE FLEET AND THE SIEGE OF A CITY.

(Fig. 172). As usual it forms an almost perfect circle, surrounded by a brick wall, and flanked with towers,

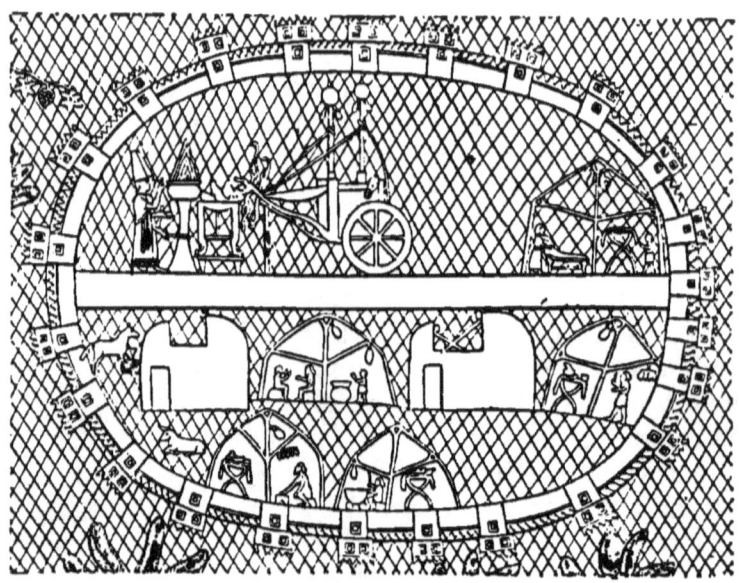

Fig. 172.—Entrenched Camp of the Assyrians.

like a real city. Every soldier is something of a workman by profession, and a few days enable them to finish the work. The interior is divided into quarters, where the tents are arranged in regular rows, like streets. One part is reserved for the worship. Two standards mounted upon a chariot represent Assur, always present in the midst of his armies: here the priests offer daily worship with the same rites as in the sanctuaries of Nineveh. Whilst one part of the assailants are resting (Fig. 173) the others continue the siege works or scour the country. In this way they

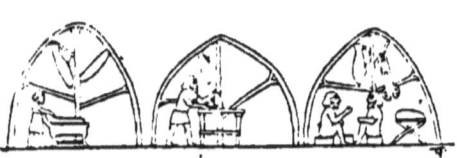

Fig. 173.—Three Tents in an Assyrian Camp.

command all the surrounding districts, and intercept all communications between Sapibel and the open country. From time to time a messenger tries to get through the investing lines, or swimming upon an inflated skin attempts to enter the city by the canal under cover of the night. If taken he is impaled, and if successful his news is so bad that it was not worth while risking his life to deliver it. The King of Babylon, alarmed by the defeat of Teumman, refuses to move; the small states of Lower Chaldea follow the example of the King of Babylon, and no one will raise even a finger to help Gambul. Dunanu is left alone to bear the whole weight of the war so lightly undertaken at the instigation of Elam.

The Assyrians, certain that no assisting army is coming to disturb them, conduct the operations of the siege with the regularity that characterises all their military organization. From the commencement of the siege they have established a girdle of slingers (Fig. 174) and archers round the city, who are charged to maintain against the besieged a perpetual conflict, and never to give them one moment's respite from morning till night, or, if possible, from night till morning. Each archer is accompanied by a spearman, who becomes his comrade, almost his second, for the remainder of the siege. They are both sheltered by a large shield of wicker-work, about six feet high, sometimes curved at the top and ended by a point, sometimes surmounted by a kind of awning at right angles with it. It is provided with a handle, placed rather high upon the inside, which enables it to be moved without too

Fig. 174.—The Assyrian Slingers.

much trouble. The spearman carries the buckler as a kind of movable rampart, which protects him and his comrade; when they are about sixty steps away from the wall he stops, plants it upon the ground, and the archer begins to shoot (Fig. 175). The archers from Gambul reply, concealing themselves behind the merlons of the curtain, or behind the round shields of the added wall. A contest of skill and vigilance then takes place, which never slackens; if an adversary exposes himself, one or two arrows are at once aimed at him. The Assyrians, although used to this style of warfare, sometimes commit an imprudence, and some men are lost every day. However, their sappers, protected by this hailstorm of arrows, drag themselves to one of the gates and try to break it down with their axes, or to set

Fig. 175.—The Archers behind their Bucklers.

Fig. 176.—The Siege of a City: in the centre an Assyrian Soldier tries to fire the Gate with a Torch.

fire to it with torches (Fig. 176). The massive panels, studded with bronze, resist these attempts, the guards from the neighbouring towers pour upon them projectiles, javelins, darts, blocks of stone, beams, and boiling water: the sappers are clothed in a kind of stuffed robe, which reaches from head to foot, but it is of no use, and they are soon forced to beat a retreat, leaving half their number upon the ground. They return at night with bundles of resinous wood and pitch, which they pile against the door, and then light; torrents of water, thrown from above, put out the fire, and this second attempt ends like the first, in the death of several of their number and the retreat of the others. Repulsed on this side, the following night they attack the tower at the southern angle, and try to undermine it so that it may fall. They take with them similar shields to those used by the archers, then lean the curved end against the wall, and beneath this shelter, like a tortoise under its shell, they attack the foundations of the wall. From the top of the tower the besieged throw beams or blocks of stone upon them, which crush them, flaming tow, which sets fire to their cloaks, but nothing daunts the workers; at last a small troop, led by Dunanu himself, secretly issues from the postern, and gliding along close under the wall surprises them in the darkness, kills some of them, puts the others to flight, then re-enters the city with the shields and some twenty prisoners. The latter are at once impaled, and on the following morning the Assyrians perceive the bodies of their comrades exposed upon the ramparts; on either side it is a struggle in which no quarter is shown, and the besieged, feeling themselves condemned, avenge themselves beforehand for the tortures they will have to endure. But, after all, these are merely feigned attacks intended to weary the enemy. Whilst this desultory fighting is carried on at the outposts, the engineers in the camp are finishing the construction of the siege machines. The battering-ram in all its forms has been in use in many parts of the world for a long time: sometimes it is a simple iron-tipped beam, carried by twenty men—this is the most rudimentary engine used in besieging cities; then there is the mounted ram, in which the beam is suspended to a framework erected at the foot of the walls and propelled with cords; lastly, there is the movable ram, which is the same as the preceding one, established upon four or six wheels, which enable it to be taken near the walls or withdrawn at pleasure. It is covered with a real carapace of fresh ox-skins or thick woollen stuff, rounded at the top so as to withstand the shock of large projectiles, and it is surmounted by a whole or half cupola over the fastenings of the cables which support the beam. This primitive shelter is frequently transformed into a kind of movable fortress, and the dome becomes a tower, where archers and soldiers stand, harassing the besieged and preventing them from setting fire to the machine with their torches.

The rams are placed in batteries at some distance from the rampart, so that some of them are directed upon a tower, others between two towers, at the weak points of the wall. The portion of ground which they are to cross is then levelled, and if in any places the soil is too soft to bear their weight, a regular paved way is made, over which they can pass safely. The besieged interfere with these preliminary works as much as they possibly can, but they cannot succeed in stopping them. The machines advance, each propelled by a hundred men. Two days are required to cross the short distance which separates them from the wall, but at last arrived within range, they commence work with activity, as though making up the time lost in their transport. At a given signal the men seize the ends of the ropes attached to the beam, and pull them all together. The first effort is always great, for the beam is heavy, the iron point of the lance or the square mass of metal with which it is provided being of considerable weight. Still, it begins to play, slowly at first, then with stronger oscillations, until the head strikes any obstacle opposed to it with great force. The wall trembles, a few bricks are detached or crushed (Fig. 177), and the shocks, continuing with great regularity, soon open a breach in each of the six points of attack. The garrison, unable to prevent the battery from being mounted, now tries to paralyse the engine or to destroy it. Chains are lowered, with running knots or hooks, which seize the head of the ram and stop its movements. The Assyrians resist, and it becomes a trial of strength, which sometimes gives an advantage to the

Fig. 177.—The Battering Rams opening the breach in the Wall.

besieged (Fig. 178). They get possession of the beam, or break it with an enormous block of stone. Still the torches, the lighted tow, the burning pitch, and the pots of fire pour upon the roofings, yet the Assyrians continue the attack quite imperturbably; when a ram is damaged, another beam is speedily fixed to it, and in a few moments the assault is recommenced.

Squadrons of men serve in relays, the flights of arrows never cease, the miners sap the foot of the towers, so that no respite is given to the defenders to enable them to concentrate their attention upon one point. Whilst the struggle rages furiously round the rams, a hundred men, chosen for their courage, enter the marshes soon after nightfall, provided with long ladders. Several of them sink in the mud; those who reach the wall plant the ladders against it, and finding them too short by some feet, yet manage, by climbing upon each other's shoulders, to reach the top. They kill the only sentinel on guard upon that side, seize the two adjacent towers, and loudly proclaim their success. The garrison, utterly discouraged, gives way, in spite of the entreaties of their leaders; a door is soon forced, and gives a free passage to the assailants, who spread

Fig. 178.—Scenes from a Siege. To the right, the archers under the shield, and the movable ram, which the besieged endeavour to disarm. In the centre, two unarmed sappers open a mine; to the left, two sappers in armour attack the foot of a wall. The river is in front.

through the town and begin to pillage it. At daybreak a few isolated groups of soldiers still resist; by noon the struggle is over, and the fall of Sapibel completes the conquest of Gambul.

The whole population is led captive into Assyria, and the city is destroyed. The houses are burnt, the walls thrown down so methodically that not one brick rests upon another; the palm-trees and fruit-trees are then cut down (Fig. 179), the dykes which protected the fields are broken, and the rubbish taken from them is used to choke the canals. Assyria does not

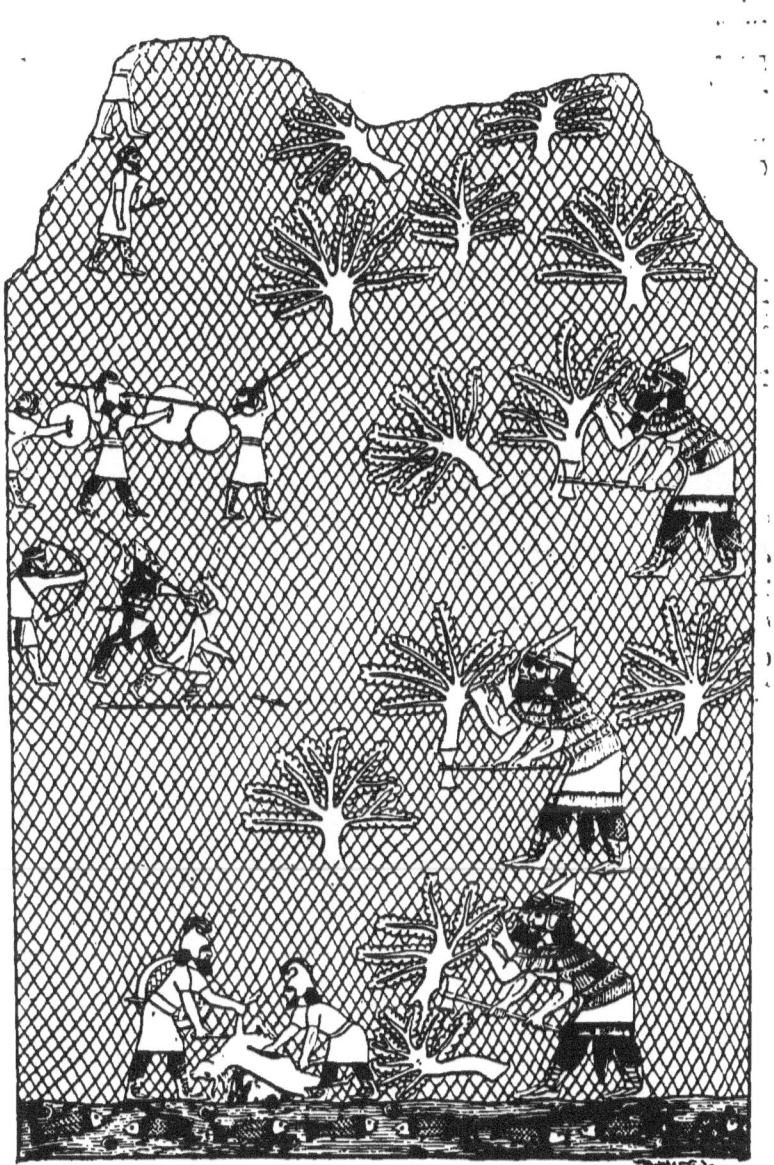

Fig. 179.—The Assyrians felling Trees in an Enemy's Country.

acknowledge that other nations have a right to make war upon her. If they resist her will they are treated as rebellious and sacrilegious subjects for whom no punishment is too severe. The only moderation she uses in her treatment of them is dictated by the amount of strength she knows or supposes them to possess. She paused after the battle of Tulliz, and was content with dividing Elam into several kingdoms which paid homage to her; but she knew that a prolonged struggle might not end to her advantage, and she never abuses her success where she fears that abuse of it may entail revenge. She razes Sapibel to the ground, and destroys almost all the population of Gambul, because she knows it can be done with impunity. The nation is too small to raise an army by itself numerically strong enough to oppose the Assyrian forces. The anger of Assur and Ishtar is never imprudent; they only give free vent to it at the expense of the weak, and the excesses in which Assyria indulges towards them amply compensates for the self-restraint which she is obliged to exercise from time to time towards the strong.

# CHAPTER XX.

### THE TRIUMPH.

Assurbanipal receives the ambassadors from Uratu—Nineveh and its palace—War is a commercial operation which enriches Assyria—The prisoners—The execution of the vanquished chiefs—Assyrian banquet and festivities—The festival in the harem—The head of Teumman—The song of triumph—Prophecy of Nahum, the Elkoshite.

WHILST these victories have been won for him, Assurbanipal has not been inactive in the palace of Arbela. He has banqueted, hunted, sacrificed to Ishtar even more often than his generals have marched, pillaged, and given battle. He has even received foreign embassies, to whom he has displayed his booty and paraded his success. Rousa, the king of Urartu, has sent his nobles to conclude a peace. To Assyria Urartu is no longer the formidable enemy that Tiglath-Pileser III. and Sargon had so much trouble in defeating. Its forces have been exhausted in the struggle, and some tribes from the west are contending with it for the cantons of the Euphrates, over which its authority has extended for many centuries. In order to concentrate all his strength against them, Rousa wishes to remain on good terms with his neighbour in Nineveh; the friendship, or, at least, the neutrality, of Assyria is well worth a few presents and a few words of praise, even of submission. Assurbanipal received the ambassadors in a public audience, and showed them the two Susian envoys, Umbadara and Nabudamiq, in chains. He wishes to give them a practical lesson, showing the danger of provoking his wrath, and, consequently, the advantages which foreign sovereigns will gain by retaining his favour. The Armenians retire, properly impressed, and after their departure Assurbanipal resumes his life of indolence and pleasure.

Day by day, couriers arrive, bringing news of some fresh success, the arrival at Duril, the hasty retreat of the Elamites, the victory of Tulliz, the death of Teumman, the accession of Ummanigas and Tammaritu, the siege and capture of Sapibel, and the speedy return of the victors with their spoil. It is customary for kings returning from war to re-enter their capital in triumph. The prisoners head the procession, then comes the tribute paid by the conquered nations, and the festival ends by the torture of the chief leaders of the rebellion. Assurbanipal makes every arrangement for the ceremony; when the day arrives, he places himself at the head of the victorious army, and leads the way into Nineveh.

The capital of Assyria is not, like Dur-Sarginu, a city built all at once, upon an arranged plan. It has grown up in the course of years, through the slow increase of buildings and men, and still retains the disorderly appearance of ancient times. It rises upon the left bank of the Tigris, at its confluence with the Khosr, and in form it resembles an irregular trapeze, much longer than it is wide. The district which borders the river is protected by a single wall, and but one wall defends the northern side; in front of it is a wide moat, filled by water from the Khosr. The southern quarters, which face the plain, and which have no natural protection, are sheltered from attack by a skilful arrangement of the ground. There is first a wall, similar to those on the other sides, and also provided with a moat; then, in front of the moat, stands a fortification shaped like a half moon, consisting of two thick walls and a second moat as wide as the first.

The road from Arbela crosses these defences, and; passing through the city, leads to the artificial mound upon which the southern palace is built, the old residence of the former kings, magnificently restored by Sennacherib. The hand of this great monarch has left many traces in Nineveh. He endowed it with aqueducts to bring fresh, clear water from the neighbouring hills; he constructed brick quays by the sides of Tigris, and, finally, in a bend of the Khosr, he erected the finest of the Assyrian palaces, the one in which his son, Esarhaddon, and his grandson, Assurbanipal, have reigned after him. The latter has ornamented the wall with representations of his hunting exploits and victories; he has also arranged a large library within it, which contains the works of ancient and modern scribes which he has collected.

The plan of the Ninevite palaces is very similar to that of Sargon's palace at Dur-Sarginu. They are reached by inclined paths, or by double staircases built in the flanks of the artificial mound which supports them. The façades have the same effect of fortresses covered with battlements and bordered with towers. The gates are decorated with masts, and open between two rows of winged bulls. The harem has separate apartments, which scarcely communicate with the main building, only a few narrow doors opening between them; gardens are annexed to them, in which cypress and cedar-trees are blended with bowers of vines and gay beds of flowers. Lastly, the storied tower rises at an angle, as though it typified the protection of the gods extended over the city lying beneath it. The Assyrians do not care to vary the type and arrangement of their monuments. The plans received from their ancestors are considered suitable for themselves, and they faithfully adopt them, at least in all the chief lines. Yet in foreign lands they have seen masterpieces of the builders' art which a people less wedded to its own traditions would have been tempted to imitate. They have entered the palaces of the Hittite kings, and have borrowed their custom of building their walls in stone up to the top; but they have stopped there, and the palaces in the Khita style, as they call them, are simple Chaldean edifices of stone instead of brick. They are acquainted with the temple of Iahveh at Jerusalem, and that of Melkarth at Tyre; they have pillaged the immense structures of Ptah at Memphis, of Amen at Thebes, but it has never occurred to them to copy their style. Esarhaddon has taken from Egypt only the type of griffon crowned with the disk of Ra (Fig. 179*), and in the palace of Assurbanipal figures may be seen in which the body of the Egyptian lion is rather heavily blended with the wings and the human head of the ancient bulls. With that exception, the buildings of the present day are still constructed according to the rules established by the Chaldeans; and the architects of Goudea, if they returned to this world, might claim for themselves the most recent work of modern architects.

Fig. 179*.—A Griffon in the Egyptian style.

The soldiers of the different regiments march through the streets amidst the acclamations of the crowd, followed by the prisoners and the booty; then the king advances upon his chariot, succeeded by more soldiers. The head of the procession is already in front of the prison, before the last lines of it have passed the gates, they are still in the suburbs. The rich booty excites general admiration. The Elamite chariots and all the material for war open the march, the horses of the Susian cavalry and the mules that belonged to the king are led past bridled and harnessed (Fig. 180) ready for service. They are of the same race as the

Assyrian horses, but are easily distinguished from the Egyptian species; this fact is confirmed by all the Ninevites who witnessed the triumph of Assurbanipal

Fig. 180.—The Horses being led past.

after his victories over Pharaoh Taharka and his son-in-law Urdamani. The head is small, but well-shaped, the nostrils widely opened, the eyes lively, the neck

Fig. 181.—A Camel and his Drivers.

and shoulders arched and fairly strong, the body is heavy, the legs delicate and muscular. A few camels taken at Gambul follow the horses (Fig. 181). These grotesque animals come from Arabia, where they are used to carry burdens and for crossing the desert.

They have only one hump, whereas the camels of the East, which are sometimes seen in Nineveh as objects of curiosity, have two. The number of oxen and small animals has greatly diminished on the road between the frontiers of Elam and Gambul and the gates of the capital. The army and the prisoners have eaten some of them, a great many have died of fatigue or have fallen victims to the beasts of prey. Those which survive are still so numerous that only part of them are admitted into the procession; the others are left outside the city in charge of the herdsmen, until they can be divided between the royal treasury and the soldiers who have assisted in the campaign.

The beasts are succeeded by bands of slaves carrying the furniture and precious objects taken from the vanquished — statues of the gods in gold or silver, vases used for the sacrifices, tripods and armchairs in chiselled bronze, all the treasures of Dunanu, all the wealth of the inhabitants of Sapibel. The bars of gold and silver may be counted by thousands; there are masses of tin, iron, and bronze, of linen and woollen garments. And this is the produce of a single expedition, the booty won by the pillage of a few provinces of Elam and the small land of Gambul. What is it, then, when a city like Tyre or a people like the Egyptians are spoiled? It is easy now to understand the Assyrians' love of war, and why their kings organize all their strength with a view to conquest. It is not simply a brutal ardour or a disinterested search for glory, but something more positive — the desire to win profit and wealth. Other nations venture upon the ocean and trade with barbarians beyond the seas; others are agricultural; others seek an honest means of winning fortune by industry and quiet commerce. The Assyrians make war. War feeds them, clothes them, exempts them from industry; to them war replaces trade, or rather war is to them merely a commercial operation, in which they risk soldiers and horses in order to win everything else.

They have fought in Chaldea, in Syria, in Elam, in Armenia, in Egypt, in Media; they will fight anywhere to fill their own coffers and the treasure-house of their prince with the wealth of the whole world.

The prisoners, marching in close column, follow the men carrying the spoil. The first rows are composed of the male and female singers who belonged to Dunanu, and sang before him in the days of his greatness, when he passed in solemn procession down the streets of Sapibel. The harp on the arm, the flute at the lips, they advance still playing, still singing the old hymns, but now under the superintendence of Assyrian soldiers and amidst the derisive applause of the crowd. The Elamites and the remnant of the peoples of Gambul follow them. The Assyrians have not, like the Egyptians, the habit of fastening their prisoners in awkward and painful attitudes, which inconvenience their movements and make them resemble grotesque marionettes. A few are handcuffed and have irons on their feet, but the majority are unchained. They advance without any distinction of rank and sex, the noble walking by the commoner, women with men, all classes merged in the same shame, in the same slavery. Their clothes, covered with mud and dirt, are merely shapeless, colourless rags, which scarcely conceal their forms. The children, still too young to understand their misfortune, watch with a mixture of fear and curiosity the multitude which hurries to see them pass. The young girls and women are in terror, wondering what their fate will be in the division of the spoil; into what hands they will fall, into those of a brutal soldier, or of an officer of rank, in those household they will at least enjoy some of the abundance and luxury to which they are accustomed. Instances have been known of kings themselves falling in love with the captives they have led in triumph behind their chariot, and more than one foreigner has entered an Assyrian harem as a slave, afterwards to reign there as a queen. The freemen look anxious and gloomy. Those who are strong and skilful in warlike exercises hope to be soon noticed and incorporated with the army; military slavery does not alarm them, and they would a hundred times rather carry arms for their conquerors than work in the fields or fulfil the menial offices exacted from domestic slaves. The men born in slavery are careless and almost gay. Service for service, it makes little difference to them whether it is at Nineveh or at Sapibel; they do not change their position, merely their owners, and many of them do not even dissimulate their cruel joy in seeing the humiliation and fall of their former masters.

One group particularly interests the Ninevites and rouses their acclamations; it is formed of the principal chiefs taken prisoners at Tulliz and during the campaign at Gambul—Dunanu, his brother Sangunu, Palia, Nabuzalli, their wives and children. Dunanu wears the head of Teumman suspended round his neck. Perhaps he secretly envies the fate of his ally, who has at least died on the field of battle, and has nothing more to fear from the cruelty of man; yet his carriage and features betray no sign of his thoughts. He walks proudly, looking neither to the right or left, his face unmoved, his head unbent, apparently neither seeing or hearing anything of the crowd that insults him, or of his wives, who weep and lament over him. The same morning, when the head of Teumman was placed upon his breast, the executioner pierced the lips or nose of his relations, passed a ring and cord through the hole, as though they were oxen, and gave the cords to soldiers, who lead the prisoners. Their conductors violently jerk at them from time to time, but so skilfully that, although they inflict acute pain, they do not tear one fragment of flesh. The courage of the unfortunate men never fails them: like their chief, they are unmoved during the long hours of the march into the city: would they not have treated Assurbanipal and his leaders in precisely the same way, if fortune had smiled upon them and they had captured Nineveh? All the nations of the world, the Egyptians themselves, although they have a reputation for clemency, delight in torturing their prisoners before executing them. Death itself, death by the sword or the club, by hanging, drowning, or any means which is rapid and almost painless, is not regarded as a real punishment: to dispatch a man with a single blow, so that he does not know he is dying, is a favour rarely granted. The rebel and the ordinary criminal have no right to so much indulgence; they must suffer pain to the very end, and invoke death frequently before it releases them.

By Assurbanipal's command, Umbadara and Nabodamiq have been placed upon the terrace of the palace, where they watch the march past with sorrow and rage. When they see the head of Teumman upon Dunanu's neck, their despair cannot be restrained. Teumman, though cruel and faithless to his adversaries, was a good and generous master. Umbadara tears his beard and sobs aloud. Nabodamiq draws the dagger left in his belt and pierces his own heart. The head of Teumman is exposed over the great gate of Nineveh, and all who enter or go out look up and greet it with insults or curses. Dunanu is flayed alive (Fig. 182), then thrown into a furnace, which consumes him. Some are stoned to death, others have their eyes put out by the king himself: he forces them to kneel before him, raises their head by the ring passed through their lips, then puts out their eyes with the point of his javelin. Sangunu is blinded, then chained between two wild pigs at the entrance of one of the city gates, where he is exposed to the insults of the passers-by, and fed with anything their pity leads them

Fig. 182.—A Prisoner being flayed alive.

to throw to him like a dog. Nabuzalli, Palia, and many others, after being tortured at Nineveh, are sent to Arbela to be sacrificed to Ishtar and die before her. They are flayed alive, their bodies are cut into quarters, and the pieces are sent to the various provinces to show that the king knows how to punish rebels. Like all Assyrian triumphs, that of Assurbanipal ended in a long butchery.

After the procession, the day is passed in a perfect frenzy of joy by the whole nation. It is customary for all the inhabitants of the city, slaves and freemen, to eat and drink at the king's expense during the festival; this is a method of giving them a share of the booty. For seven days the palace gates are open to all comers. Many-coloured stuffs suspended over the walls by means of ropes have transformed the courts into immense banqueting-halls. The crowd is coming and going from morning till night; the people instal themselves upon state beds or seats, and ask for whatever they like; the slaves have orders to give them anything they wish for, and to bring to each person whatever he desires as many times as he asks for it. Women and children are admitted to these festivals as well as men. The soldiers kept in barracks by their duty are not forgotten; the king sends them the food and wine they cannot fetch for themselves in so great profusion that they have nothing to regret. The loaves disappear by thousands, by thousands also the oxen, sheep, goats, and birds of all kinds are sacrificed to satisfy the public appetite. But what they eat is nothing to what they drink. The Assyrian is sober in ordinary life, but he does not know how to stop if he once allows himself any excess. Wines of Assyria and Chaldea, wines from Elam, wines from Syria and Phœnicia, wines from Egypt, amphoræ and skins are emptied as soon as opened, without visibly quenching the universal thirst. After one or two days no brain is strong enough to resist it, and Nineveh presents the extraordinary spectacle of a whole city in different degrees of intoxication; when the festival is over, several days are required before it resumes its usual aspect. This would be the time for a resolute enemy to suddenly attack it, when the disorder is at its height and the army, like the people, has lost all consciousness. Tradition relates that more than one powerful city has perished in this way during a festival, having scarcely any strength left for resistance. Whilst the people are becoming tipsy outside, Assurbanipal feasts the leading chiefs and the ministers of state within the

Fig. 183.—The King's Guests at Table.

palace. They are seated upon double chairs, two on each side of a small table, face to face (Fig. 183). The chairs are high, without any backs or footstool upon which the guests can rest either elbows or feet; the honour of dining with the king must always be paid for by some fatigue. The tables are covered with fringed cloths, upon which the dishes are placed by the slaves. Unlike the common people, the nobles eat but little, so that few dishes of meat are set before them, but cakes and fruits of different kinds, grapes, dates, apples, pears, and figs are brought in continual relays

B B

by long lines of slaves (Figs. 184 and 185). On the other hand, they drink a great deal—with more refinement, perhaps, than the common people, but with equal avidity. Upon this occasion the king has distributed the most precious vases in his treasury, cups of gold and silver, the majority of them moulded or chased in the form of a lion's head. Many of them were formerly sacred vessels which the priests of vanquished nations used in their sacrifices; some are from Babylon or Carchemish, some were taken from

Fig. 184.—Slaves bringing Fruit.

Tyre or Memphis, whilst others belonged to the temples at Samaria and Jerusalem. By using them for a profane occasion, the Assyrians insult the gods to whose service they belong, so that to the pleasure of drinking is added that of humiliating the foreign deities in the sight of Assur whom they had resisted.

The wines, even the most delicate, are not drunk in their natural state; they are mixed with aromatics and various drugs, which give them a delicious flavour and add tenfold to their strength. This operation is performed in the hall, under the eyes of the revellers

Fig. 185.—Slaves bringing Wine, Cakes, and Fruit.

An eunuch standing before a table pounds in a stone mortar the intoxicating substances, which he moistens

Fig. 186.—The Cup-bearers taking the Wine from the Large Bowl.

from time to time with some essence. His comrades have poured the contents of the amphoræ into immense bowls of chased silver, which reach to their chests. As soon as the perfumed paste is ready they put some of it into each bowl and carefully dissolve it. The cup-bearers bring the cups, draw out the wine, and serve the guests (Fig. 186). Even the sentinels at the doors receive their share, and, standing spear or club in hand, pledge each other as they mount guard (Fig. 187). The only persons who do not drink, or who drink very little, through the necessity of retaining their sobriety, are the eunuchs—who stand behind the guests to fan them—the servants, and the musicians. No festival is complete without the presence of singers, and the king's musicians conscientiously perform their finest melodies. Perhaps some one listened to them at the beginning of the feast, but now that the great silver bowls have been filled and emptied several times, their music is literally wasted. They may sing out of tune or remain silent, just as they please, no one will listen or care.

Fig. 187.—The Sentinels, Cup in hand.

Assurbanipal presided over the first of these banquets; he has deigned to drink the same wine which has been prepared for his nobles, then he retired into the harem, in order to pass the days of festival there. The women's house opens upon one of those gardens, planted with sycamores, cypresses, and poplars, in which the queens of Assyria, condemned by their rank to strict seclusion, gratify themselves by a semblance of the country; fountains, supplied by machines which raise the waters of the Khosr to the top of the mound, flow beneath the trees. The queen, who also wishes to celebrate the Assyrian victories, has begged her husband to dine with her, and he has graciously accepted an invitation which made her tremble as she gave it. The festival couch is placed beneath the shade of a trellis, with its mattress and embroidered coverings; a small table, loaded with golden dishes and cups, is placed near the head of the couch; then opposite the table stands the high chair with a back and footstool, upon which the queens have the right to sit in the presence of their lord (Fig. 188). The king reclines upon the couch, accepts a cupful of perfumed wine, and, raising his eyes, sees facing him a deformed object of blackish tint hanging to the bough of a tree. It is the head of

Fig. 188.—Assurbanipal drinking with the Queen in the Gardens of the Harem; the head of Teumman is hanging to one of the branches of the second tree to the left.

Teumman, which the queen has sent for from the gate of Nineveh, and which she has hung in her garden, so that Assurbanipal should look at it during the festival and rejoice over his triumph. He gazes at it ironically, salutes it with his cup, looks again, and cannot satiate himself with the pleasure of gazing at it; behind him the musicians of the harem sing his praises, accompanying themselves with their harps.

The court poet has placed the recital of the hero's life and exploits, from the hour of his birth until the day of his triumph, in his own mouth. 'In the midst of joy and gaiety, I am come into the harem, into the splendid hall, the sanctuary of royalty, where Sennacherib, the father of the father of my father, was formerly son of a king, then king; where Esarhaddon, my father, was born, grew up, and reigned as lord over Assyria; where all the kings were born, and where their families have grown up, sons and daughters; where I, at last—I, Assurbanipal—I was nourished in the wisdom of Nebo; where I learnt the knowledge of all that has been written, through the medium of all the learned men; where I learnt to shoot with the bow, to ride, to drive a chariot, to handle the reins. By the command of the great gods, whose name I have always invoked, whose praise I have always celebrated, who ordained me to exercise the dignity of king, I have devoted all my care to the enrichment of their temples. This is why they have overwhelmed me with prosperity, and have placed mine enemies beneath my yoke. I am a strong warrior, beloved of Assur and Ishtar, the child of royalty. Since Assur, Sin the moon-god, Shamash the sun-god, Ramman, Bel, Nebo, Ishtar of Nineveh, Ishtar of Arbela, Adar, Nergal, and Nouskou have been gracious unto me, Ramman has always granted fertilising rains to me, Hea has always opened the arcana of his waters; the wheat has grown to five cubits, and its ears of corn are always one cubit long; during my reign, abundance has overflowed; during all the years of my reign, the divine blessing has been poured out upon me like a heavy dew. The gods have raised me higher than any king ever ascended before me. Whilst Assur and Ishtar support me, who can prevail against me? My power is everlastingly founded by their hands, the duration of my race is established; they shall reign for many days, and for everlasting years.'

At this time, Nahum, the Elkoshite, the prophet of Judah, had a vision relating to Nineveh, and the word of the Eternal came unto him, saying: 'Woe to the bloody city! it is all full of lies and rapine; the prey departeth not! The noise of the whip, and the noise of the rattling of wheels, and prancing horses and jumping chariots; the horsemen charging, and the flashing sword and the glittering spear; and a multitude of slain, and a great heap of carcases; and there is no end of their corpses; they stumble upon their corpses.

'Behold, I am against thee, saith the Lord of Hosts. . . . . And it shall come to pass that all they that look upon thee shall flee from thee, and say, "Nineveh is laid waste; who will bemoan her? Whence shall I seek comforters for thee?"

'Art thou better than No-amen, that was situate among the rivers, that had the waters round about her; whose rampart was the sea, and her wall was of the sea? Ethiopia and Egypt were her strength, and it was infinite; Put and Lubim were thy helpers. Yet was she carried away, she went into captivity; her young children also were dashed in pieces at the top of all the streets, and they cast lots for her honourable men, and all her great men were bound in chains.

'Thou also shalt be drunken, thou shalt be hid; thou also shalt seek a stronghold because of the enemy. All thy fortresses shall be like fig-trees with the first-ripe figs; if they be shaken they fall into the mouth of the eater. Behold, thy people in the midst of thee are women; the gates of thy land are set wide open unto thine enemies; the fire hath devoured thy bars.

'Draw thee water for the siege, strengthen thy fortresses; go into the clay and tread the mortar, make strong the brick kiln. Then shall the fire devour thee, the sword shall cut thee off, it shall devour thee like the canker-worm. Make thyself many as the canker-worm, make thyself many as the locust. Thou hast multiplied thy merchants above the stars of heaven. The canker-worm spoileth, and flieth away. .

'Thy crowned are as the locusts, and thy marshals as the swarms of grasshoppers which camp in the hedges in the cold day; but when the sun ariseth they flee away, and their place is not known where they are. Thy shepherds slumber, O king of Assyria; thy worthies are at rest, thy people are scattered upon the mountains, and there is none to gather them.

'There is no assuaging of thy hurt; thy wound is grievous. All that hear the bruit of thee clap the hands over thee; for upon whom hath not thy wickedness passed continually?'

LONDON:
Printed by STRANGEWAYS & SONS, Tower Street, Cambridge Circus, W.C.

www.ingramcontent.com/pod-product-compliance
Lightning Source LLC
Chambersburg PA
CBHW032017220426
43664CB00006B/282